YUCATAN BEFORE AND AFTER THE CONQUEST

by

FRIAR DIEGO DE LANDA

WITH OTHER RELATED
DOCUMENTS, MAPS AND
ILLUSTRATIONS

Translated with notes by
WILLIAM GATES

DOVER PUBLICATIONS, INC.
NEW YORK

Published in Canada by General Publishing Company, Ltd., 30 Lesmill Road, Don Mills, Toronto, Ontario.

Published in the United Kingdom by Constable and Company, Ltd., 10 Orange Street, London WC2H 7EG.

This Dover edition, first published in 1978, is an unabridged republication of the work originally published as Publication Number 20 by The Maya Society, Baltimore, in 1937, in an edition of 80 copies. Many of the illustrations were originally hand tinted; all are black and white in the present edition.

The work is a translation of *Relación de las cosas de Yucatan*, a manuscript of 1566.

International Standard Book Number: 0-486-23622-6
Library of Congress Catalog Card Number: 77-91231

Manufactured in the United States of America
Dover Publications, Inc.
180 Varick Street
New York, N.Y. 10014

There are so few instances to be found in the world today of balanced, constructive and honest programs in the life of the nations, that when one appears like that of Mexico in her present solution of her centuries-old problem of peasant farm lands and its allied practical needs of social and economic education, working, succeeding and actually rebuilding a nation of self-respecting and self-keeping citizens, and at the same time restoring the Indian race to a contributing position in the life of America, it calls for any recognition one can give. So thus this volume, whose story goes to the root of the historic questions involved, calls by its very nature to be

Dedicated

To His Excellency

Lázaro Cárdenas

President of Mexico

CONTENTS

INTRODUCTION

The position of Diego de Landa in history rests upon two of his acts, one the writing of the book that is herewith published in English for the first time, and the other the famous Auto de fé of July 1562 at Maní, at which, in addition to some 5000 'idols,' he burned as he tells us twenty-seven hieroglyphic rolls, all he could find but could not read, as 'works of the devil,' designed by the evil one to delude the Indians and to prevent them from accepting Christianity when it should in time be brought to them. Both acts were monumental, one to the ideas of his time, and the other as the basis and fountain of our knowledge of a great civilization that had passed.

It is perhaps not too strong a statement to make, that ninety-nine percent of what we today know of the Mayas, we know as the result either of what Landa has told us in the pages that follow, or have learned in the use and study of what he told. Landa left for us there the knowledge of their days and months, and the ceremonial festivals for planting, hunting and their other daily activities; the same preparations for a prosperous New Year by the favor and protection of the powers of the earth and sky, the devotions, new resolutions and the dismissal of the scapegoat of the old year and invocation of a coming better one, all as we do when we clean house and decorate for the coming of Santa Claus and his reindeer — who would certainly have been 'demons' to him had he found their images among the Mayas: in short, the many social and communal functions in which their life was expressed.

These things were told him possibly by Gaspar Antonio Chi (of whom we shall read later), but more probably by Nachi Cocom as stated by Landa himself, and whose bones he later dug up and cast into the fields on the suspicion that he had practised ancient Maya customs after he had been baptised; and from them we learned the structure of their yearly social calendar, and therefrom got our start.

He knew of their greater " count of ages," but only that such a count existed. He did not understand it, but left a one-line formula which, used as a mathematical and chronological key, opened to us their greatness in that science, and their almost perfect astronomy.

He also told us, as learned probably through Chi and derived from the Xiu sources of western Yucatan, much of the history of the northern part of the peninsula, after the fall of what we have called the Old Empire.

If ninety-nine hundredths of our present knowledge is at base derived from what he told us, it is an equally safe statement that at that Auto de fé of

'62, he burned ninety-nine times as much knowledge of Maya history and sciences as he has given us in his book.

Landa's fame thus rests on the repercussions of his conduct as provincial of the Franciscan order in Yucatan, and on this book, both events preceding his appointment as bishop.   It is also quite fair to add that it is to Bishop Toral, a man of wholly different character, who arrived in Yucatan on the very heels of this event at Maní, released the prisoners Landa had incarcerated and forced Landa's own return to Spain for trial before the Council of the Indies, that we actually owe the present book.   For it was written in Spain as a matter of self-support, as is clearly shown in chapters XVII and XVIII, and the final Paragraph 12, his epilogue and appeal.   Had he remained in Yucatan he would probably never have written his *Relación de las Cosas de Yucatan;* it would not there have been necessary to his plans and objectives.

The present translation is a revision of one I made for my own use over twenty years ago.   The constant calls, and still more the need, for an English edition, caused me to take it up seriously a year ago.   From the first I planned to illustrate the work as herewith appears, with line drawings of things or places referred to in the text.   Soon the material for this and for comments piled up so that only one way out resulted: first, an edition of Landa, restricted as to notes to just enough to let the general reader (as distinct from the specialist) into the subject, and help to visualize the life of the people he was reading about;   restricted also as to illustrations to *Landa's* Yucatan. After that another, broader work to follow, covering the whole field of ' Maya,' and the Yucatan that Landa did not know.

A further step was promptly called for, in connection with this present work; this was to use the other, largely unpublished and almost entirely uncoordinated material in my own collection, to make of this a composite volume, picturing the Yucatan and its people of whom Landa wrote, as they were in his time;   also *his* position in their history.   This brought in the Xiu Papers, with all their highly valuable information, non-existent elsewhere.

On this came an obvious, though previously shadowy aid to the whole, namely a Maya *map,* or better termed, a map of Mayadom, as found by Landa and the Spaniards who preceded him by the seven years from 1542 to 1549.   The names and general boundaries of the various chiefdoms at that initial time were known, and in fact are named in Landa.   *The key to Yuca-tecan history at and before that time lies in an understanding of the true relation between the two halves of this map.*   By adding to what Landa tells us (from western, Xiu sources of history) the information to be gathered in a detailed digest of what is scattered through the Reports called for by the Crown, of 1579-81, a picture of the ' Things of Yucatan ' comes out, much

wider than, and complementary to Landa's Relation, and supremely illumi-
nating as to not only the state of the country when he left it with his death,
but also as to his part in what was done to impose Spain and her ways on them,
as their spiritual creditor, in place of their own " founders and progenitors,
who had begotten them in sin," as he tells us in his epilogue.

This we may summarize by quoting Ancona, in his *History of Yucatan*.
There he says that the Provincial Landa and his Franciscans, supported by the
Auditor Tomás López with his Ordinances and his direct authorization for
the town removals so bitterly complained of, made for " more convenient
doctrination and ecclesiastical supervision," had turned the whole country
into " a Franciscan monastery," effectively independent and superior to the
regular Church authorities.   And further, that Landa returning in 1573
as bishop, in succession to Toral (who had been so unable to make headway
against the dominating Franciscan friars intrenched in their great, Indian-
labor built structures, that he had at last retired back to Mexico, where he
died, in 1571) — that Landa, Bishop, set more store by his provincialate in
the Franciscan order than in his bishopric, which he used the rather to support
his Franciscan ideology.

Then finally came a fortunate turning up of the unpublished Tax List of
1549, the very year that Landa arrived in Yucatan as a simple Franciscan
friar.   Without this as a concrete documented background for the population
figures then, more than half the value of the 1579 Relations would not have
come out.

A few shorter pieces of documentation, published and unpublished, came
up to fit in place.   The first is the delicious bit of political ' back-up ' play
shown by the *multiple* set of ' form letters,' ostensibly signed by a number
of native caciques, to be sent to the king asking him to send back their beloved
friar Landa and other Franciscans.   One of these was printed 60 years ago
in the great volume of *Cartas de Indias,* and since supposed to stand alone as
an expression of love especially for Landa himself;   the fact being that this
was but one of a number, all the Indians' names signed for them in the same
hand as the letters, a second instance of which appears in facsimile immediately after the text of the Relation and its final epilogue.   This has not before
been known, or published.   It is also followed by another long letter, signed
by the very Francisco de Montejo Xiu, governor of Maní, he who first came
of his own accord to yield to Montejo in January 1542, together with other
governors of high standing, disavowing these " procured " duplicate letters
as false, and then relating what had in fact been done to their people.

Finally I have added two more official documents of the time, without
whose inclusion no sure and clear envisioning of the forces at play, and their
work *and results* would have been possible.   One is the Ordinances of Tomás

López, Auditor and Judge of the High Court of Guatemala and the Confines, himself a Franciscan friar and later one of those to sit in judgment on and finally absolve their co-member, friar Diego de Landa, of any illegality or wrong in doing what López, assuming the imperial authority, had told the friars in Yucatan they *should* do, in the matter of full ecclesiastical regimentation of daily and social life, and punishment as by inquisition for any violation on the part of the Indians of the friars' orders.   These ordinances are given, in condensed form, at the end.

Also the declaration required to be read by all Spanish captains at once on landing for the purpose of conquest, regardless of whether the native inhabitants were present to hear, or if so could understand the words as spoken;   the last part of this proclamation was quoted by Stephens, but it is here given in full.   In this amazing declaration lies the key to the whole course of affairs in Spanish America to the present day, from the landing of the first conquistadores.   And it is exactly at issue in the world today.   Philip II, seeking not merely world supremacy but world ownership, relied for the *legality* of his course on the Bull dividing the new found world between the kings of Spain and Portugal, which authority in turn rested on the 'keys of Peter,' and the principle of divine vice-gerency;   just as we today rest on recognized international *law* in matters of search and freedom of the seas.   The Indian race, as still too little recognized, represented the *active* principle of communalism, which is not 'common ownership,' but a community-approved principle of social cooperation in the vital necessities of production and distribution — something we are today in the white race groping for as a dim but needed goal.   It is simply social peace, not senseless and destructive economic war, that costs all sides more than they gain, in the mere ambition to control.

And today, as Spain struggles, the same Mexico and Yucatan are *effectively* giving scope and freedom to that age-long ingrained Indian principle of town community action;   a system that through freedom to work and produce without being robbed, gives spur to the desire to learn how to work better, produce better, in — yes — social security.   The peasant farmer, on *his own* land, educated to his station, does not have to deny 'God' because he goes to a local school to learn better how to treat his 'great mother' the land, or to work a motor.   To the Indian, far more truly religious than we are, 'God' is the beneficent (and *therefore* divine) overruling force that shines on all and aids nature to produce, in her (and his) ceaseless struggle to produce and grow;   for there can be no production without hard labor, nor growth without struggle.   And the hardest of the struggle is with those who want to control others.   All this is the problem of the town removals, and the López Ordinances;   its natural revolt is in the Mexico of today, where she is after these same 400 years actually making her great Indian population (which *is* Mexico) a self-reliant farm citizenry, not economic (nor human) slaves, but an economic asset in a country of immense possibilities.

We have said that Landa's fame rests on two facts, the Auto at Maní and his book, the latter the incidental result of that Auto and its results. Both are monumental, in widely different yet connected ways. It is exactly these questions of ideology that are today at universal issue on the world stage. In our small research region we are trying to learn what we can of the great American past culture and civilization of the Maya race, to restore to view their forms of life and sciences before obscurity descended on them, by supposedly divinely ordered autos de fé. And the syllogism is complete, and it is not attacking religion to question history or use logic so as not to evade patent, or confessed facts that lie below the whole.

The Czar *owned* Russia, owned it; by law every acre, every thing, every person, belonged to him, to dispose of. With us the State, which is the corporate body of the whole people, has the same ultimate right in emergency to enlist all the people and impound all resources, for the *common* safety; the fountain of the law here, in England since the earliest days, and on the continent since the French Revolution, is the people. In the system of the Czar, of Metternich, of the Holy Roman Empire, and of Philip II and Spain, it rests on the assertion of divine right, in complete exclusivism through the keys of Peter. Thus the Proclamation required to be made by each Spanish captain on landing was not only utterly logical, but necessary. *And,* when each captain landed, Montejo or other, he believed fully in the *legality* of his act, and of that proclamation, harsh as it seems to us today. So also did Landa and López and their Franciscans, believe their acts (however abhorrent to our sensibilities today) were implacably necessary in order to root out the ' demon's ' control over the Americas. The syllogism is simply:

God created the universe and the world, even to putting the salt into the rain-water to fill the lagoons on the north shore of Yucatan; therefore he owned it, and also made provision for its conduct and salvation, that identical thing which Landa in his epilogue calls the " justice and *peace* " ! ! that Spain brought to America. Then he appointed his Church to guide and *govern* it, not only factually but necessarily universal and exclusive. When Philip II issued his famous decree condemning at one stroke the entire population of Holland to death, he was entirely logical just as much so as when Mussolini, claiming the Mediterranean says there shall not be a center of opposite ideology maintaining itself at Barcelona. For there is only one possible answer to the principle of ' divine right ' and that is the denial that it is of divine origin.

We are told by all that in the oldest days, under the almost legendary Itzá rule, the Mayas worshipped *One* Supreme ' God,' formless, and without images. As to the Egyptian with his life-giving Nile, his wheat fields and Ra, the life-giving sun, to the American, ' god ' was the ever-acting beneficent force above and behind nature, and life, life of every kind. The Mayas had two actual words that show this: **bail** is the physicality of things, and **lail** the ' inner essence,' in Spanish the *ser interior,* the inner being. Now when by centuries of slavery, and the wiping out of those who taught him in this, the **ah-miatzil** or scientists and the **chilánes** or proclaimers, you reduce his conception of ' God ' to that of a being who *gave* him and his lands to the King of Spain, telling him that that is God, and there is no ' God ' save that; then when after centuries of powerlessness and with all ' news ' of any other view shut out, and *kept* out by the Bull of Paul III, given as in his favor, in 1537, he at last comes to the era of the *científico* rule under Díaz, is ground by it to the last degree of exploitation and loss of even the individual farm and town ownerships that had survived somehow through the ' years of darkness and evil ' the Chumayel manuscript tells us about, *and then revolts,* nothing is more certain than that for a while he will revolt against the whole scheme, and for a while say " there is no God," as Job was urged to do. But you can no more make the Indian an atheist than his comforters could Job; it just cannot be done. And thus it is no more nor less than a sin against man to tell the Indian that his ' commun*al*ism,' his restored cooperative social order, which *is* social order, is ' communism,' the denial of private ownership, and atheism; the two concepts have no relation, except through the false syllogism of universality and exclusivism, to support the ' divine right ' claim.

That the principle itself is at issue appears in our very present ' affaire Landa,' in the work of Molina Solís. Outside of Justin Winsor's *Narrative and Critical History,* we have hardly a work in the United States to compare with his on the *History of Yucatan,* for pure scholarship in the real sense, for fair and unbiassed treatment of his facts. Himself an element in the aristocratic Díaz régime, with his family made wealthy by the new-found ' green gold,' the sisal hemp that with cattle and sugar turned the last screws on Indian independence, he is unsparing in his condemnation of Landa, both humanely and legally. And yet he defends and believes in the López Ordinances for the ecclesiastical regimentation of all Indian life, for the plain reason that he believed in that ideology. My personal remembrances of him are those of a charming scholar, a delightful man, and I imagine too a lovable man (not at all like Audomaro, who just was *not*). I think he was kindly (a rather rare quality), and that in his heart he worshipped that which we refer to as ' God,' but he wrapped it up, legalistically, in the keys of Peter; hence the accepted ' beneficence ' of the López regulations. Of course he also thought of the Indians as a subject, certainly inferior race, really bene-fitted by having Spanish people in charge for the reformation of their lack of a civilized life.

As will appear somewhat in the Xiu Papers to follow in this volume, once the Landas and Pachecos had been curbed in their worst excesses (even by complete depopulation in much of eastern Yucatan) and the Mayas, power-less, had accepted without forgetting, things did not go so unbearably badly in the back-waters of Yucatan; and even at the coming of colonial independ-ence there came the Sanjuanistas, of white local blood, declaring that the country did and should belong to the Mayas. The uprising of 1847, Santa Ana and the seizure and sale of Mayas in Cuba to recoup quite cynically the State treasury, passed. But then came the needs of our modern machine and corporate age. In imitation of our Homestead Laws, to allow individual settlement on quarter sections of government lands, under Díaz came a pat-terned law of ' denunciation to private ownership of vacant lands.' But the object and results were different; any one could denounce any amount, by posting a notice in the near cabildo. Soon the Indian lands they had farmed individually or collectively from before the Conquest, passed before their owners had heard of the ' notice,' to create the great landed cattle ranches of the north, the hemp haciendas of Yucatan, the sugar lands of Morelos, where at the time of the Madero revolt practically every bit of arable land in the whole state was *owned* by a few great landholders, and the Church. And that struck the issue. Were there excesses? Of course; excessive abuse of concentrated power, and especially with the throttling power of great corporate extension, affecting production and distribution on a nation-wide scale (whether divine-royal or business-corporate) always at the end brings excesses in the outburst. After which excesses subside, comes the conflict of ideologies.

It is thus by understanding Landa, the Proclamation and the Ordinances, and the town-burnings and removals of 1550, that we can understand better *their reactions* today, on both continents: the one Spain took and failed to hold, and the one in which she fights in herself the same conflict of national ideas. People call them ' religious issues,' and make a religious war out of them, in defense of power just as they were in Yucatan; but they are not so in final fact, not matters of religion but only of dogma, on the surface, and of social and economic rights here on earth, where we have to live and work to produce.

It is also by seeing the same ideologies, supported by the same elements on the two sides, before us today, that we can further form a better idea of what the Yucatan of pre-Landa Mayadom was, and suffered. The story is implicit in the Map.

Our own view of the subject would not be complete, nor would we be historically just to Diego de Landa himself, did we not here give the legal grounds on which rested the ecclesiastical controversy that caused his being sent to Spain for trial before the Council. These are wholly clear, are undisputed and attested by the surviving original documents and letters.

At the beginning Leo X and Adrian VI gave various privileges to the religious orders, whose members are usually referred to as *los religiosos*, ' the religious,' or members of the orders, as distinguished from the priests or regular clergy of the apostolic church; the first were *fraters,* friars, brothers of the Orders, the second were padres, fathers of their flocks. The Orders were governed by their custodians, provincials, and general; the second constituted the consecrated hierarchy, the priests, bishops and at their head the Supreme Pontiff, deriving in ' apostolic succession,' from the apostles, and in whose hands thus lay the ' power to bind and to loose,' to excommunicate and to absolve. This passing down of a consecrated succession is and always has been an essential part of any priesthood, Roman, Brahmanical, or ' pagan.' The religious orders, being of later human constitution, though accepted divine approval as ' missionary bodies,' with the task of conversion and teaching as a preparation for the consecration of baptism, did not share the ' apostolic ' succession, as integral in the church constitution as is the principle of heredity in a peerage or monarchy. Thus in the Middle Ages when the system was complete, and unquestioned until the Reformation, and both spiritual and temporal sovereignty came through the single channel, the consecration by anointing of the monarch was as necessary upon his succession as it was to the bishop upon his appointment; and this is what gives point to the Provincial, Landa's message to Bishop Toral on his landing at Campeche in August 1562, that if he had been consecrated, he, Landa would recognize him; otherwise not. The following events, and the whole Landa controversy, with its far-reaching consequences, are only understandable in the light of the above facts.

These orders and privileges of Leo and Adrian were then amplified by Paul III, in the Bull of Feb. 15, 1535. Then later that year, in November the bishops of Mexico, Oaxaca and Guatemala met and wrote the Emperor to solicit the ' plenary authority ' for them through his ambassador at Rome. This *autoridad omnimoda,* or plenary authority, then involved the right of the bishops, the consecrated apostolic body as above, to call on the civil power for aid in rooting out heresy, the particular task of the Holy Office, the Inquisition. It was the illegal assumption of this authority, especially when accompanied by such brutalities on the Indians, who were by ecclesiastical law not subject to the Inquisition, being ' infants in the faith,' just as minors of tender age are not under criminal but only paternal care, which sent Landa to Spain for trial.

The members of the orders had meanwhile been seeking for themselves special ' emergency ' rights for the use of plenary authority in distant places, where the episcopal hierarchy was afar off or unavailable, or not yet appointed. (It corresponded quite to our own emergency legislation, sought ' even if of doubtful constitutionality,' on the basis of the 'public good,' and the hope that once granted it might somehow stick and come to justify itself, and be credited with returning prosperity, and the expulsion of the ' demon ' of depression.) In the interval, however, in June 1537 Paul III sent out another Bull, especially in the Indians' *favor* and protection. This concluded:

That under pain of excommunication by sentence carried, *latae sententiae*, no apostate shall presume to go to these parts (the Indies), so that the *Indians* be not infected and perverted by bad examples. The *bishops* shall see that all such apostates are expelled from their dioceses, that they may not deprave and deceive souls tender in the faith.

Elsewhere the ' apostates ' are referred to as *'ateistas luteranos.'* This rule that no apostate, and above all no 'judaizing heretic,' could come to or remain in Spanish America under penalty of expulsion or death, remained the law until colonial independence, and the same total intolerance was even one of the three major principles of the short Iturbide reactionary ' Empire ' in Mexico. But also, it was this very Bull on which the religious friars sought to rest their emergency Inquisitional claims, by an interpretation they claimed as its necessary meaning and expansion. But in this they never gained their point, although over in Mexico a certain friar, one Augustin de la Coruba, hunting for a ' concealed ' idol, assumed the *autoridad omnimoda,* constituted himself inquisitor, built a great fire in the plaza and threatened to burn the town governor and the *whole town* alive, unless they showed him the idol.

The matter then came to formal consideration, and on April 27, 1539, the four bishops met in Mexico, among other things took note of the claims by the friars to authority in derogation of the bishops, and ordered that *whipping and flogging should not be used to enforce obedience to the church, or in matters of faith.* All three of the Orders were also present, and signed the procedure. While this did not of course abolish the Inquisition itself, it put a definite ban on all the acts of the friars with which we have to do in the present work. This was then two years before the youth Diego de Landa entered the Franciscan order, at the age of 17; also before Montejo reached Ti-ho, established Merida, and "by the aid of the Xius of Maní, began the tributes." See besides the letter of this same Kukum, Montejo Xiu, the Lord of Maní, and others, to the king, in 1567.

Nevertheless, in the Audiencia at Guatemala was the Franciscan, Tomás López, and Landa having procured copies of the above-mentioned Bulls of Leo and Adrian, the friars of his convent at Izamal reported to the Audiencia that in the service of God it was necessary that they have the aid of the public officials in punishing cases which the bishops were under obligation to take on, and they got from the Audiencia a decree allowing the friars to act in the bishop's place, in the matters in the said Bulls. This the friars did; appeals to Mexico were denied, on the ground that only appeal to Rome could be had. Landa also established prisons in the other convents than his own, and appointed judges of the Holy Office, ordering that they procede *por via de inquisición.* On this then came on the events we are considering. Declaring himself "*apostolic* judge," (see above), and inquisitor under the said Bulls of 1535, he proceeded without process or previous informations, or any other steps, to imprison all Indians whom he *thought might be guilty of idolatry.* See the letter of the notary Contreras to Toral, that all this was without previous informations, and based on forced confessions under torture and fear of death; also his report on those *killed under torture,* with their names; also the many left without arms or hands to eat with, to say nothing of those who fled or hung themselves. And further the letter of Father Bienvenida on these events, and the letters herein at pages 119 to 125, for the effects on the country.

Then Toral arrived, himself a Franciscan, but officially as bishop. Lodged in a Franciscan convent he was so treated that he had to remove to the house of a civilian. Of his action we have told elsewhere; it is to be read in his letter to Bienvenida, commissary general of the Franciscans in Guatemala, and especially in Toral's letter of March 3, 1564, to the king, still in the royal archives (if Franco's guns have not yet destroyed them). Therein he says:

Most of the caciques imprisoned in the monastery at Mérida, and all of the towns in revolt. Remained to investigate until the end of April; freed the innocent from prison and sent them home, although many died in the city, and others when they got home, from the tortures imposed. Remitted the slavery of others, up to ten years service to Spaniards, as such slaves; also removed the sambenitos the friars had compelled them to wear. They had been condemned of things they were innocent of, solely on their own confessions under torture and fear of death; justice and right availed nothing, the cause being that the friars " were men of little learning and less charity " — *pocas letras y menor caridad.*

Landa, sent to Spain for trial, was condemned severely by the Council of the Indies, but his case was referred to a committee of learned doctors, including his own Tomás López, and after the necessary delays, he was absolved. Thus from 1562 to 1573 he remained in Spain, until, Toral having died in

Mexico as related above, in 1572 the "learned friar Diego," his work written, returned as bishop to his provincialate of Yucatan.

Then, still untamed, and "absolved," he again began his efforts for conversion, and the eradication of the ancient ways. First he sent Fuente Ovejuna out, who continued the floggings, "in matters of faith." Then himself followed with his own visits, resulting again in appeals for the Indians to Mexico for *amparo*, 'relief.' This the Royal Audiencia granted, on August 12, 1574, setting out therefor the *royal cédula* of four years before, before Landa had become bishop or left Spain, under date of Sept. 4, 1570, prohibiting the friars from having prison cells in the monasteries, shaving the heads or flogging, and ordering those held in prison set free.

In 1557 the conference at Maní took place, settling the boundaries of the western Maya chiefdoms, those of Maní, of Canul and Maxcanú, of those of Sotuta, and of Calotmul in Cochuah; see pages 132-4.

We have said above that all Indian life has been communal, in those activities that supply the essentials of existence, and also in those seasonal and other festivals that express them, become a full and socially satisfying part of the life and ways, and put joy into the labor of supplying these needs. This social order is founded on the natural use of nature's resources, adjusted to the environment; it creates the 'honorable tea, the honorable rice' of the Chinese, just as in more sophisticated communities it creates the afternoon tea without which life is not, to the Briton; it is the most conservative of all human forces, just because it is rooted in nature herself, and you can change the external expression of religion easier than you can shift this; it obeys the Galton law and becomes the personality of the local life, because it *is* the local life. It renders obeisance to the earth, the waters and the sky by which the community lives.

Now the food of the Indian race, at least of North and Middle America, is maize, which quickly exhausts the nitrogen, and in the usual milpa agriculture of burning over, and without restorative crop rotations to renew the soil (such as the new education of the Mexican rural Government schools is now introducing) requires long fallow periods of grown-up 'bush,' and changes of site. Thus for more centuries than our history knows, the agricultural town units of this region have had *town-owned* communal districts, called their *ejidos*, sufficient for, and near enough to, the town to whose members belongs the right of *use*. With those town-lands, the Indian is a freeman; take them away as was done in the reachable and exploitable parts of Mexico under the Díaz period, the people become wage-paid serfs of the soil and the hacienda. They must take what is offered them, take what is done to them, or try to escape (where?) and leave the place that has been home to them and theirs. But that home stability, as with the French peasant whose ancestors have farmed the land he still *owns*, or the Chinese in like case, for actually hundreds and many hundreds of years, spells sturdy strength and peace, with a genuine reverence for the sun and the soil and the waters; break it up, and it spells the unrest of him who has no home to keep him, with the pleasure of its building and its keeping, and its protection, to him, and by him; and then in necessary sequence, however delayed, revolt.

One Maya town I have at various times visited, the one in fact which sent forth its surplus to found other town units (among them **Chan-kom**, or ' Little Valley '), held its town titles, known and recorded in its own archives, each by name, to *twenty-seven* such *ejidos*. Now take that picture, and those facts in mind, and consider the unspeakable sudden uprootings of the townsfolk, houses and goods burned over their heads that six, seven, thirteen even, such self-sustaining towns might be moved to " more convenient doctrination " centers and be at hand to build the convents on the sites of their ancient shrines. It is there that lies the inner story of Landa's Yucatan, " before and after the conquest," as he found it, and as he left it, in the fragmentary story of the thirty years from '49 to '79, to which this volume is devoted.

The original manuscript of Landa's Relation has long disappeared; as shown by the irregular numbering of the chapters (practically none of whose headings are in the manuscript we have, but are due to Brasseur and for their convenience have been kept) and references to omitted statements or sections, it must have been materially longer. The copy we have is a shortened transcript, although bearing what is quite surely the original date of the year it was written, 1566; see for the evidence of this the chapter on the annual calendar.

The present copy also had long been unknown until it was discovered in Madrid by the untiring Brasseur de Bourbourg, to whom we owe the preservation of more original documents on Maya, or Mayance, languages and history than we do to all others combined. It was translated, annotated, with a long introduction, by him in Paris in 1864. This however stopped at sec. XLII, on the Edifices.

A new annotated French translation was published in 1928-9, but it also, due to the untimely death of its scholarly editor Jean Genet, stopped with sec. XLI, on the system of writing. Two Spanish, unannotated editions appeared, one in Madrid in 1884 as an appendix in a now very scarce volume containing a translation of a work by the French Americanist, Léon de Rosny, and the other in the second volume of the *Relaciones de Yucatan*, to which we refer at length in our final chapter on the period from '49 to '79. No edition has yet appeared in English.

The illustrations herein have been drawn from whatever sources were apt and available. Some are from unpublished photographs by Teoberto Maler, taken 50 years ago, which I have had for over twenty years; most of the small marginals from the Dresden and Madrid hieroglyphic codices, with a few from the Aztec; the two of structures at Maní were redrawn after Catherwood; others from illustrations we have courteously been allowed to use by the American Museum of Natural History, the University Museum at Philadelphia, and the U. S. National Museum, who have with a very gracious liberality taken for me photographs of many objects needed to illustrate artifacts, models, etc.; also the like courtesies shown by the Field Museum, the Carnegie Institution at Washington, Mr. T. A. Willard of Beverly Hills, and Major George Oakley Totten of Washington. To Dr. Elizabeth Stewart finally, I owe the identification of the Maya plant names appearing in the text.

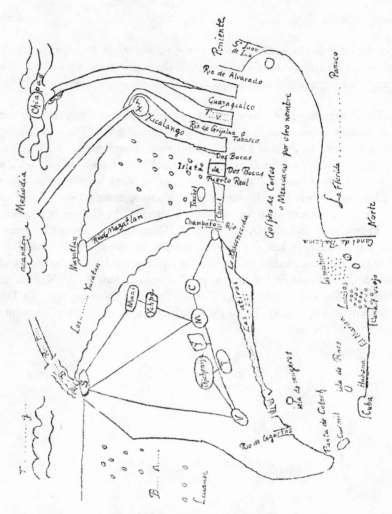

Key to above Map

The wording in full is as follows, place names being extended as here given.

From the Point of Cotoch to Puerto Real is 130 leagues in length. The Point of Cotoch is one less than *xx* degrees. The mouth of Puerto Real is more than *xxiii* degrees. From Yucatan to the island of Cuba is *ix* leagues.

Cuzmil is an island 15 leagues long and *v* wide in *xx* degrees of this part of the equinoctial.

The island of Mugeres is *xiii* or *xiiii* leagues below the point of Cotoch, separated from *toracolvo* (?) two leagues. Chicheniza is ten leagues from Izamal and *xi* from Valladolid.

S: Salamanca. **V**: Valladolid. **Chicheniza**: an ancient settlement of Yucatan and where Montejo first settled. **T**: town of Tikoch. **Y**: Yzamal, ancient town. **M**: Merida which anciently was Tiho. **C**: ancient town called Calkini. **Mani**: city of the king and *bue*°. **Ychpa**: the ancient city of Ychpa.

Tg: Land they call of war. **EB**: Straits of Bacalar. **RT**: Rivers of Tahiza. **Los Y**: The uninhabited part of Yucatan. **BA**: Baia de Ascension. **Las atiras**: The strips that traverse the length of the coast, Zilam, Kichal, Caukel and Alzibo. **TV**: Tavasco, villa de la Victoria. **La Florida** and its rivers and ports discovered as far as Panuco.

YUCATAN

BEFORE AND AFTER THE CONQUEST

BY

FRIAR DIEGO DE LANDA

SEC. I. DESCRIPTION OF YUCATAN. VARIETY OF SEASONS.

Yucatan is not an island, nor a point entering the sea, as some thought, but mainland. This error came about from the fact that the sea goes from Cape Cotoche along the Ascension passage to the Golfo Dulce on the one side, and on the other side facing Mexico, by the Desconocida before coming to Campeche, and then forming the lagoons by Puerto Real and Dos Bocas.

The land is very flat and clear of mountains, so that it is not seen from ships until they come very close; with the exception that between Campeche and Champotón there are some low ranges and a headland that is called Los Diablos.

As one comes from Veracruz toward Cape Cotoch, one finds himself at less than 20 degrees, and at the mouth of Puerto Real it is more than 23; from one point to the other it should be over a hundred and thirty leagues, direct road. The coast is low-lying, so that large ships must stay at some distance from the shore.

The coast is very full of rocks and rough points that wear the ships' cables badly; there is however much mud, so that even if ships go ashore they lose few people.

The tides run high, especially in the Bay of Campeche, and the sea often leaves, at some places, half a league exposed; as a result there are left in the seaweed and mud and pools many small fish that serve the people for their food.

A small range crosses Yucatan from one corner to the other starting near Champotón and running to the town of Salamanca in the opposite angle. This range divides Yucatan into two parts, of which that to the south toward Lacandón and Taiza* is uninhabited for lack of water, except when it rains. The northern part is inhabited.

This land is very hot and the sun burns fiercely, although there are fresh breezes like those from the northeast and east, which are frequent, together

---

* Tah-Itzá, the country of the Itzás, around Lake Petén.

with an evening breeze from the sea. People live long in the country, and men of a hundred and forty years have been known.

The winter begins with St. Francis day,* and lasts until the end of March; during this time the north winds prevail and cause severe colds and catarrh from the insufficient clothing the people wear. The end of January and February bring a short hot spell, when it does not rain except at the change of the moon. The rains come on from April until through September, during which time the crops are sown and mature despite the constant rain. There is also sown a certain kind of maize at St. Francis, which is harvested early.

SEC. II. ETYMOLOGY OF THE NAME OF THIS PROVINCE. ITS SITUATION.

This province is called in the language of the Indians **Ulumil cuz yetel ceh,** meaning ' the land of the turkey and the deer.' It is also called **Petén,** meaning ' island,' an error arising from the gulfs and bays we have spoken of.†

When Francisco Hernández de Córdoba came to this country and landed at the point he called Cape Cotoch, he met certain Indian fisherfolk whom he asked what country this was, and who answered **Cotoch,** which means ' our houses, our homeland,' for which reason he gave that name to the cape. When he then by signs asked them how the land was theirs, they replied **Ci uthan,** meaning ' they say it,' ‡ and from that the Spaniards gave the name Yucatan. This was learned from one of the early conquerors, Blas Hernández, who came here with the admiral on the first occasion.

In the southern part of Yucatan are the rivers of Taiza (Tah-Itzá) and the mountains of Lacandón, and between the south and west lies the province of Chiapas; to pass thither one must cross four streams that descend from the mountains and unite with others to form the San Pedro y San Pablo river discovered by Grijalva in Tabasco. To the west lie Xicalango and Tabasco, one and the same province.

Between this province of Tabasco and Yucatan there are two sea mouths breaking the coast; the largest of these forms a vast lagoon, while the other is of less extent. The sea enters these mouths with such fury as to create a great lake abounding in fish of all kinds, and so full of islets that the Indians put signs on the trees to mark the way going or coming by boat from Tabasco to Yucatan. These islands with their shores and sandy beaches have so great a variety of seafowl as to be a matter of wonder and beauty; there is an infinite amount of game: deer, hare, the wild pigs of that country, and

---

* October 4th.   † **Petén** properly means district, region, circuit.
‡ In common use today in Yucatan, meaning ' he speaks nicely, well.'

monkeys as well, which are not found in Yucatan. The number of iguanas is astonishing. On one island is a town called **Tixchel.**

To the north is the island of Cuba, with Havana facing at a distance of 60 leagues; somewhat further on is a small island belonging to Cuba, which they call Isla de Pinos. At the east lies Honduras, between which and Yucatan is a great arm of the sea that Grijalva called Ascension Bay; this is filled with islets on which many boats are wrecked, especially those in the trade between Yucatan and Honduras. Fifteen years ago a ship laden with many people and goods foundered, and all were drowned save one Majuelas and four others, who seized hold of a great piece of wood from the ship, and thus went three or four days without reaching any of the islets until their strength gave out and all sank except Majuelas. He came out half dead and recovered himself eating snails and shellfish; then from the islet he reached the mainland on a balsa or raft which he made as best he could out of branches. Having come to land, and while hunting for food, he came upon a crab that bit off his thumb at the first joint, and caused him intense pain. Thence he set out through difficult bush to try to reach Salamanca, and when night came he climbed a tree from which he saw a great tiger waylay and kill a deer; then when morning came he ate what the tiger had left.

In front of Yucatan, somewhat below Cape Cotoch, lies **Cuzmil** (Cozumel), across a 5-league channel where the sea runs with a strong current between the mainland and the island. Cozumel is an island fifteen leagues long by five wide. The Indians are few in number, and of the same language and customs as those of Yucatan. It lies at the 20th degree of latitude. Thirteen leagues below Point Cotoch is the Isla de las Mugeres, 2 leagues off the coast opposite **Ekab.**

Photo by Maler

ISLA DE LAS MUGERES

SEC. III. CAPTIVITY OF GERONIMO DE AGUILAR. EXPEDITION
OF HERNANDEZ DE CORDOBA AND GRIJALVA TO YUCATAN.

It is said that the first Spaniards to come to Yucatan were Gerónimo de Aguilar, a native of Ecija, and his companions. These, in 1511, upon the break-up at Darien resulting from the dissensions between Diego de Nicueza and Vasco Núñez de Balboa, followed Valdivia on his voyage in a caravel to San Domingo, to give account to the admiral and the governor, and to bring 20,000 ducats of the king's. On the way to Jamaica the caravel grounded on the shoals known as the Viboras, where it was lost with all but twenty men. These went with Valdivia in a boat without sails, and only some poor oars and no provisions, and were at sea for thirteen days. After nearly half of them had died of hunger, the rest reached the coast of Yucatan at a province called that of the Maya, whence the language of Yucatan is known as **Mayat'an,** meaning the ' Maya speech.'

These poor fellows fell into the hands of a bad cacique, who sacrificed Valdivia and four others to their idols, and served them in a feast to the people. Aguilar and Guerrero and five or six others he saved to fatten. These broke their prison and came to another chief who was an enemy of the first, and more merciful; he made them his slaves, and his successor treated them with much kindness. However, all died of grief, save only Gerónimo de Aguilar and Gonzalo Guerrero. Of these Aguilar was a good Christian and had a breviary, by which he kept count of the feast days and finally escaped on the arrival of the Marquis Hernando Cortés, in 1519.

Guerrero learned the language and went to Chectemal (Chetumal), which is Salamanca de Yucatan. Here he was received by a chief named **Nachan Can,** who placed in his charge his military affairs; in these he did well and conquered his master's enemies many times. He taught the Indians to fight, showing them how to make barricades and bastions. In this way, and by living as an Indian, he gained a great reputation and married a woman of high quality, by whom he had children, and he made no attempt to escape with Aguilar. He decorated his body, let his hair grow, pierced his ears to wear rings like the Indians, and is believed to have become an idolater like them.

During Lent of 1517 Francisco Hernández de Córdoba sailed from Cuba with three ships to procure slaves for the mines, as the population of Cuba

---

* The ghastly chapter of the fate of the peaceful population of Cuba has been elsewhere told, and we have here one of its early evidences. But the Cubans were fortunate—it was at least quick total extermination. The Mayas were to live through 400 years of seizures for sale abroad, resettlements and forced removals from their towns, to receive their conquerors' religion, or to add to his wealth and ease.

was diminishing.* Others say he sailed to discover new lands. Taking Alaminos as a pilot he landed on Isla de las Mugeres, to which he gave this name because of the idols he found there, of the goddesses of the country, **Aixchel, Ixchebeliax, Ixhunié, Ixhunieta,** vestured from the girdle down, and having the breasts covered after the manner of the Indians. The building was of stone, such as to astonish them; and they found certain objects of gold, which they took. Arriving at Cape Cotoch they directed their course to the Bay of Campeche, where they disembarked on Lazarus Sunday, whence they called the place Lazaro. They were well received by the chief and the Indians marveled at seeing the Spaniards, touching their beards and persons.

At Campeche they found a building in the sea near to the land, all square and in steps, on the top of which was an idol with two fierce animals devouring his flanks; also a great thick serpent swallowing a lion; the animals were covered with the blood of sacrifices. At Campeche they learned of a large town nearby, which was Champotón; landing there they found a chief named **Moch-Covoh,** a warlike man who called his people together against the Spaniards. Francisco Hernández was much disturbed seeing in this what must happen; but not to show a less spirit he put his men in order and had the artillery fired from the ships. The Indians however, notwithstanding the strange sound, smoke and fire of the guns, attacked with great cries; the Spaniards resisted, inflicting severe wounds and killing many. Nevertheless the chief so inspired his people that they forced the Spaniards to retire, killing twenty, wounding fifty, and taking alive two whom they afterwards sacrificed. Francisco Hernández came off with thirty-three wounds, and thus returned downcast to Cuba, where he reported that the land was good and rich, because of the gold he found on the Isla de las Mugeres.

These stories moved Diego Velásquez, governor of Cuba, as well as many others, so that he sent his nephew Juan de Grijalva with four ships and 200 men. With him went Francisco de Montejo, to whom one ship belonged, the expedition sailing on the 1st of May, 1518.

They took with them the same Alaminos as pilot, and landed on the island of Cozumel, from which the pilot descried the coast of Yucatan which with Francisco Hernández he had previously coasted along, on the right hand going south. Desiring to see whether it was an island, they turned left and followed by the bay they called Ascension, because of entering it on that day. Then turning back they followed the whole coast until they reached Champotón for the second time; landing here for water, one man was killed and fifty wounded, among them Grijalva, who received two arrows and lost a tooth and a half. In this maner they departed and named the harbor the Puerto de Mala Pelea. On this voyage they discovered New Spain, Pánuco and Tabasco, where they stayed for five months, and also tried to make a landing at Champotón.   This the Indians resisted with such spirit as to come out close to the ships in their canoes, in order to shoot their arrows.   So they made sail and departed.

When Grijalva returned from his voyage of discovery and trade in Tabasco and Ulúa, the great captain Hernando Cortés was in Cuba; and he on the news of such a country and such riches, conceived the desire of seeing it, and even of acquiring it for God, for his king, for himself, and for his friends.

SEC. IV.   EXPEDITION OF CORTES TO COZUMEL.   LETTER TO AGUILAR AND HIS FRIENDS.

Hernando Cortés sailed from Cuba with eleven ships, the largest being of 100 tons burden, placing in them eleven captains, and himself being one of these.   He took along 500 men, some horses, and goods for barter, having Francisco de Montejo as a captain and Alaminos as chief pilot of the armada. On the admiral's ship he set a banner of white and blue in honor of Our Lady, whose image, together with the cross, he always placed wherever he destroyed idols.   On the banner was a red cross surrounded by a legend reading: *Amici sequamur crucem, et si habuerimus fidem, in hoc signo vincemus.*

With this fleet and no further equipment he set sail and arrived at Cozumel with ten ships, one becoming separated in a storm; he however recovered it later on the coast.   They arrived at Cozumel on the north, where they found fine buildings of stone for the idols, and a fine town; but the inhabitants seeing so great a fleet and the soldiers disembarking, all fled to the woods.

On reaching the town the Spaniards sacked it and lodged themselves. Seeking through the woods for the natives they came on the chief's wife and children.   Through an Indian interpreter named Melchior, who had been with Francisco Hernández and Grijalva, they learned it was the chief's wife, to whom and the children Cortés gave presents and caused them to send for the chief.   Him on his arrival he treated very well, gave him some small gifts and returned to him his wife and children, with all the things that had been taken in the town; and begged him to have the Indians return to their houses, saying that when they came everything that had been taken away from them would be restored.   When they were thus restored, he preached to them the vanity of idols, and persuaded them to adore the cross; this he placed in their temples with an image of Our Lady, and therewith public idolatry ceased.

Here Cortés learned that there were bearded men six days away, in the power of a chief, and persuaded the Indians to send a messenger to summon them.   With difficulty he found one that would go, because of the fear they had of the chief of the bearded men.   He then wrote this letter:

Noble sirs: I left Cuba with a fleet of eleven ships and 500 Spaniards, and laid up at Cozumel, whence I write this letter. Those of the island have assured me that there are in the country five or six men with beards and resembling us in all things. They are unable to give or tell me other indications, but from these I conjecture and hold certain that you are Spaniards. I and these gentlemen who go with me to settle and discover these lands urge that within six days from receiving this you come to us, without making further delay or excuse. If you shall come we will make due acknowledgment, and reward the good offices which this armada shall receive from you. I send a brigantine that you may come in it, and two boats for safety.

The Indians took this letter wrapped in their hair, and gave it to Aguilar. But the Indians delaying beyond the time appointed, those on the ships believed them killed, and returned to the port of Cozumel. Cortés then seeing that neither the Indians nor the bearded men returned, set sail the next day. On that day, however, a ship sprung a leak and it was necessary to return to port. While the repairs were being made Aguilar, having received the letter, crossed the channel between Yucatan and Cozumel in a canoe; when those of the fleet seeing him approach went to see who it was, Aguilar asked whether they were Christians. When they answered Yes, and Spaniards, he wept for joy and falling on his knees gave thanks to God. He then asked the Spaniards if it was Wednesday.

The Spaniards took him all naked as he was to Cortés, who clothed him and treated him with much affection; and Aguilar related there * his peril and labors, and the death of his companions, and how it was impossible to send word to Guerrero in so short a time, he being more than eighty leagues away.

Aguilar having told his story, and being an excellent interpreter, Cortés renewed the preaching of the adoration of the cross, and put the idols out of the temples; and they say that this preaching by Cortés made such an impression on those of Cuzco † that they came out to the shore saying to the Spaniards who passed: " Maria, Maria, Cortés, Cortés."

Cortés departed thence, touched Campeche in passing, but did not make a stop until he reached Tabasco. Here among other presents and Indian

---

* The pleasant Sunday supplement story of the beautiful maiden, and the temptation arranged for Aguilar by the chief, which of course must have first been given currency by Aguilar himself, as related by Cogolludo, has probably been repeated by every succeeding chronicler. It is a bit hard to visualize, even when buttressed by his reported words on meeting Cortés' men, asking the Spaniards if they were Christians, and then verifying his devotion to his breviary by asking if it was Wednesday. But beside it should be set off a curiously surviving manuscript, dated Mexico, 1554, in support of a petition for payment for military services under Cortés, by one Cristóbal Doria, of Oaxaca, the husband by a " legitimate church marriage" with Luisa, the natural daughter of Gerónimo de Aguilar, had by him, " an unmarried bachelor, and free," by an unnamed Tarascan woman.

† So in the ms., but clearly an error for Cuzamil.

women which those of Tabasco gave to him was one who was afterwards
called Marina. She was from Xalisco, a daughter of noble parents, stolen
when small and sold in Tabasco, and later sold in Xicalango and Champotón,
where she learned the language of Yucatan. By this she was able to understand Aguilar, and thus God provided Cortés with good and faithful inter-
preters, through whom he acquired knowledge and intimacy with Mexican
matters. With these Marina was well posted, having mingled with Indian
merchants and leading people, who spoke of them daily.

SEC. V. PROVINCES OF YUCATAN. ITS PRINCIPAL ANCIENT STRUCTURES.

Some old men of Yucatan say that they have heard from their ancestors
that this country was peopled by a certain race who came from the East,
whom God delivered by opening for them twelve roads through the sea.
If this is true, all the inhabitants of the Indies must be of Jewish descent
because, the straits of Magellan having been passed, they must have spread
over more than 2000 leagues of territory now governed by Spain.

The language of this country is all one, a fact which aided greatly in its
conversion, although along the coasts there are differences in words and
accents. Those living on the coast are thus more polished in their behavior
and language; and the women cover their breasts, which those further inland
do not.

The country is divided into provinces subject to the nearest Spanish settle-
ment. The province of **Chectemal** and **Bak-halal** is subject to Salamanca.
The provinces of **Ekab**, of **Cochuah** and of **Cupul** are subject to Valladolid.
Those of **Ahkin-Chel** and of **Izamal**, of **Sututa**, of **Hocabaihumun**, of
Tutuxiu, of **Cehpech**, and of **Chakan**, are attached to the city of Mérida;
Camol (Canul), **Campech**, **Champutun** and **Tixchel** are assigned to San
Francisco de Campeche.

There are in Yucatan many edifices of great beauty, this being the most
outstanding of all things discovered in the Indies; they are all built of stone
finely ornamented, though there is no metal found in the country for this
cutting. These buildings are very close to each other and are temples, the
reason for there being so many lying in the frequent changes of the population, and the fact that in each town they erected a temple, out of the
abundance of stone and lime, and of a certain white earth excellent for
buildings.

These edifices are not the work of other peoples, but of the Indians themselves, as appears by stone figures of men, unclothed but with the middle

covered by certain long fillets which in their language are called **ex,** together with other devices worn by the Indians.

While the author of this work was in that country, there was found in a building that had been demolished a large urn with three handles, painted on the outside with silvered colors, and containing the ashes of a cremated body, together with some pieces of the arms and legs, of an unbelievable size, and with three fine beads or counters of the kind the Indians use for money. At Izamal there were eleven or twelve of these buildings in all, with no memory of their builders; on the site of one of these, at the instance of the Indians, there was established the monastery of San Antonio, in the year 1550.

Photo by George Oakley Totten

THE CENOTE OF SACRIFICE AT CHICHEN ITZA

The next most important edifices are those of Tikoch and of Chichén Itzá, which will be described later. Chichén Itzá is finely situated ten leagues from Izamal and eleven from Valladolid, and they tell that it was ruled by three lords, brothers that came to the country from the West. These were very devout, built very handsome temples, and lived unmarried and most honorably. One of them either died or went away, whereupon the others conducted themselves unjustly and wantonly, for which they were put to death. Later on we shall describe the decorations of the main edifice, also telling of the well into which they cast men alive as a sacrifice; and also other precious objects. It is over seven stages down to the water, over a hundred feet across and marvelously cut in the living rock. The water appears green, which they say is caused by the trees that surround it.

SEC. VI. CUCULCAN. FOUNDATION OF MAYAPAN.

The opinion of the Indians is that with the Itzás who settled Chichén Itzá there ruled a great lord named **Cuculcán,** as an evidence of which the principal building is called Cuculcán.

THE PYRAMID OF KUKULCAN

As restored by the Mexican Government, under the direction of Don Eduardo Martinez

They say that he came from the West, but are not agreed as to whether he came before or after the Itzás, or with them. They say that he was well disposed, that he had no wife or children, and that after his return he was regarded in Mexico as one of their gods, and called **Cezalcohuati** [Quetzalcóatl]. In Yucatan also he was reverenced as a god, because of his great services to the state, as appeared in the order which he established in Yucatan after the death of the chiefs, to settle the discord caused in the land by their deaths.

This Cuculcán, having entered into an agreement with the native lords of the country, undertook the founding of another city wherein he and they might live, and to which all matters and business should be brought. To this end he chose a fine site eight leagues further inland from where Mérida now lies, and some fifteen or sixteen from the sea. They surrounded the place with a very broad wall of dry stone some eighth of a league in extent, leaving only two narrow doorways; the wall itself was low. In the middle of the enclosure they

MAYAPAN

built their temples, calling the largest Cuculcán, the same as at Chichén Itzá. They built another circular temple, different from all others in the country, and with four entrances; also many others about them, connected one with the other. Within the enclosure they built houses for the lords alone, among whom the country was divided, assigning villages to each according to the antiquity of their lineage and their personal qualifications. Cuculcán did not call the city after himself, as was done by the **Ah-Itzaes** at Chichén Itzá (which means the ' Well of the Ah-Itzaes '), but called it Mayapán, meaning the ' Standard of the Mayas,' the language of the country being known as Maya. The Indians of today call it **Ich-pa,** meaning ' Within the Fortifications.'

After Catherwood

ROUND TOWER AT MAYAPAN

Cuculcán lived for some years in this city with the chiefs, and then leaving them in full peace and amity returned by the same road to Mexico. On the way he stopped at Champotón, and there in memorial of himself and his departure he erected in the sea, at a good stone's throw from the shore, a fine edifice similar to those at Chichén Itzá. Thus did Cuculcán leave a perpetual memory in Yucatan.

CARACOL AT CHICHEN ITZA

As uncovered under the care of the Carnegie Institution of Washington

SEC. VII. GOVERNMENT, PRIESTHOOD, SCIENCES, LETTERS AND BOOKS IN YUCATAN.

On the departure of Cuculcán the chiefs agreed that for the permanence of the state the house of the Cocoms should exercise the chief authority, it being the oldest and richest, or perhaps because its head was at that time a man of greater power. This done, they ordained that within the enclosure there should only be temples and residences of the chiefs, and of the High Priest; that they should build outside the walls dwellings where each of them might keep some serving people, and whither the people from the villages might come whenever they had business at the city. In these houses each one placed his mayordomo, who bore as his sign of authority a short thick baton, and who was called the **Caluac**. This officer held supervision over the villages and those in charge of them, to whom he sent advices as to the things needed in the chief's establishment, as birds, maize, honey, salt, fish, game, clothing and other things. The **Caluac** always attended in the chief's house, seeing what was needed and providing it promptly, his house standing as the office of his chief.

It was the custom to hunt out the crippled and the blind in the villages, and give them their necessities. The chiefs appointed the governors and, if worthy, confirmed their offices to their sons. They enjoined upon them good treatment of the common people, the peace of the community, and that all should be diligent in their own support and that of the lords.

Upon all the lords rested the duty of honoring, visiting and entertaining Cocom, accompanying and making festivals for him, and of repairing to him in difficult affairs. They lived in peace with each other, and with much diversion according to their custom, in the way of dances, feasts and hunting.

The people of Yucatan were as attentive to matters of religion as of government, and had a High Priest whom they called **Ahkin May**, or also **Ahaucan May**, meaning the Priest **May**, or the High Priest **May**. He was held in great reverence by the chiefs, and had no allotment of Indians for himself, the chiefs making presents to him in addition to the offerings, and all the local priests sending him contributions. He was succeeded in office by his sons or nearest kin. In him lay the key to their sciences, to which they most devoted themselves, giving counsel to the chiefs and answering their inquiries. With the matter of sacrifices he rarely took part, except on great festivals or business of much moment. He and his disciples appointed the priests for the towns, examining them in their sciences and ceremonies; put in their charge the affairs of their office, and the setting of a good example to the people; he provided their books and sent them forth. They in turn attended to the service of the temples, teaching their sciences and writing books upon them.

They taught the sons of the other priests, and the second sons of the chiefs, who were brought to them very young for this purpose, if they found them inclined toward this office.

The sciences which they taught were the reckoning of the years, months and days, the festivals and ceremonies, the administration of their sacraments, the omens of the days, their methods of divination and prophecies, events, remedies for sicknesses, antiquities, and the art of reading and writing by their letters and the characters wherewith they wrote, and by pictures that illustrated the writings.

3 ix, cauac, kan, muluc   Dresden, ḃ. 64

a   b   c   d

16 6   16 9   16 12   16

They wrote their books on a long sheet doubled in folds, which was then enclosed between two boards finely ornamented; the writing was on one side and the other, according to the folds. The paper they made from the roots of a tree, and gave it a white finish excellent for writing upon. Some of the principal lords were learned in these sciences, from interest, and for the greater esteem they enjoyed thereby; yet they did not make use of them in public.

* The text figure shows the general arrangement of the texts in both the Dresden and Madrid codices; that in the Paris codex and on the monuments was quite different.

Here, in section, or tzolkin 64 of the Dresden, we see the figure of Itzamná in four different activities, in each accompanied by one of the four major food animals, the turkey, iguana, fish and deer. Above each are four glyphs, the first identical save for the subfix element in the fourth column; this may be taken as an introductory to an invocation, or chanting rhythm, such as actually found in one of our most important Maya manuscripts, the *Ritual of the Bacabs*. The four glyphs across in the second line represent the North, West, South and East. In the next position we see the head as of a ' lord,' wearing a ceremonial banded headdress, preceded by the known signs for the four colors attached to the four Directions: White, Black, Yellow, Red. In the bottom row the repeated glyph of Itzamná, accepted as such from its constant occurrence above his figure as shown here.

Finally, since the *composition* of the original codex of which the existing ' Dresden codex ' is rather clearly a copy, is to be placed from its own internal evidence as relating to the moon and eclipse calculations finally worked out probably at Copan, about the year 750 A. D., the uncertainties involved in any effort to read this in the modern forms of Yucatecan Maya (or other), are just about as great as should one ignorant of historical English try to treat the text of Beowulf as if it showed the spoken English of today.

Sec. XIII. Arrival of the Tutul-xius and the alliance they made with the lords of Mayapan. Tyranny of Cocom, the ruin of his power and of the city of Mayapan.

The Indians relate that there came into Yucatan from the south many tribes with their chiefs, and it seems they came from Chiapas, although this the Indians do not know; but the author so conjectures from the many words and verbal constructions that are the same in Chiapas and in Yucatan, and from the extensive indications of sites that have been abandoned. They say that these tribes wandered forty years through the wilderness of Yucatan, having in that time no water except from the rains; that at the end of that time they reached the Sierra that lies about opposite the city of Mayapán, ten leagues distant. Here they began to settle and erect many fine edifices

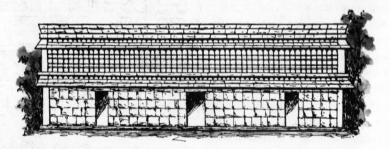

Photo by Maler

EIGHTH CENTURY STONE RESIDENCE IN THE SIERRA DISTRICT

in many places; that the inhabitants of Mayapán held most friendly relations with them, and were pleased that they worked the land as if they were native to it. In this manner the people of the **Tutul-xiu** subjected themselves to the laws of Mayapán, they intermarried, and thus the lord Xiu of the Tutul-xius came to find himself held in great esteem by all.*

* The historical problem involved in this paragraph is far from settled. The word **xiu** is the common term for 'plant' in both Aztec and Maya, and we are told that the Tutul-xius were Mexicans. Their significant symbol was a plant, just as that of the Cocoms was the **kambul** or pheasant. They were called foreigners by the Cocoms, but they certainly became the dominant element in western Yucatan, and finally at the fall of Mayapán claimed to be the defenders of 'true Maya,' and the present paragraph is clearly a Xiu 'apologia.' Nevertheless the evidence for very strong Mexicanization of customs and religion around the year 1000 is unquestioned, although the language does not seem to have been affected, as was English by the Normans. And finally, Landa's statement as to the closer similarity between Yucatecan Maya and the language of the Chiapans is definitely correct, Tzeltal and Maya being the two branches of the Mayance family most nearly alike.

These tribes lived in such peace that they had no conflicts and used neither arms nor bows, even for the hunt, although now today they are  excellent archers. They only used snares and traps, with which they took much game. They also had a certain art of throwing darts by the aid of a stick as thick as three fingers, hollowed out for a third of the way, and six palms long; with this and cords they threw with force and accuracy.†

They had laws against delinquents which they executed rigorously; such as against an adulterer, whom they turned over to the injured party that he might either put him to death by throwing a great stone down upon his head, or he might forgive him if he chose. For the adulteress there was no penalty save the infamy, which was a very serious thing with them. One who ravished a maiden was stoned to death, and they relate a case of a chief of 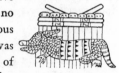 the Tutul-xiu who, having a brother accused of this crime, had him stoned and afterwards covered with a great heap of rocks. They also say that before the foundation of the city they had another law providing the punishment of adulterers by drawing out the intestines through the navel.

The governing Cocom began to covet riches, and to that end negotiated with the garrison kept by the kings of Mexico in Tabasco and Xicalango, that he would put the city in their charge. In this way he introduced the Mexicans into Mayapán, oppressed the poor, and made slaves of many. The chiefs would have slain him but for fear of the Mexicans. The lord of the Tutul-xiu never gave his consent to this. Then those of Yucatan,    seeing themselves so fixed, learned from the Mexicans the art of arms, and thus became masters of the bow and arrow, of the lance, the axe, the buckler, and strong cuirasses made of quilted cotton,‡ together with other implements of war. Soon they no longer stood in awe of nor feared the Mexicans, but rather held them of slight moment. In this situation several years passed.

This Cocom was the first who made slaves; but out of this evil came the use of arms to defend themselves, that they might not all become slaves. Among the successors of the Cocom dynasty was another

one, very haughty and an imitator of Cocom, who made another alliance
with the Tabascans, placing more Mexicans within the city, and began
to act the tyrant and to enslave the common people.   The chiefs then
attached themselves to the party of Tutul-xiu, a man
patriotic like his ancestors, and they plotted to kill
Cocom.   This they did, killing at the same time all of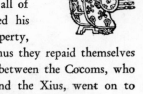
his sons save one who was absent;   they sacked his
dwelling and possessed themselves of all his property,
his stores of cacao and other fruits, saying that thus they repaid themselves
what had been stolen from them.   The struggles between the Cocoms, who
claimed that they had been unjustly expelled, and the Xius, went on to
such an extent that after having been established in this city for more than
five hundred years, they abandoned and left it desolate, each going to his
own country.

SEC. IX.   CHRONOLOGICAL MONUMENTS OF YUCATAN.   FOUNDATION OF THE KINGDOM OF SOTUTA.   ORIGIN OF THE CHELS.   THE THREE PRINCIPAL KINGDOMS OF YUCATAN.

According to the reckoning of the Indians it has been 120 years since the
abandonment of Mayapán.   On the site of that city are to be found seven or
eight stones each ten feet in height, round on one side, well carved and bearing several lines of the characters they use, so worn away by the water as to
be unreadable, although they are thought to be a monument of the foundation
and destruction of the city.   There are others like them at Zilán, a town on
the coast, except that they are taller.*   The natives being asked what they

† The dart thrower, hulche in Maya, atlatl in Mexican, is a weapon common throughout
ancient America generally.   The text illustrations above are all taken from the Madrid Maya
codex, except the last, which is Mexican.   In the first a deer is caught by a spring trap set
at a stream;   in the next an armadillo is caught in a box trap, and in the next a turkey in a
net or noose.   The two hunters both carry hulches, the first as he sets out and the other as
he returns with the deer on his back.   The last figure is an Aztec warrior.

‡ A curious error in the Landa manuscript occurs here, stating that they wore " heavy
coats of salt and cotton."   The garment is the well-known ichca-huipil, corrupted in Yucatan to escuypil, of heavy quilted or ' tied ' cotton strong enough to withstand arrows.   Now
in Maya taab (with double a) means ' to tie,' while tab (short a) means ' salt.'   The error
in the text would seem to have come from a mistranslation by Landa of what was told to him
in Maya.

* The date at Mayapán has been read as katun 10 Ahau, meaning that the event took place
in the 20-year period preceding Oct. 7, 928, or else again in 1185 or 1441.   It could hardly
be the latter, since Mayapán had just previously been destroyed, as correctly stated by Landa;
if the earlier, it might easily record the foundation.   The Zilán date reads 7 Muluc, 2 Kayab,
denoting 891, as most probable.

were, answered that it was the custom to set up one of these stones every twenty years, that being the number by which they reckon their periods. This however seems to be without warrant, for in that event there must have been many others; besides that there are none of them in any other places than Mayapán and Zilán.

The most important thing that the chiefs who stripped Mayapán took away to their own countries were the books of their sciences, for they were always very subject to the counsels of their priests, for which reason there are so many temples in those provinces.

That son of Cocom who had escaped death through being away on a trading expedition to the Ulúa country, which is beyond the city of Salamanca, on hearing of his father's death and the destruction of the city, returned in haste and gathered his relatives and vassals; they settled in a site which he called **Tibulon,** meaning ' we have been played with.' † They built many other towns in those forests, and many families have sprung from these Cocoms. The province where this chief ruled was called **Sututa.**

The lords of Mayapán took no vengeance on those Mexicans who gave aid to Cocom, seeing that they had been influenced by the governor of the country, and since they were strangers. They therefore left them undisturbed, granting them leave to settle in a place apart, or else to leave the country; in staying, however, they were not to intermarry with the natives, but only among themselves. These decided to remain in Yucatan and not return to the lagoons and mosquitos of Tabasco, and so settled in the province of Canul, which was assigned them, and where they remained until the second Spanish wars.

They say that among the twelve priests of Mayapán was one of great wisdom who had an only daughter, whom he had married to a young nobleman named **Ah-Chel.** This one had sons who were called the same as their father, according to the custom of the country. They say that this priest predicted the fall of the city to his son-in-law; they tell that on the broad part of his arm the old priest inscribed certain characters of great import in their estimation. With this distinction conferred on him he went to the coast and established a settlement at Tikoch, a great number of people following him. Thus arose the renowned families of the Chels, who peopled the most famous province of Yucatan, which they named after themselves the province of **Ahkin-Chel.** Here was Izamal, where the Chels resided; and they multiplied in Yucatan until the coming of the admiral Montejo.

† Landa is in error here; the proper spelling as given in the 1579 Relations, is **Tibolon,** ' at the Nine,' as **Tiho,** the site of Merida, ' At the Five.' Also **ti-bul on** means only ' we gambled,' and not ' we were played with,' a meaningless term here; also Maya place names are simple or compound nouns, not verbal phrases like this.

Between these great princely houses of the Cocoms, Xius and Chels there was a constant feud and enmity, which still continues even though they have become Christians.   The Cocoms call the Xius strangers and traitors, murdering their natural lord and plundering his possessions.   The Xius say they are as good as the others, as ancient and as noble;   that they were not traitors but liberators, having slain a tyrant.   The Chel said that he was as good as the others in lineage, being the descendant of the most renowned priest in Mayapán;   that as to himself he was greater than they, because he had known how to make himself as much a lord as they were.   The quarrel extended even to their food supply, for the Chel, living on the coast, would not give fish or salt to the Cocom, making him go a long distance for it;   and the Cocom would not permit the Chel to take any game or fruits.

SEC. X.   VARIOUS CALAMITIES FELT IN YUCATAN IN THE PERIOD
    BEFORE THE CONQUEST BY THE SPANIARDS: HURRICANE,
    WARS, ETC.

These tribes enjoyed more than twenty years of abundance and health, and they multiplied so that the whole country seemed like a town.   At that time they erected temples in great number, as is today seen everywhere;   in going through the forests there can be seen in the groves the sites of houses and buildings marvelously worked.

Succeeding this prosperity, there came on one winter night at about six in the evening a storm that grew into a hurricane of the four winds.   The storm blew down all the high trees, causing great slaughter of all kinds of game;   it overthrew the high houses, which being thatched and having fires within for the cold, took fire and burned great numbers of the people, while those who escaped were crushed by the timbers.

The hurricane lasted until the next day at noon, and they found that those who lived in small houses had escaped, as well as the newly married couples, whose custom it was to live for a few years in cabins in front of their fathers or fathers-in-law.   The land thus then lost the name it had borne, that " of the turkeys and the deer," and was left so treeless that those of today look as if planted together and thus all grown of one size.   To look at the country from heights it looks as if all trimmed with a pair of shears.

Those who escaped aroused themselves to building and cultivating the land, and multiplied greatly during fifteen years of health and abundance, the last year being the most fertile of all.   Then as they were about to begin gathering the crops there came an epidemic of pestilencial fevers that lasted for twenty-four hours;   then on its abating the bodies of those attacked swelled and broke out full of maggoty sores, so that from this pestilence many people died and most of the crops remained ungathered.

After the passing of the pestilence they had sixteen other good years, wherein they renewed their passions and feuds to the end that 150,000 men were killed in battle.   With this slaughter they ceased and made peace, and rested for twenty years.   After that there came again a pestilence, with great pustules that rotted the body, fetid in odor, and so that the members fell in pieces within four or five days.

Since this last plague more than fifty years have now passed, the mortality of the wars was twenty years prior, the pestilence of the swelling was sixteen years before the wars, and twenty-two or twenty-three after the destruction of the city of Mayapán.   Thus, according to this count, it has been 125 years since its overthrow, within which the people of this country have passed through the calamities described, besides many others after the Spaniards began to enter, both by wars and other afflictions sent by God;   so that it is a marvel there is any of the population left, small as it is.

SEC. XI. PROPHECIES OF THE COMING OF THE SPANIARDS. HISTORY OF FRANCISCO DE MONTEJO, FIRST ADMIRAL OF YUCATAN.

As the Mexican people had signs and prophecies of the coming of the Spaniards and the end of their power and religion, so also did those of Yucatan some years before they were conquered by Admiral Montejo.   In the district of Maní, in the province of Tutul-xiu, an Indian named **Ah-cambal**, filling the office of **Chilán,*** that is one who has charge of giving out the responses of the demon, told publicly that they would soon be ruled by a foreign race who would preach a God and the virtue of a wood which in their tongue he called **vahom-ché,** meaning a tree lifted up, of great power against the demons.

The successor of the Cocoms, called Don Juan Cocom after he became a Christian, was a man of great reputation and very learned in matters and affairs of the country, very wise and well informed.   He was on familiar terms with the author of this book, Fray Diego de Landa, recounting to him many ancient things, and showing him a book which had belonged to his grandfather, the son of the Cocom whom they killed in Mayapán.   In this was painted a deer, and his grandfather had told him that when there should come into the land large deer (for so they called the cows), the worship of the gods would cease; and this had been fulfilled, because the Spaniards brought along large cows.

---

* **Ah-cambal** means ' one who learns, a pupil.'   **Chilán** means ' orator.'

The admiral Francisco de Montejo was a native of Salamanca, and came to the Indies after the settling of the city of San Domingo, in the Island of Española, after having lived for a time in Sevilla, where he left an infant son whom he had there. He came to the island of Cuba, where he gained a livelihood and made many friends by his fine qualities, among these being Diego Velásquez the governor of the island, and Hernando Cortés. The governor having determined to send his nephew Juan de Grijalva to redeem the territory of Yucatan and to discover new lands, after the news brought by Francisco Hernández de Córdova of how rich the land was, he decided to have Montejo go with Grijalva. He being wealthy supplied one of the ships and much provisioning, and was thus one of the second party of Spaniards that discovered Yucatan; having seen the coast of Yucatan he resolved to enrich himself there instead of in Cuba.

Learning the determination of Hernando Cortés, he followed him with his person and fortune, Cortés giving him command of a ship and making him its captain. In Yucatan they then met Gerónimo de Aguilar, from whom Montejo acquired knowledge of the language of the country and its matters. Cortés having landed in New Spain began at once to make settlements, calling the first town Vera Cruz, after the blazon of his banner. Montejo was appointed as one of the royal alcaldes of the town, acquitting himself discreetly, and being so publicly named by Cortés when he returned from the trip he made around the coast. For this he was sent to Spain as one of the Procurators of the state of New Spain, that he might convey to the King his fifths, together with a relation of the countries discovered, and the things about taking place there.

When Francisco de Montejo arrived at the Court of Castile, Juan Rodríguez de Fonseca, Bishop of Burgos, was president of the Council of the Indies, and he was wrongly informed to Cortés' prejudice, by Diego Velásquez, the governor of Cuba, who claimed likewise the governorship of New Spain. The majority of the Council thinking that Cortés seemed to be asking money of the King instead of sending it, and Montejo finding that on account of the absence of the Emperor in Flanders the affair went ill, he persevered for seven years from the time he left the Indies (which was in 1519), until he re-embarked in 1526. By his perseverance he challenged the president and Pope Adrian who was regent for the kingdom, and talked with the Emperor to the effect that he gave his approval and disposed of the affairs of Cortés as justice required.

SEC. XII. MONTEJO SAILS FOR YUCATAN AND TAKES POSSESSION
OF THE COUNTRY. THE CHELS CEDE TO HIM THE SITE OF
CHICHEN ITZA. THE INDIANS FORCE HIM TO LEAVE.

During the time that Montejo was at Court he got for himself the conquest
of Yucatan, although he might have had other things, and received the title
of Admiral. He then went to Sevilla, and took with him a nephew thirteen
years of age, bearing his own name. He also found his son, twenty-eight
years of age, and took him along. He arranged a marriage with a rich
widow of Sevilla, and was thus able to gather 500 men whom he embarked
in three ships; setting sail he made port at Cozumel, an island of Yucatan.
The Indians there did not oppose him, having been made friendly by the
Spaniards under Cortés. There he learned many words of their language,
and how to make himself understood by them, after which he sailed to
Yucatan. Here he took possession, one of his Ensigns saying, banner in
hand: "In the name of God I take possession of this land for God and the
King of Castile."

In this way he sailed down the coast, which was then well populated, until
he landed at Conil, a town of the coast; the Indians were alarmed at seeing
so many horses and men, and sent word to all the country of what was
happening, watching the purpose of the Spaniards.

The Indians of the province of **Chicaca** [**Chuaca**] came to visit the admiral
in peace and were well received; among them came a man of great strength
who, taking a cutlass from a young negro who bore it, tried to kill the admiral
with it. The latter defended himself and the Spaniards came up and stopped
the trouble; but they learned that it was necessary to proceed on their guard.

The admiral sought to learn what was the largest city and found it to be
Tikoh [**Tikoch**], a city of the Chels, situated on the coast further down
along the course the Spaniards were taking. The Indians thinking they were
on their way to leave the country, were not aroused, nor did they oppose their
march. In this way they came to Tikoch, and found it a much larger and
finer city than they had supposed. It was fortunate that the chiefs of that
country were not the Covohes of Champotón, who were always braver than
the Chels. The latter with their priesthood, which still exists today, were
not as haughty as the others, and hence allowed the admiral to make a settlement for his people, giving him the site of Chichén Itzá for the purpose, an
excellent place seven leagues away. From this position he set out to the
conquest of the country, a task rendered easy by the non-resistance of the
people of **Ahkin-Chel,** and the assistance of those of **Tutul-xiu,** by reason
whereof the others offered little resistance.

In this way the admiral asked for men to build at Chichén Itzá, and in a short time he built a town, making the houses of wood and the roofs of certain palms and long grass used by the Indians. They say the smallest allotment contained 2000 or 3000 Indians. He also began to fix rules for the natives touching their services to the city, although he was moderate in his demands upon the Indians, and kept his plans hidden for the time.

SEC. XIII. MONTEJO LEAVES YUCATAN WITH ALL HIS PEOPLE AND RETURNS TO MEXICO. HIS SON, FRANCISCO DE MONTEJO, AFTERWARDS PACIFIES YUCATAN.

The Admiral Montejo did not carry out his settlement as he planned . . . . . of one who has enemies,* because it was quite far from the sea for entry from and departure for Mexico, and for receiving goods from Spain. The Indians feeling it a hardship to serve strangers where they had been the lords, began to be hostile on all sides, although he defended himself with his horses and men, and killed many. Nevertheless the Indians grew stronger every day, so that he found provisions failing, and at last one night he left the city, leaving a dog tied to the clapper of a bell, near some bread just out of his reach. The day preceding he had harassed the Indians by skirmishes that they might not follow. The dog in trying to reach the bread kept the bell ringing, keeping the Indians uncertain and expecting an attack. When they discovered the ruse, they were furious at what had been played on them, and sought to pursue the Spaniards in all directions, but not knowing what road they had taken. The party that followed in the direction they had gone caught up with the Spaniards, making a great hue and cry as if in a chase of fugitives. Six of the horsemen waited for them in the open and ran many of them down; one of the Indians seized hold of a horse by the leg, and stayed him as if he were a sheep. The Spaniards came to **Zilán** [**Dzilán**], a beautiful place, whose chief was a youth of the Chels, and had become a Christian and a friend of the Spaniards; he treated them well. This was near Tikoch, which with all the other towns of that region was under the sway of the Chels; here they remained some months in safety.

The admiral seeing that here they would be unable to receive aid from Spain, and that in case of an uprising by the Indians they would be lost, decided to go to Campeche and Mexico with all his people. From Dzilán to Campeche it was forty-eight leagues, densely populated, so that when he made known his purpose to **Namux Chel**, the chief of Dzilán, the latter offered to make the road safe and to accompany him. The admiral also arranged with the chief of Yobain, an uncle of him of Dzilán, for the company of his two

* A break in the original here.

sons, well disposed youths. Thus with these three youthful cousins, he of Dzilán on horse and the others *en croupe,* they arrived safely at Campeche and were received there in peace, there taking leave of the Chels who returned to their homes, though the chief of Dzilán died on the way. Thence they departed for Mexico, where Cortés had assigned a quota of Indians to the admiral, notwithstanding his absence.

On arriving at Mexico with his son and nephew, the admiral instituted a search for his wife, Doña Beatrix de Herrera, whom he had married secretly at Sevilla, and a daughter he had had by her, named Beatrix de Mendoza. Some say he refused to recognize her, but Don Antonio de Mendoza, the Viceroy of New Spain, intervened and reconciled them. Thereupon the Viceroy sent him as governor of Honduras, where he married his daughter to the licentiate Alonso Maldonado, president of the Audiencia of the Confines; then after some years they removed to Chiapas, and from there he sent his son, duly empowered, to Yucatan, conquering and reducing it to submission.

This Don Francisco, son of the admiral, was brought up at the court of the Catholic king, and was taken along by his father on his return to the Indies for the conquest of Yucatan; whence he went with him to Mexico. The Viceroy and the Marquis Don Hernando Cortés thought well of him, and he went with the Marquis on the trip to California. On his return the Viceroy made him governor of Tabasco and he married a lady named Doña Andrea del Castillo, who had come to Mexico as a young girl with her parents.

SEC. XIV. STATE OF YUCATAN AFTER THE DEPARTURE OF THE SPANIARDS. DON FRANCISCO, SON OF THE ADMIRAL MONTEJO, RE-ESTABLISHES THE SPANISH RULE IN YUCATAN.

After the departure of the Spaniards from Yucatan, a drought followed in the land, and the corn having been consumed during the wars with the Spaniards they suffered much from famine and were reduced to eating the bark of trees, especially of a certain kind called **cumché (kunché),** the inside of which is soft and mellow. On account of this famine the Xius of Maní undertook to make a solemn sacrifice to the idols, taking certain male and female slaves to cast into the pool at Chichén Itzá. To do this they had to pass by the town of the Cocom chiefs, their mortal enemies, but thinking that ancient quarrels would be forgotten in such times they sent to ask permission to pass through the country. The Cocoms deceived them with a favorable answer, but having lodged them all together in one great building they set fire to it, and slew those who escaped. From this great wars fol-

lowed.* There was also a plague of locusts for five years, so great that no
green thing was left and such a famine ensued that they fell dead on the roads,
and when the Spaniards returned they did not recognize the country. However, four good years followed and bettered the situation somewhat.

This Don Francisco set out for Yucatan along the rivers of Tabasco, and
entered by the lagoons of Dos Bocas. The first place he touched was Champotón, whose chief Moch-Covoh had received Francisco Hernández and
Grijalva so ill. The chief however having died, Don Francisco met no opposition, but was on the contrary supported with his company for two years by
the people of the place; during this time he could not advance because of
the resistance he encountered. Later he went to Campeche, where he found
the inhabitants very friendly, so that with their help and that of the people of
Champotón he accomplished the conquest. For their fidelity he promised
that the King would reward them, a promise which up to the present time the
King has not fulfilled.

Such resistance as he met was not strong enough to prevent Don Francisco
from reaching Tiho with his army; here he founded the city of Mérida, and
leaving the baggage there he set out to continue the conquest, sending captains
in different directions. Don Francisco sent his cousin Francisco de Montejo
to Valladolid to pacify the natives, who had rebelled somewhat, and to settle
the city as it now is. In Chectemal [Chetumal] he founded the city of
Salamanca [de Bacalar]; Campeche he already had occupied. He established
in orderly manner the services of the Indians and the rule of the Spaniards,
before the coming of his father the admiral to assume control. The latter
on arriving from Chiapas with his wife and household was well received at
Campeche, and gave his own name to the city, as San Francisco; and then
went on to the city of Mérida.

SEC. XV. CRUELTIES OF THE SPANIARDS TOWARD THE INDIANS. HOW THEY EXCUSED THEMSELVES.

The Indians took the yoke of servitude grievously. The Spaniards held the
towns comprising the country well partitioned, but there were some among
the Indians who kept stirring them up, and very severe punishments were
inflicted in consequence, resulting in the reduction of the population. Several
principal men of the province of Cupul they burned alive, and others they
hung. Information being laid against the people of Yobain, a town of the
Chels, they took the leading men, put them in stocks in a building and then

* This is the famous event of 1536, the death of Ahpulá Napot Xiu, the ' rain-bringer,' at
Otzomal; see the Maya Chronicles and the Xiu Papers at page ... herein.

set fire to the house, burning them alive with the greatest inhumanity in
the world. I, Diego de Landa, say that I saw a great tree near the village
upon the branches of which a captain had hung many women, with their
infant children hung from their feet. At this town, and another two leagues
away called Verey, they hung two Indian women, one a maiden and the other
recently married, for no other crime than their beauty, and because of fearing
a disturbance among the soldiers on their account; also further to cause the
Indians to believe the Spaniards indifferent to their women. The memory of
these two is kept both among the Indians and Spaniards on account of their
great beauty and the cruelty with which they were killed.

The Indians of the provinces of Cochuah and Chetumal rose, and the
Spaniards so pacified them that from being the most settled and populous it
became the most wretched of the whole country. Unheard-of cruelties were
inflicted, cutting off their noses, hands, arms and legs, and the breasts of their
women; throwing them into deep water with gourds tied to their feet,
thrusting the children with spears because they could not go as fast as their
mothers. If some of those who had been put in chains fell sick or could not
keep up with the rest, they would cut off their heads among the rest rather
than stop to unfasten them. They also kept great numbers of women and
men captive in their service, with similar treatment. It is affirmed that Don
Francisco de Montejo was not guilty of any of those cruelties nor approved
them, but condemned them severely, yet was unable to do more.*

In their defense the Spaniards urge that being so few in numbers they could
not have reduced so populous a country save through the fear of such terrible
punishments. They offer the example from the history of the passage of
the Hebrews to the land of promise, committing great cruelties by the command of God. On the other hand, the Indians were right in defending their
liberty and trusting to the valor of their chiefs, and they thought it would
so result as against the Spaniards.

They tell of a Spanish cross-bowman and an Indian archer, who being both
very expert sought to kill each other, but neither could take the other
unawares. The Spaniard feigning to be off guard, put one knee to the
ground, whereupon the Indian shot an arrow that entered his hand and going

---

* This reduction of Cochuah and Chetumal was entrusted to Captain Gaspar Pacheco and
his son, who had already served against the Zapotecs. For sheer lusting cruelty for its own
sake, their record there vies with that of Pedro de Alvarado among the Quichés of Guatemala.
For another side of the story, that of the burning and destruction of entire towns to concentrate the Indians near the great central monasteries, and the conduct of the *Franciscans
and Landa himself* in their assumption of Inquisition powers, see elsewhere.

up the arm separated the bones from each other. At the same moment the Spaniard shot his cross-bow and struck the Indian in the chest. He, feeling himself mortally wounded, cut a withe like an osier only much longer, and hung himself with it that it might not be said that a Spaniard had killed him. Of such instances of valor there are many.

Sec. XVI. State of the country before the conquest. Royal decree in favor of the Indians. Health of the admiral Montejo. His descendants.

Before the Spaniards subdued the country the Indians lived together in well ordered communities; they kept the ground in excellent condition, free from noxious vegetation and planted with fine trees. The habitation was as follows: in the center of the town were the temples, with beautiful plazas, and around the temples stood the houses of the chiefs and the priests, and next those of the leading men. Closest to these came the houses of those who were wealthiest and most esteemed, and at the borders of the town were the houses

Photo by Eric Thompson

of the common people. The wells, where they were few, were near the houses of the chiefs; their plantations were set out in the trees for making wine, and sown with cotton, pepper and maize. They lived in these communities for fear of their enemies, lest they be taken in captivity; but after the wars with the Spaniards they dispersed through the forests.

Either led on by their evil way or from their bad treatment by the Spaniards, the Indians of Valladolid conspired to slay the Spaniards when they separated to collect the tribute. In one day they killed 17 Spaniards and 400 servants belonging to those they killed and to the others they left alive. Then they sent arms and feet through the whole country in token of what they had done, in order to arouse the rest. These however would not respond, and so the admiral was able to send aid to the Spaniards of Valladolid and to punish the Indians.

The admiral had difficulties with those of Mérida, particularly through the royal decree which deprived the governors of their Indians. An actuary came to Yucatan, took his Indians from the admiral and placed them under the royal protection. After this a Residencia was instituted before the Royal Audience of Mexico, which ordered him before the Royal Council of the Indies in Spain. There he died, full of years and labors, leaving his wife Doña Beatrix richer than himself; also his son Don Francisco de Montejo, married in Yucatan, and his daughter Doña Catalina, married to the licentiate Alonso Maldonado in Honduras, president of the Audience of Honduras and San Domingo in the island of Hispaniola; also Don Juan de Montejo, a Spaniard, and Don Diego, a son by an Indian woman.

Don Francisco, after he turned over the government to his father the admiral, lived in his home as a simple citiezn, so far as public life went, but much honored by all as having conquered, partitioned and ruled the country. He went to Guatemala to close his Residencia and returned to his home. As children he had Don Juan de Montejo, who married Doña Isabel a native of Salamanca, Doña Beatriz de Montejo who married her uncle, his father's first cousin, and Doña Francisca de Montejo who married Don Carlos de Avellano, a native of Guadalajara. He died after a long sickness, having seen all of his children married.

SEC. XVII. ARRIVAL OF THE SPANISH FRANCISCAN FRIARS IN YUCATAN. PROTECTION THEY GAVE TO THE NATIVES. THEIR CONTESTS WITH THE SPANISH MILITARY ELEMENT.

Friar Jacobo de Testera, a Franciscan, came to Yucatan and began to instruct the Indian children. The Spanish soldiery, however, wanted to use the services of the youths to such an extent that it left no time for them to learn the catechism; they also hated the friars for rebuking their evil conduct toward the Indians. As a result of this friar Jacobo returned to Mexico, where he died. Afterwards friar Toribio Motolinia sent two friars from Guatemala, and from Mexico friar Martin de Hojacastro sent other friars, all of whom settled in Campeche and Mérida, with the approval of the admiral and his son Don Francisco, who built them a monastery at Mérida, as has been stated. They undertook to learn the language, which was very difficult. The one who succeeded the best was friar Luís de Villalpando, who commenced to learn it through signs and small stones; he reduced it to a certain form of grammar and wrote a Christian catechism in the language.* But he suffered many hindrances, both on the part of the Spaniards who, being absolute masters, wanted everything directed to their own profit and

tributes, as well as on the part of the Indians who wanted to persist in their
idolatries and debaucheries. Especially was the labor heavy because of the
Indians being scattered through the forests.*

The Spaniards took it ill that the friars built monasteries; they drove
the young Indians from their domains that they might not come to catechism,
and twice they burned the monastery at Valladolid, which was built of wood
and straw, so that it became necessary for the friars to go and live among the
Indians. When the Indians of that province rebelled they wrote to the
Viceroy Don Antonio that it was through their fondness for the friars; as
to this the Viceroy investigated and proved that the friars had not yet come
into the province at the time of the uprising. They spied at night on the
friars, causing great scandal with the Indians, pried into their lives, and
deprived them of the alms given.

In the face of this danger the friars sent one of their people to a very
upright judge, Cerrato, president of Guatemala, to whom he made report of
what had happened. The latter, seeing the disorder and unchristian conduct
of the Spaniards, how they levied all the tribute they possibly could, against
the King's orders, besides requiring personal service for every sort of labor
even to the transport of burdens, established a certain scale of taxation, which
while enough was still bearable, and by which it was specified what property
should belong to the Indian after his tribute to his master was paid, instead of
everything belonging absolutely to the Spaniards.

From this they appealed, and from fear of the tax they took from the
Indians even more than before. The friars went back to the Audiencia and
also sent to Spain, succeeding so far that the Audiencia of Guatemala sent
an Auditor, who fixed the land tax and abolished the personal service. Some
of them he forced to marry, breaking up the houses full of women they had.
This man was the licentiate Tomás López, a native of Tendilla. All this
caused a great increase of the animosity against the friars, infamous libels
were spread about them, and the men ceased to attend the masses.

This very hatred caused the Indians to feel well toward the friars, seeing
the troubles they took disinterestedly, and securing their freedom; so far did
this go that they undertook nothing without consulting the friars and getting
their counsel. And all this aroused further envy against the friars on the

* This grammar and 'doctrina' was then apparently reformed by Landa, then made the
basis of that by Coronel, as printed in 1620. The grammar, of which only one copy has
survived, in the present writer's collection, was then enlarged in the grammar of Gabriel de
San Buenaventura, as printed in 1684. There is a persistent assertion that he also composed
a large vocabulary which was printed in Mexico City in 1571, and that one copy of this has
also survived; but the fact remains yet to be verified. It is also very unlikely that Landa

part of the Spaniards, who declared they did all this to get the government of the Indies in their own hands and themselves enjoy all the things they had deprived the Spaniards of.*

Sec. XVIII. Vices of the Indians. Studies of the friars in the language of the country. Their teachings to the Indians. Conversions. Punishments of apostates.

The vices of the Indians were idolatry, divorce, public orgies, and the buying and selling of slaves, and because of being kept from these things they came to hate the friars. The ones however who, apart from the Spaniards, were most averse to the friars were the priesthood, as being a class who had lost their office and its emoluments.

The method taken for indoctrinating the Indians was by collecting the small children of the lords and leading men, and establishing them around the monasteries in houses which each town built for the purpose. Here all in each locality were gathered together, and their parents and relatives brought them their food. Then among these children they gathered them in for catechism, from which frequent visiting many asked for baptism, with much devotion. The children then, after being taught, informed the friars of idolatries and orgies; they broke up the idols, even those belonging to their own fathers; they urged the divorced women and any orphans that were enslaved to appeal to the friars. Even when they were threatened by their people they were not deterred, but answered that it was for their honor, since it was for the good of their souls. The admiral and the royal judges always backed up the friars in gathering the Indians to catechism, and in punishing those who returned to their old life. At first the lords gave up their children with ill grace, fearing that they wished to make little slaves of them as the Spaniards had done, so that they gave many young slaves in place of their own children; but when they understood the matter they sent them with good grace. In this way the children made remarkable progress in the schools, and the others in the catechism.

They learned to read and write in the Indian tongue, forming a grammatical system, so as to study it like the Latin. They found that six of our letters, D, F, G, Q, R, S, were not used or needed at all. Others however they had to double, and some to add, in order to understand the many meanings of

---

would not have mentioned it, or that Villalpando could have produced such a work in the eight years of his conversion activities and travels, between his arrival in 1544 and his death at some time between 1551 and 1553; as given by Cogolludo.

* As to this whole chapter see the Appendix to this volume.

some words. Thus **pa** means ' to open,' and **ppa,** spoken by tightly compressing the lips, means ' to break '; **tan** means ' lime,' or ' ashes,' and **tan (t'an)** uttered forcibly between the tongue and upper teeth means a 'word,' or ' to speak.' Apart from having different characters for these things, there was no need for inventing new forms of letters, but only to make use of the Latin ones, common to all.

They also gave orders that they should leave their homes in the forests and gather as formerly in proper settlements, that they might be more easily instructed and not make the fathers so much trouble. For their support they also made contributions at the paschal and other festivals, and also contributed to the churches through two aged Indians, appointed for the purpose. Thus they supplied the needs whenever they went visiting among them, and also adorned the churches.

After the people had been thus instructed in religion, and the youths benefitted as we have said, they were perverted by their priests and chiefs to return to their idolatry; this they did, making sacrifices not only by incense, but also of human blood. Upon this the friars held an Inquisition, calling upon the Alcalde Mayor for aid; they held trials and celebrated an Auto, putting many on scaffolds, capped, shorn and beaten, and some in the penitential robes for a time. Some of the Indians out of grief, and deluded by the devil, hung themselves; but generally they all showed much repentance and readiness to be good Christians.[*]

Sec. XIX. Arrival of Bishop Toral and release of the imprisoned Indians. Voyage of the Provincial of San Francisco to Spain to justify the conduct of the Franciscans.

At this point fray Francisco Toral, a Franciscan friar, and a native of Ubeda, who had been for twenty years in Mexico and then come as Bishop of Yucatan, arrived at Campeche. He, giving ear to the charges of the Spaniards and the complaints of the Indians, undid the friars' work, and ordered the prisoners released. The provincial feeling himself aggrieved thereat, determined to go to Spain, after first lodging complaint in Mexico. He thus

---

[*] Landa evades saying here that it was under his own leadership and assumed authority that this assumption of full inquisitional rights, with a calling on the plenary civil power, went on. The present work was written by him while in Spain, not voluntarily but under formal charges, and quite certainly to increase his own credit politically. As an outcome, both sides won: the law was affirmed with full clearness, and the friars told not to violate it further; while Landa was officially let off, and then allowed to go back as bishop.

arrived at Madrid, where the Council of the Indies censured him severely for having usurped the office of bishop and inquisitor. In defense he asserted the privileges held by his order in those territories by the grant of Pope Adrian, at the instance of the Emperor; as well as the support ordered to be given him by the Royal Audience of the Indies, the same as given to the bishops. These defenses alienated the members of the Council yet more, and they decided to refer him and his papers, as well as those which had been sent by the Bishop, against the friars, to fray Pedro de Bobadilla, Provincial of Castile, to whom the King wrote commanding investigation and the performance of justice. Fray Pedro, being ill, committed the examination of the affair to Fray Pedro de Guzmán, of his own order, a man learned and experienced in inquisitorial matters.

To him, then, were presented the opinions of seven learned persons of the kingdom of Toledo, namely: Don fray Francisco de Medina and fray Francisco Dorantes, of the Franciscan order; master frayle Alonso de la Cruz, an Augustinian friar who had spent thirty years in the Indies; the licentiate Tomás López who had been an Auditor in Guatemala in the New Kingdom, as well as a judge in Yucatan; D. Hurtado, professor of canon law; D. Méndez, professor of the Sacred Scriptures; and D. Martínez, Scotist professor at Alcalá. These declared that the Provincial had acted rightly in the matter of the Auto and other things for the punishment of the Indians. This being reviewed by fray Francisco de Guzmán, he wrote fully upon it to the Provincial, fray Pedro de Bobadilla.

The Indians of Yucatan deserve that the King should favor them for many reasons, and especially for the readiness they have shown in his service. While he was occupied in Flanders the princess Doña Juana his sister, who was then regent of the kingdom, wrote a letter asking the assistance of those in the Indies. This an Auditor of Guatemala bore to Yucatan, and having gathered the chiefs together, he directed a friar to preach upon what they owed to his majesty, and what was asked of them. Having finished his discourse, the Indians rose to their feet and said that they recognized their obligation to God for having given them so noble and Christian a king, and that they were grieved not to live where they might serve him in person; wherefore whatever in their poverty they had that he desired, they placed at his service; and if that did not suffice, they would sell their children and wives.

SEC. XX. CONSTRUCTION OF THE HOUSES OF YUCATAN. OBE-DIENCE AND RESPECT OF THE INDIANS FOR THEIR CHIEFS. HEADGEAR AND WEARING OF GARMENTS.

In building their houses their method was to cover them with an excellent thatch they have in abundance, or with the leaves of a palm well adapted to that purpose, the roof being very steep to prevent its raining through. They then run a wall lengthways of the whole house, leaving certain doorways into the half which they call the back of the house, where they have their beds. The other half they whiten with a very fine whitewash, and the chiefs also have beautiful frescos there. This part serves for the reception and lodging of guests, and has no doorway but is open along the whole length of the house. The roof drops very low in front as a protection against sun and rain; also, they say, the better to defend the interior from enemies in case of necessity.

Photo by Eric Thompson

The common people build the chiefs' dwellings at their own expense. The houses having no doors, it is held a grave offense to do any wrong to another's house; in the back, however, they have a small door for household uses. They sleep on beds made of small rods, covered with mats, and with their mantles of cotton as covering. In the summer they sleep in the front part of the house on the mats, especially the men. Away from the house the entire village sows the fields of the chief, cares for them, and harvests what is required for him and his household; and whenever they hunt and fish, or at the salt gathering time, they always give a part to the chief; in these matters everything is always in common.

If the chief should die his eldest son would succeed him, but the others would always be much respected, favored and held as lords. The leading men, lower than the chief, are favored in all these matters according to who they are, or the favor shown them by the chief. The priests live upon their benefices and offerings. The chiefs govern the town, settling suits, ordering and adjusting the affairs of the commonwealths, doing all through the hands of the leading men. These latter are much honored and obeyed, especially the wealthy, the chiefs visiting them and holding court at their houses for the settlement of affairs and business, this being done principally at night.

Whenever the chiefs leave the town they have a great company in attendance, and the same when they leave their houses.

The Indians of Yucatan are people of good physique, tall, robust and of great strength, and commonly are all bow-legged from having in their infancy been carried astride the mother's hip when they are taken somewhere. It was held as a grace to be cross-eyed, and this was artificially brought about by the mothers, who in infancy suspended a small plaster from the hair down between the eyebrows and reaching the eyes; this constantly binding, they finally became cross-eyed. They also had their heads and foreheads flattened from infancy by their mothers. Their ears were pierced for earrings and much scarified from the sacrifices. They did not grow beards and say that their mothers were used to burn their faces with hot cloths to prevent the growth. Nowaday beards are grown, although they are very rough, like hogs' bristles.

They allowed their hair to grow like the women; on top they ringed it, making a good tonsure. Thus it grew long below but short on the crown; it was braided and wound around the head, with an end left behind like a queue. All the men used mirrors, and the women not; and to call a man a cuckold they said his wife had put the mirror in his hair behind his head. They bathed a great deal, not troubling to cover themselves before the women, except such as they might do with the hand. They were devoted to perfumes, having bouquets of flowers and odorous plants, arranged with much care and art. They painted their faces and bodies red, disfiguring themselves, though to them it seemed handsome.

Their clothing was a strip of cloth a hand broad that served for breeches and leggings, and which they wrapped several times about the waist, leaving one end hang in front and one behind. These ends were embroidered by their wives with much care and with featherwork. They wore large square mantles, which they threw over the shoulders. They wore sandals of hemp or deerskin tanned dry, and then no other garments.[*]

[*] The foregoing portrait of Nezahualpilli, king of Tezcoco, attributed to Ixtlilxochitl, although Mexican, illustrates well the garments here described.

Sec. XXI.   Food and drink of the Indians of Yucatan.

Their principal sustenance is maize, of which they prepare various dishes and drinks;   and even drunk as they do it, it serves as their food and drink. The Indian women put the maize to soak the night before in lime and water, and in the morning it is soft and half-cooked, having in the process lost the husk and nib.   They next grind it on stones, and when half ground make it into great balls and loads for the use of laborers, travelers and sailors.   In that shape it keeps for several months, except for souring.   Of this they then take a lump and dissolve it in a vessel or gourd formed by the rind of a fruit that grows on a tree, whereby God has provided them with vessels;   out of this they drink the liquor and then eat the rest, it being of excellent taste and very nourishing.   From the maize that is more fully ground they take away the milk and thicken it at the fire, making a sort of curd for morning use; and this they drink hot.   Upon what is left from the morning they put water for drinking through the day, since they are not accustomed to drink water alone.   They also toast the maize and then grind and mix it with water into a very refreshing drink, putting into it a little Indian pepper or cacao.

Out of maize and ground cacao they make a sort of froth that is very delicious, and with which they celebrate their festivals.   From the cacao they extract a grease that is much like butter, and from this together with maize they prepare another agreeable and much esteemed drink.   Still another is made from the substance of the ground maize, raw, which is also fresh and tasty.   They prepare many kinds of bread, good and healthful, except that it is not good to eat when cold;   so that the Indian women are kept busy with making it twice a day.   They have not learned how to make flour that can be kneaded like wheat flower, and when they do make it as one makes wheat bread, it is good for nothing.   They make ragouts of vegetables and venison, and of wild and domestic fowls of which there are plenty, and of fish of which there are plenty.   Thus they have good provisions, especially since they are raising Spanish pigs and fowls.

In the mornings they take their hot drink with pepper, as we have said: through the day the cold drinks and in the evening the ragouts.   When they have no meat they make their sauces of pepper and vegetables.   The men and women do not eat together, but eat apart, on the ground;   or if there is much, with a mat for a table.   They live well when they have it, and endure hunger equally well when they have not, getting along on very little.   After eating they wash their hands and mouth.

SEC. XXII. PAINTING AND TATTOOING OF THE INDIANS. THEIR ORGIES, WINES AND BANQUETS. THEIR COMEDIES, MUSIC AND DANCES.

They tattoo their bodies and are accounted valiant and brave in proportion to its amount, for the process is very painful. In doing it the craftsman first covers the part he wishes with color, and then delicately pierces the pictures in the skin, so that the blood and color leaves the outlines on the body. This they do a little at a time, on account of the pain and because of the disorders that ensue; for the places fester and form matter. But for all this they ridicule those who are not tattooed. They set much store on amiability and the showing of graces and natural accomplishments; today they eat and drink as we do.

The Indians are very dissolute in drinking and becoming intoxicated, and many ills follow their excesses in this way. They kill each other; violate their beds, the poor women thinking they are receiving their own husbands; they treat their own fathers and mothers as if they were in the houses of enemies; they set fire to their houses, and so destroy themselves in their

CORN FESTIVAL - DRESDEN CODEX

drunkenness. When the carouse is general, and for the sacrifices, all contribute to it; when private, the cost is borne by the entertainer, with the aid of his parents. Their wine they make of honey and water and the root of a certain tree they grow for the purpose, and which gives the wine strength and a very disagreeable odor. At their dances and merry-makings they eat seated two by two, or in fours. After the eating the cup-bearers, who have had to remain sober, help themselves from great jars until they are overcome, and their wives have great trouble in getting their drunken husbands home.

They often spend on one banquet all they have made by many days of trading or scheming. They have two methods of making these feasts; the first of these (that of the chiefs and leading men) obliges each guest to return an invitation to his host; to each guest the host must give a roast fowl and cacao and drinks in abundance, and after the banquet it is the custom to present each with a mantle to wear, with a small stand

FIGURINE
FROM ISLA JAINA

and a cup, as fine as the host can afford. If one of the
guests has died, the obligation to give the return invitation
lies on his house or parents.

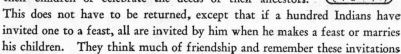

The other kind is between kinsfolk, when they marry
their children or celebrate the deeds of their ancestors.
This does not have to be returned, except that if a hundred Indians have
invited one to a feast, all are invited by him when he makes a feast or marries
his children. They think much of friendship and remember these invitations
even when separated far from each other. At the banquets
the drink is passed by beautiful women, who, after handing
the goblet, turn the back until it is emptied.

The Indians have delightful ways of entertainment; particularly they have actors who perform with great skill, to such
an extent as that they hire themselves to the Spaniards for
nothing other than to observe the jests the Spaniards pass with
their servants, their wives, and on themselves over their good
or bad serving; all of this they act later with as much art as
attentive Spaniards could.

They have small drums which they strike with the hand,
and another drum of hollow wood that gives a deep, mournful
sound. This they hit with a longish stick at the end of which
is a ball of a certain gum that exudes from a tree. They have
long, thin trumpets of hollow wood, the end of which is
formed of a large twisted gourd. They have another instru-
ment made of a whole tortoise with its shells, from which the
flesh has been removed; this they strike with the palm of the hand, giving
a mournful, sad sound.

They have whistles of cane and of deer bones, also large conchs and reed
flutes; with these instruments they accompany the dancers. Two of their
dances are especially virile and worth seeing; one is a game of reeds, whence
they call it **colomché,** the word having that meaning [a ' palisade of sticks '].
To perform it they make a large circle of dancers, whom the music accom-
panies, and in time with which two come into the circle; one of these dances
erect, holding a handful of reeds, while the other dances squatting, both keeping time around the circle. The one with the reeds throws them with all his
force at the other, who with great skill catches them with a small rod. When
all are thrown they return, keeping time, into the circle, and others come
out to do the same.

There is another dance in which 800 Indians, or more or less, dance with
small flags in a great war measure, among all of them not one being out of

time. They are heavy in their dances, since they do not cease dancing for the entire day, food and drink being brought to them. The men do not dance with the women.

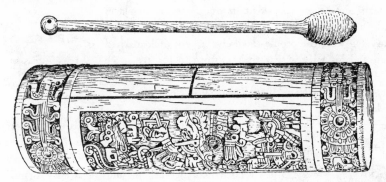

The **tunkul** or Mexican **teponaztli**; beaten with a rubber-tipped stick it can be heard for five or six miles.

The other cuts show a musical Corn Festival as pictured in the Dresden Codex; a **pax** or Mexican huehuetl, to be beaten with the flat palms; a clay figurine of a dancer, from Isla Jaina, off the west coast; a deity seated on the earth, blowing a pipe (this and the **pax** from the Madrid Codex); a clay pipe in the form of a lizard.

Sec. XXIII. Industry, commerce and money. Agriculture and seeds. Justice and hospitality.

Among the occupations of the Indians were pottery and wood-working; they made much profit from forming idols of clay and wood, in doing which they fasted much and followed many rites. There were also physicians, or better named, sorcerers, who healed by use of herbs and their superstitious practices. It was so also with all their other occupations.

Their favorite occupation was trading, whereby they brought in salt; also cloths

and slaves from Tabasco and Ulúa. In their bartering they used cacao and stone counters which they had for money, and with which they bought slaves and other fine and beautiful stones, such as the chiefs wore as jewels on festal occasions. They had also certain red shells for use as money and jewels for wearing; these they carried in network purses. In their markets they dealt in all the products of the country; they gave credit, borrowed and paid promptly and without usury.

The commonest occupation was agriculture, the raising of maize and the other seeds; these they kept in well-constructed places and in granaries for sale in due time. Their mules and oxen were the people themselves. For each married man and his wife it was their custom to plant a space of 400 feet, which was called **hun vinic** [one man], a plot measured with a 20-foot rod, 20 in breadth and 20 in length.

  The Indians have the excellent custom of helping each other in all their work. At the time of planting, those who have no people of their own to do it join together in bands of twenty, or more or less, and all labor together to complete the labor of each, all duly measured, and do not stop until all is finished. The lands today are in common, and whoever occupies a place first, holds it; they sow in different places, so that if the crop is short in one, another will make it up. When they work the land they do no more than gather the brush and burn it before sowing. From the middle of January to April they care for the land and then plant when the rains come. Then carrying a small sack on the shoulders they make a hole in the ground

The growing plant springs from the head of the god Itzamna. The plant, springing from the earth, withers and is revived. The Corn deity holds forth the growing plant, springing from the sign **ik**, or Breath, Life. (All the figures shown on this page are from the Madrid Codex, which has chiefly to do with farm ceremonies.)

Itzamná plants the tree in the earth. Itzamná drops the seed in the earth and animals attack it. Worms attack the Corn-god, seated on the earth. Birds of prey feed on the dying Corn-god (note the closed eye).

with a stick, dropping in five or six grains, and covering them with the same
stick.   When it rains, it is marvelous how they grow.   In hunting also, they
unite in bands of fifties, or more or less; the flesh of the deer they grill over
rods to keep it from spoiling; then when they come back to the town they
first make their presents to the chief and then distribute all as between friends.
In fishing they do the same.

The Fire-dog, or heat rays from the sun, burns the growth, while the Corn-god, with arms
bound, is dying.   Next, Itzamná waters the growing maize, denoted by the kan-sign.   The
hunter ties up the deer.

In making visits the Indians always carry a gift, according to their quality,
and the one visited returns the gifts with another.   During these visits third
persons present speak and listen attentively to those talking, having due regard
for their rank; notwithstanding which all use the ' thou.'   Those of less
position must, however, in the course of the
conversation, repeat the title or dignity of the
one higher in rank.   They have the custom of
assisting one who delivers a message by respond-
ing with a cadence of the voice, a sort of aspirate
in the throat, as if to say ' it is well,' or ' be it
so.'   The women are brief in what they say,
nor do they have the habit of negotiating on

their own account, especially if poor; for this the chiefs scoffed at the friars
for giving ear to poor and rich without distinction.
    For offenses committed by one against another the chief of the town
required satisfaction to be made by the town of the aggressor; if this was
refused it became the occasion of more trouble.   If they were of the same
town they laid it before the judge as arbitrator, and he ordered satisfaction
given; if the offender lacked the means for this, his parents or friends helped
him out.   The cases in which they were accustomed to require such amends
were in instances of involuntary homicide, the suicide of either husband or
wife on the other's account, the accidental burning of houses, lands of
inheritance, hives or granaries.   Other offenses committed with malice called
for reparation through blood or blows.

The Yucatecans are very generous and hospitable; no one enters their houses without being offered food and drink, what drink they may have during the day, or food in the evening. If they have none, they seek it from a neighbor; if they unite together on the roads, all join in sharing even if they have little for their own need.

SEC. XXIV. METHOD OF COUNTING OF THE YUCATECANS. GENE-
ALOGIES. INHERITANCES AND TUTELAGE OF THE ORPHANS.
THE SUCCESSION OF THE CHIEFS.

They count by fives up to twenty, by twenties to a hundred and by hundreds to four hundred; then by 400's up to 8000. This count is much used in merchandising the cacao. They have other very long counts, extended to infinity, counting twenty times 8000, or 160,000; then they multiply this 160,000 again by twenty, and so on until they reach an uncountable figure. They do all their counting on the ground or a flat surface.*

They make much of knowing the origin of their lineages, especially if they come from one of the houses of Mayapán; this they learn from their priests, it being one of their sciences, and they boast much about one of their lineage who has distinguished himself. The name of the father is transmitted to his sons, but not to his daughters. Both sons and daughters received the name of their father and their mother, the father's as the proper name, and the mother's as the given one; thus the son of Chel and Chan was called Na-Chan Chel, meaning the son of so and so. For this the Indians consider all of the same name as related, and treat them accordingly; and thus when they go to a part of the country where they are unknown, and are in need, they make known their names, and if there are any of the same they are received and treated with good will and affection. Thus also no man or woman marries another of the same name, because this was for them a great infamy. Today they use their baptismal names.

Daughters did not inherit equally with their brothers, except as a matter of favor or good will, in which case a part of the whole was given them. The rest was divided equally, except where one had helped more in the accumulation of the property, in which case he received an equivalent before

* Maya numeration went on to the 6th power of 20, with terms for each period, as we have for our decimal progression, ten, hundred, thousand, million. But whereas we had to adopt the Latin *mil*, or 1000, to get a term for the fourth place, the Mayas had a separate and distinct term for each multiple up to the sixth: **kal, bak, pic, kinchil, calab, alau**, the highest calendrical term being an **alau** of years, or 64,000,000.

the division. If the children were all daughters, then the cousins or other nearest kin inherited. Where the heir was not of sufficient age to receive the property, they entrusted it to the nearest relative as guardian or tutor, who supplied the mother with what she needed for his bringing up; for it was not their custom to place the property in the mother's control; or they even took the children from her care where the tutors were the brothers of the deceased. When the heirs reached their majority, the guardians rendered them the property; if this was not done it was held as in great dishonor, and became the cause of violent quarrels. The transfer was made in the presence of the chiefs and leading men, deducting what had been spent for their care; the heirs received nothing of the harvests, or the products of the hives or cacao trees, because of the labor involved in keeping them up.

When the chief died, if he left no sons to succeed him, but left brothers, the eldest or most capable became the ruler; meanwhile the heir was instructed in the customs, the ceremonies and everything he would need to know when he became of age. These brothers, even when the heir came to his position, still controlled affairs through their lives. In the case of there being no brothers of a deceased chief, the priests and leading men chose a man fitted for this position.

SEC. XXV. DIVORCES FREQUENT AMONG THE YUCATECANS. NUPTIAL CUSTOMS.

In the olden times they married at the age of twenty, but now at that of twelve or thirteen. For this reason they divorce the more easily because they marry without love, and ignorant of married life and the duties of married people; and if their parents could not persuade them to return to their wives, they hunted them another, and others and others. With equal ease men with children left their wives with no anxiety lest another might take them as wives, or that they themselves might later return to them. Nevertheless, they are very jealous, and do not lightly suffer infidelity on their wives' part; and now that they see that the Spaniards kill their wives for this reason, they are beginning to maltreat and even to kill them. In cases of divorce, small children stayed with their mothers, while the grown-up went with their father and the girls with their mother.

Even though divorce was so common and familiar a thing, the old people and those of better customs condemned it, and there were many who never had but the single wife; nor did they ever marry one bearing their own name on the father's side, for this was considered a very bad thing. Equally wrong was it held that a man should marry his sister-in-law, the widow of a brother.

Neither did they marry their step-mothers, their wives' sisters, nor their mothers' sisters, all these being regarded as wrong. But with all other kinsmen on their mothers' side, even first cousins, it was held legitimate.

The fathers were at great care to seek in good season wives for their sons, of equal rank and condition; and for the men to seek their wives themselves was regarded as undignified, as well as for the parents of the woman to make advances. In these matters they left the preparatory steps in the charge of other persons to care for; these then negotiated, dealt together, discussed the dowry or the settlement (which was not large). This the youth's father gave to the prospective father-in-law, while the girl's mother prepared garments for the bride and for the child.

The day of the marriage having arrived, they all gathered at the house of the fiancée's father, where a repast had been prepared. The guests met with the young couple and their relatives; the priest assured himself that the latter had given the matter all due consideration, gave the young man his wife, if it was settled for him to receive her that night; and after this the banquet took place. From that day the son-in-law remained in his father-in-law's house for five or six years, working for him; if he failed in this, he was driven from the house, but the mothers arranged always for the wife to supply her husband with his food, as a mark of the marriage.

The marriage of widowers and widows took place without any festival or ceremonies; the man simply went to the woman's house, was admitted and given to eat, and with this it was a marriage. The result of this was that they separated as easily as they came together. The Yucatecans never took more than a single wife, although in other places they frequently took a number together. At times the parents contracted marriages for their sons even when they were young children, and were regarded as their fathers-in-law until they came of age.

SEC. XXVI. METHOD OF BAPTISM IN YUCATAN; HOW IT WAS CELEBRATED.

Baptism is not found anywhere in the Indies save here in Yucatan, and even with a word meaning to be born anew or a second time, the same as the Latin *renascer*. Thus in the language of Yucatan sihil means 'to be born anew,' or a second time, but only however in composition; thus caput-sihil means to be reborn.* Its origin we have been unable to learn, but it is some-

---

* Sihil means 'to be born' simply; caput-sihil 'to be born a second time,' and is the specific term in Maya for baptism, being distinct from caput-cuxtal, 'to come to life a second time.'

thing they have always used and for which they have had such devotion that
no one fails to receive it; they had such reverence for it that those guilty of
sins, or who knew they were about to sin, were obliged to confess to the
priest, in order to receive it; and they had such faith in it that in no manner
did they ever take it a second time. They believed that in receiving it they
acquired a predisposition to good conduct and habits, protection against being
harmed by the devils in their earthly affairs, and that through it and living
a good life they would attain a beatitude hereafter which, like that of
Mahomet, consisted in eating and drinking.

Their custom of preparing for baptism was as follows: the Indian women
raised the children to the age of three, placing for the boys a small white
plaquet, fastened to the head in the hair of the tonsure; the girls wore a
thin cord tied very low about the waist, to which was attached a small shell
over the private parts; to remove these two things was regarded among them
as a sin and disgraceful, until the time of the baptism, which was given
between the ages of three and twelve; until this ceremony was received they
did not marry.

Whenever one desired to have his child baptised, he went to the priest and
made his wish known to him, who then published this in the town, with the
day chosen, which they took care should be of good omen. This being done,
the solicitant, being thus charged with giving the fiesta, selected at his dis-
cretion some leading man of the town to assist him in the matter. Afterwards they chose four other old and honored men to assist the priest on the
day of the ceremony, these being chosen with the priest's cooperation. In
these elections the fathers of all the eligible children took part, for the fiesta
was a concern of all; those so chosen were called **Chacs.** For the three days
before the ceremony the parents of the children, as well as the officials, fasted
and abstained from their wives.

On the day, all assembled at the house of the one giving the fiesta, and
brought all the children who were to be baptized, and placed them
in the patio or court of the house, all clean and scattered with
fresh leaves; the boys together in a line, and the girls the same,
with an aged woman as matron for the girls, and a man in charge
of the boys.*

* The marginal illustration is from the Madrid Codex, in a clause where the act is repeated
in like style in four illustrations, and obviously refers to child baptism, the only place in
either codex where the ceremony seems to be referred to. Clearly the actual ceremony was
far more elaborate and impressive, this being one of the many cases where the scanty details
related by Landa, and the isolated references we have so far been able to identify in the codices
and the few post-Conquest Maya manuscripts, like the Chumayel, just barely supplement and
touch each other enough to show how much existed, and how full the civilization was, and
how little we yet know of it — as it actually was, and how it was lived.

When this was done the priest proceeded to the purification of the house, expelling the demon. To do this they placed four benches in the four corners of the patio, on which the four **chacs** seated themselves, with a long cord tied from one to the other, in such fashion as that the children were corraled in the middle, after which those parents who had fasted stepped over the cord, into the circuit. Afterwards, or previously, they placed in the middle another bench on which the priest seated himself, with a brazier and a little ground maize and incense. Then the boys and girls came to him in order, and he put a little of the ground maize and incense into the hand of each, and they threw it into the brazier. When all had done this, they took up the brazier and the cord held by the **chacs**; they also threw a little wine in a vase and then gave it all to an Indian to carry away from the village, enjoining him not to drink the wine or to look behind him on his return; and in this manner they said that the demon had been exorcised.

After this they swept the patio and took away the leaves that were scattered at the beginning, which were of a tree called **sihom,** and scattered others of a tree called **copó,** laying down mats while the priest changed his vestures. He next entered wearing a tunic of red feathers, worked with other vari-colored feathers, and with other long feathers pendant from the ends; on his head he wore a sort of miter of the same feathers, while beneath the tunic there hung to the ground strips of cotton like tails. He carried a hyssop made of a short, finely decorated stick, and the tails of certain serpents like rattlesnakes;* all this with neither more nor less gravity than that of a pope crowning an emperor, and a serenity that was a marvel to behold. The **chacs** then went to the children and placed on the heads of all white cloths which their mothers had brought for the purpose. They asked of the largest ones whether they had done any bad thing, or obscene conduct, and if any had done so, they confessed them and separated them from the others.

When this was done the priest called on all to be silent and seated, and began to bless the children, with long prayers, and to sanctify them with the hyssop, all with great serenity. After this benediction he seated himself, and the one elected by the parents as director of the fiesta took a bone given him by the priest, went to the children and menaced each one with the bone on the forehead, nine times. After this he wet the bone in a jar of water he carried, and with it anointed them on the forehead, the face, and between the fingers of their hands and the bones of their feet, without saying a word. This liquor was confected out of certain flowers and ground cacao, dissolved

There is a confusion in this section, between child and adult baptism, which latter having necessarily been of a different ceremonial nature, is not given by Landa.

* See illustration of this aspersarium on page 79.

† **Suhuy nok**, or ' virgin cloth,' as still known in Yucatan.

in virgin water, as they call it, taken from the hollows of trees or of rocks in the forest.

After this unction the priest rose, removed the white cloths from their heads, as well as others they wore suspended from the shoulders containing a few feathers of very beautiful birds and some grains of cacao, all of which were collected by one of the **chacs.** Then with a stone knife the priest cut away the small bead or counter each had worn fastened to his head. After this the other assistants of the priest brought a bunch of flowers and a pipe such as the Indians smoked; with these they menaced each child nine times, and then gave him the bouquet to smell and the pipe to smoke. After this they gathered the presents brought by the mothers, which were things to eat, and gave these to each child to eat there. Then they brought a fine chalice of wine and quickly offered it to the gods, invoking them with devout prayers to receive this small gift from the children; this chalice they then gave to another officiant called **cayom,** that he might empty it at a single draught; for him to stop to take breath in this was regarded as something sinful.

When this was over the girls took their leave first, their mothers removing the cord and shell they had worn about the girdle in sign of their chastity; this gave license for them to be married, when such might seem best to their parents. Then the boys took their leave, and the fathers came bearing the heap of mantles they had brought, and gave them with their own hands to the assistants and the officiants. The fiesta then ended with long eating and drinking; and this fiesta was called **em-ku,** which means ' the descent of the god.' The one then who had instituted and borne the cost of the ceremony, in addition to his three previous days of abstinence and fast, was obliged to continue this for yet other nine days; this they did inviolably.

Sec. XXVII.   Kind of confessions among the Indians. Abstinences and superstitions.   Diversity and abundance of idols.   Duties of the Priests.

The Yucatecans naturally knew when they had done wrong, and they believed that death, disease and torments would come on them because of evildoing and sin, and thus they had the custom of confessing to their priests when such was the case. In this way, when for sickness or other cause they found themselves in danger of death, they made confession of their sin; if they neglected it, their near relatives or friends reminded them of it; thus they publicly confessed their sins to the priest if he was at hand; or if not, then to their parents, women to their husbands, and the men to their wives.

The sins of which they commonly accused themselves were theft, homicide, of the flesh, and false testimony; in this way they considered themselves in safety. Many times, after they had recovered, there were difficulties over the disgrace they had caused, between the husband and wife, or with others who had been the cause thereof.

The men confessed their weaknesses, except those committed with their female slaves, since they held it a man's right to do with his own property as he wished. Sins of intention they did not confess, yet considered them as evil, and in their counsels and sermons advised against them.

Those widowed did not marry for a year thereafter, nor know one of the other sex for this time; those who infringed this rule were deemed intemperate, and they believed some ill would come on them.

In some of the fasts observed for their fiestas they neither ate meat nor knew their wives. They always fasted when receiving duties in connection with their festivals, and likewise on undertaking duties of the State, which at times lasted as long as three years; those who violated their abstinence were great sinners.

So given were they to their idolatrous practices that in times of necessity even the women and youths and maidens understood it as incumbent on them to burn incense and pray to God that he free them from evil and overcome the demon who was the cause of it.

Even travelers on the roads carried incense with them, and a little plate on which to burn it; and then wherever they arrived at night they erected three small stones, putting a little incense on each, and three flat stones in front of these, on which they burned incense, praying to the god they called Ekchuah * that he bring them safely back home; this ceremony they performed every night until their return, unless there were some other who could do this, or even more, on their account.

Ekchuah
ON HIS TRAVELS

The Yucatecans had a great number of temples, sumptuous in their style; besides these temples in common the chiefs, priests and principal men also had their oratories and idols in their houses for their private offerings and prayers. They held Cozumel and the well at Chichén Itzá in as great veneration as we have in our pilgrimages to Jerusalem and Rome; they visited them to offer gifts, especially at Cozumel, as we do at our holy places; and when they did

---

* The figure in the text, from the Madrid codex, shows the North Star god (so called) in the usual habiliments of Ekchuah, the headbands, corded hamper and pouch, on his travels, also bearing a flint-tipped spear. Ekchuah is the recognized god of the merchants, the beyom or 'traveling man.' He is in nearly every case shown with his body painted black, as well as his glyph here in the margin. As such he occurs seventeen times in the Madrid codex, devoted to daily or mundane affairs, and only once in the Dresden.

not visit they sent offerings. When traveling also, and passing an abandoned temple, it was their custom to enter for prayers and burn incense.

So many idols did they have that their gods did not suffice them, there being no animal or reptile of which they did not make images, and these in the form of their gods and goddesses. They had idols of stone (though few in number), others more numerous of wood, but the greatest number of terra cotta. The idols of wood were especially esteemed and reckoned among their inheritances as objects of great value. They had no metal statues, there being no metals in the country. As regards the images, they knew perfectly that they were made by human hands, perishable, and not divine; but they honored them because of what they represented and the ceremonies that had. been performed during their fabrication, especially the wooden ones.

The most idolatrous of them were the priests, the **chilánes**, the sorcerers, the physicians, the **chacs** and the **nacónes**. It was the office of the priests to discourse and teach their sciences, to indicate calamities and the means of remedying them, preaching during the festivals, celebrating the sacrifices and administering their sacraments. The **chilánes** were charged with giving to all those in the locality the oracles of the demon, and the respect given them was so great that they did not ordinarily leave their houses except borne upon litters carried on the shoulders. The sorcerers and physicians cured by means of bleeding at the part afflicted, casting lots for divination in their work, and other matters. The **chacs** were four old men, specially elected on occasion to aid the priest in the proper and full celebration of the festivals. There were two of the **nacónes;** the position of one was permanent and carried little honor, since it was his office to open the breasts of those who were sacrificed; the other was chosen as a general for the wars, who held office for three years, and was held in great honor; he also presided at certain festivals.

SEC. XXVIII. SACRIFICES AND SELF-MORTIFICATIONS, BOTH CRUEL AND OBSCENE, AMONG THE YUCATECANS. HUMAN VICTIMS SLAIN BY ARROWS, AND OTHERS.

At times they sacrificed their own blood, cutting all around the ears in strips which they let remain as a sign. At other times they perforated their cheeks or the lower lip; again they made cuts in parts of the body, or pierced the tongue crossways and passed stalks through, causing extreme pain; again they cut away the superfluous part of the member, leaving the flesh in the form of ears. It was this custom which led the historian of the Indies to say that they practised circumcision.

At other times they practised a filthy and grievous sacrifice, whereby they gathered in the temple, in a line, and each made a pierced hole though the member, across from side to side, and then passed through as great a quantity of cord as they could stand; and thus all together fastened and strung together, they anointed the statue of the demon with the collected blood. The one able to endure the most was considered most valiant, and their sons of tender age began to accustom themselves to this suffering; it is frightful to see how much they were dedicated to this practice.

The women made no similar effusions of blood, although they were very devout. Of every kind of animal obtainable, birds of the sky, animals of the earth, fishes of the sea, they used the blood to anoint the face of the demon; they also gave as presents whatever other thing they had. Of some animals they took out the heart and offered that; others were offered whole, some living, some dead, some raw, some cooked. They also made large offerings of bread and wine, and of all the kinds of food and drink they possessed.

To make these sacrifices in the courts of the temples there were erected certain tall decorated posts; and near the stairway of the temple there was a broad, round pedestal, and in the middle a stone, somewhat slender and four or five palms in height, set up; at the top of the temple stairs there was another similar one.

Apart from the festivals which they solemnized by the sacrifices of animals, on occasions of great tribulation or need the priests or **chilánes** ordained the sacrifice of human beings. For this purpose all contributed, for the purchase of slaves. Some out of devotion gave their young sons. The victims were feted up to the day of the sacrifice, but carefully guarded that they might not run away, or defile themselves by any carnal acts; then while they went from town to town with dances, the priests, the **chilánes** and the celebrants fasted.

When the day of the ceremony arrived, they assembled in the court of the temple; if they were to be pierced with arrows their bodies were stripped and anointed with blue, with a miter on the head. When they arrived before the demon, all the people went through a solemn dance with him around the wooden pillar, all with bows and arrows, and then dancing raised him upon it, tied him, all continuing to dance and look at him. The impure priest, vestured, ascended and whether it was man or woman wounded the victim in the private parts with an arrow, and then descended and anointed the face of the demon with the blood he had drawn; then making a sign to the dancers, they began in order as they passed rapidly, dancing, to shoot an arrow to the victim's heart, shown by a white mark, and quickly made of his chest a single point, like a hedgehog of arrows.

If his heart was to be taken out, they conducted him with great display and concourse of people, painted blue and wearing his miter, and placed him on the rounded sacrificial stone, after the priest and his officers had anointed the stone with blue and purified the temple to drive away the evil spirit. The **chacs** then seized the poor victim and swiftly laid him on his back across the stone, and the four took hold of his arms and legs, spreading them out. Then the **nacon** executioner came, with a flint knife in his hand, and with great skill made an incision between the ribs on the left side, below the nipple; then

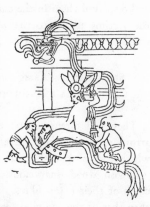

he plunged in his hand and like a ravenous tiger tore out the living heart, which he laid on a plate and gave to the priest; he then quickly went and anointed the faces of the idols with that fresh blood.

At times they performed this sacrifice on the stone situated on the top step of the temple, and then they threw the dead body rolling down the steps, where it was taken by the attendants, was stripped completely of the skin save only on the hands and feet; then the priest, stripped, clothed himself with this skin and danced with the rest. This was a ceremony with them of great solemnity. The victims sacrificed in this manner were usually buried in the court of the temple; but it occurred on occasions that they ate the flesh, distributing portions to the chiefs and those who succeeded in obtaining a part; the hands, feet and head went to the priests and celebrants; and these sacrificial victims they then regarded as sainted. If they were slaves captured in war, their masters kept the bones,

* The above illustration, after a drawing by Ann Axtell Morris from a wall-painting at Chichén Itzá, is almost exactly reproduced on a repoussé gold piece recovered from the great cenote, in which the incision in the chest is also shown, of which we unfortunately cannot show a reproduction, but which may be seen on display at the Peabody Museum in Cambridge. A further striking similarity is also to be found in the illustration on page 21 of the Gomesta manuscript, apparently a death but not a sacrificial scene, where the man's body lies tied and prone (not supine) on a table, facing into the head of a serpent which stretches coiled almost as in the above picture. An identity of symbolism (which does not in the least have to indicate either origin or transmission, as a certain school seems to derive everything Maya straight from Egypt because of other similarities) is perhaps somewhat curiously present in the Chinese honorific expression for one's decease: "He has mounted the dragon," and invoked the great mystery.

The sacrificial flint knife, with inlaid mosaic handle representing two intertwined serpents, as shown on the next page, was also brought up from the sacred cenote at Chichén Itzá. It is reproduced by courtesy of Mr. T. A. Willard, from his *City of the Sacred Well*.

and displayed them in the dances, as a mark of victory. At times they threw the victims alive into the well at Chichén Itzá, believing that they would come forth on the third day, even though they never did see them reappear.

SEC. XXIX. ARMS OF THE YUCATECANS. MILITARY CHIFTAINS. MILITIA AND SOLDIERS. CUSTOMS OF WAR.

They had offensive and defensive arms. The offensive were bows and arrows carried in their quivers, tipped with flints and very sharp fishes' teeth, which they shot with great skill and force. The bows were of a beautiful yellowish wood, marvelously strong and more straight than curved, with cords of their hemp fibres. The length of the bow is always somewhat less than that of the one who carries it. The arrows are made of reeds that grow in the lagoons, and more than five palms long, in which is fixed a piece of thin wood, very strong, in which again is fastened the flint. They do not know or use poisons, though from no lack of them. They had hatchets of a certain metal and of this shape, fastened in a handle of wood. These served them both as arms in war, and then at home for working wood. The metal being soft, they gave it an edge by beating with a stone. They had short lances a man's height in length, pointed with very hard flint; besides these they had no other arms.
For defense they had shields made of split and woven reeds, and covered with deer hide. They wore protective jackets of cotton, quilted in double thicknesses,* which were very strong. Some of the chiefs and captains wore helmets of wood, but these were not common. With these arms they went to war, adorned with feathers, and with skins of tigers and lions, when they possessed them. They had two captains, one perpetual and hereditary, the other elected for three years with a great deal of ceremony. This latter was selected to celebrate the festivals of the month **Pax**, which falls on the 12th of May; and during a war he commanded the second corps of the army.
This captain was called **nacon**; during these three years he was forbidden to hold converse with women, even with his wife, or to eat met. They held him in great respect, and supplied him with fish and iguanas, which are a sort of edible lizards; during this period he must not become drunk, and

---

* Landa here again makes the curious mistake before noted, of stating that they wore strong quilted coats of cotton and *salt*, in two layers. (See page 16.)

The illustration of a copper axe on the preceding page is from the Landa manuscript itself. The axes in the margin above are from Aztec and shown to have been of copper both by the

the vessels and household articles for his use were kept apart; he was not served by a woman, and mingled little with the towns-folk.

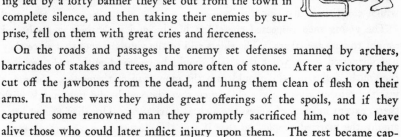

The three years passed as stated. These two captains arranged matters for wars, and put things in their order. In each district there were men chosen as the soldiery, and when the occasion came they presented themselves with their arms; these were called the **holcánes,** and if there were not enough of them, others were collected; they were then given instructions and divided. Marching led by a lofty banner they set out from the town in complete silence, and then taking their enemies by surprise, fell on them with great cries and fierceness.

On the roads and passages the enemy set defenses manned by archers, barricades of stakes and trees, and more often of stone. After a victory they cut off the jawbones from the dead, and hung them clean of flesh on their arms. In these wars they made great offerings of the spoils, and if they captured some renowned man they promptly sacrificed him, not to leave alive those who could later inflict injury upon them. The rest became captives of war in the power of those who took them.

These **holcánes** received no pay except in time of war, and then they were given certain money by the captains, but not much, because it came from their own funds; or if they lacked the needful, the town helped them. The town also supplied their food, which the women prepared for them; this they carried on their backs for the lack of animals, and thus the wars were of short duration. After the war the soldiers harassed the people in the districts greatly, under color of the war, while this lasted, requiring services and gifts; if any of them succeeded in killing some captain or chief he was greatly honored and feted.

SEC. XXX. PENALTIES AND PUNISHMENTS FOR ADULTERERS, HOMICIDES AND THIEVES. EDUCATION OF THE YOUNG MEN. CUSTOM OF FLATTENING THE HEADS OF CHILDREN.

From Mayapán these people retained the custom of punishing adulterers in the following manner. The investigation having been made and the man convicted of adultery, the leading men gathered at the chief's house and brought the adulterer tied to a piece of wood, delivering him to the husband

distinctive color, and place-names elsewhere. The three lower figures are all from the Madrid Maya codex, showing a warrior with hulché, or throwing stick, and spears; the god Ekchuah with knapsack and long lance, and the war-god putting fire and sword to a building.

of the woman. If he pardoned him he went free, if not, he killed him by dropping a large stone on his head, from a height. For the woman a sufficient punishment was the infamy, which was great; and commonly for this he left her.

The penalty for homicide, even when involuntary, was death at the hands of the relatives, unless he paid himself off. A thief had to reimburse the value, and was besides enslaved, however small the theft, which was a reason why they had so many slaves, especially in times of hunger. Because of this the friars made special effort to baptise them, that they might be set at liberty. If the thief was one of the chiefs or leading men, they assembled and having seized him scarified both sides of his face from the beard to the forehead, which constitutes a major dishonor.

The young men respected the elders highly, and took their counsels and sought to pass as mature. The elders said to the younger ones that since they had witnessed more, what they said should be received with credit, so that the youths following this would gain the more respect themselves. So much was the respect given to the elder men that the youths did not mingle with them, except in cases of necessity, such as marriages. Also they visited little among the married people; so that it was the custom to have in each town a large building, whitewashed and open on all sides, where the young men gathered for their pastimes. They played ball, and a certain game with beans like dice, and many others. Here they nearly always slept, all together, until they were married.

And since I have heard it said that in other parts of the Indies they were guilty of unnatural offenses in these houses, I have not learned of their doing this in this country, nor do I believe they did so; this because they say that those addicted to this pestilential vice care nothing for women, as these people did. For it was their habit to bring to these places the public women and make use of them; and it is said that among them the poor creatures who took up this mode of life, although they were paid therein, were so beset by the number of the youths that they were harassed even to death.

They painted their bodies black before marriage, but were not tattooed until after, except slightly. As to other things they always accompanied their fathers, and so became as great idolaters as they; and they helped them much in their labors.

The Indian women raised their children both harshly and wholly naked. Four or five days after the child was born they laid it on a small cot made of rods, face down, with the head between two pieces of wood, one on the occiput and the other on the forehead, tying them tightly, and leaving it suffering for several days until the head, thus squeezed, became permanently flattened, as is their custom. This however caused so great distress and risk for the poor infants that they were at times in danger of death; and the author hereof saw one where the head was pressed back of the ears, which must have been happened to many.

They were brought up entirely naked, but at about four or five years of age they gave them a wrap for sleeping, and strips of cloth to cover themselves as their fathers did; the little girls also began to cover themselves from the girdle down.   They suckled much, for the mothers never ceased to give them milk as long as they could, until three or four years old; from this there has resulted so many robust people in the country.

For the first two years they grew up marvelously pretty and fat; after that, due to the constant bathing by their mothers, and the heat of the sun, they became tanned.   But during the whole of their childhood they were jolly and lively, always armed with bows and arrows, and playing with each other. Thus they grew up until they began to behave as youths, taking on more importance, and leaving children's things.

SEC. XXXI.   CLOTHING AND ORNAMENTS OF THE INDIAN WOMEN.

The Indian women of Yucatan are in general of better build than the Spaniards, larger and well formed.   They lack the large haunches of negresses.   Those who are beautiful are quite vain of it, and indeed they are not bad looking; they are dark-skinned, caused more by their constant bathing and by the sun, than naturally; they do not powder their faces as our women do, regarding this as immodest.   They have a habit of filing their teeth, saw fashion, as a matter of elegance; this is done for them by the old women, using certain stones and water.

They pierce the cartilage of the nose within, to take a stone of amber for adornment.   They also pierce the ears for rings, in the manner of their husbands; they tattoo the body from the waist up, leaving the breasts for nursing reasons, the patterns being more delicate and beautiful than those of the men.   They bathe constantly, like the men, in cold water, but with little reserve, going stripped into the places where they go for water.   They also bathe in hot water, heated by fire; this is however rather for sake of health than cleanliness.

Their custom is to rub themselves with a red ointment, like their husbands; those who can do so add an odoriferous and very sticky gum which I take to be liquidambar, and which they call **istahté**.   This ointment they apply to a sort of briquet like soap, decorated with fancy designs, rubbing it on their breasts, arms and shoulders, until they are very gallant and odorous, as they feel; it lasts a long time without disappearing, according to the quality of the ointment.

They wear the hair very long, which they used to and still do arrange in very fine tresses, parted in two parts, and made use of to build up the coiffure. When the young girls go to be married, their mothers go to such pains in arranging their hair, and use such skill, as that I have seen many with their coiffures as fine as those of the most coquettish Spanish women. The little girls, not grown up, wear theirs in two or four plaits which become them well.

The Indian women of the coast, of the province of Bak-halal and of Campeche, are more modest in their costume; besides the skirt which they wear from the waist down, they cover the breasts with a double mantle fastened below the armpits. As to the others, their sole garment is a long wide sack, open at the sides, reaching to the thighs and there fastened by its own ends; besides this they have only the mantle in which they always sleep, and which when on the road they carry doubled and rolled, and wrapped up.

SEC. XXXII.   CHASTITY AND EDUCATION OF THE INDIAN WOMEN
OF YUCATAN.   THEIR CHIEF QUALITIES AND THEIR HOUSE-
HOLD ECONOMY.   THEIR DEVOTION AND THE SPECIAL
OBSERVANCES AT THE TIME OF CHILDBIRTH.

The women vaunted themselves as chaste, and with reason, because before they knew our nation they were such to a marvel; of this they have two examples. The captain Alonso López de Avila, father-in-law of the admiral Montejo, captured a handsome and graceful Indian girl during the war at Bacalar. She, in fear of death for her husband, had promised him never to yield herself to another, and for this nothing could persuade her, even the fear of death, to consent to violation; so that they threw her to the dogs.

As for myself, I once received the complaints of a baptized Indian woman, against a baptised man who followed her impetuously for her beauty; after she had repeatedly rejected him, without avail, he came one night in her husband's absence and when his pleas and offer of gifts remained without effect, attempted force, being a powerful man. For the whole night she fought him off, with such grief to herself as that she came to me; and it had been as she said.

The women were in the habit of turning their shoulders toward the men in passing them, and of turning to the side on the roads; this also they did in giving a man drink, until he had finished it. They taught their daughters the things they knew, and raised them excellently in their mode; they repri-manded them, instructed them and made them work; if they misbehaved they punished them by boxing their ears or slapping their arms. If they raise their eyes they reprove them severely, and put pepper on them, which causes great pain; if they are immodest they whip them, and put pepper on the other part, as a punishment and affront. It is also a grave reproach to tell the young girls they are like women brought up without a mother.

They are very jealous and at times lay hands on those women that have aroused their suspicions; again they are quick to anger and irritation on this score, though in other ways very mild; so that they are wont to pull their husbands' hair for the least infidelity. They are great workers and good in all the domestic economies, for on them rest the most, and most important, work of alimentation, housekeeping and education of their children, and the payment of the tributes; with all this they bear heavier burdens if it is necessary, working the fields and harvesting the crops. They are great economists, watching at night in what time is left them after their domestic labors, attending the markets to buy and sell their things.

They raise both Spanish and native fowls for sale, and for eating. They raise birds for their pleasure and for the feathers for adornment on their finer clothes; also raising other domestic animals, among these even offering their breast to the deer, which they have so tame that they never run away into the woods, even when they take them there and back, and raise them there.

They help each other mutually in their working and spinning, paying for this work in the same way as do their husbands on their farms; and while at this they ever have their jokes and tell their stories, at times with a bit of grumbling. They hold it disgraceful to look at the men and laugh at them, so this fact alone is enough to cause trouble, and with no other grounds to bring them into disrepute.

The most of their dances they do by themselves, although in some they dance with the men; among these the **naual** dance, one not very modest. Their fecundity is great, and they bear the children in good time; they are excellent nurses, first because their hot morning drink produces plenty of milk, and again because their constant grinding of the maize without tying up the breasts causes them to grow large and thus to hold a great deal of milk.

They also become intoxicated in their banquets, which they have among themselves, but not so much as do the men. They desire many children, and she who lacks them invokes their idols with gifts and prayers; and today they pray to God for them. They are

3 cib, lamat, ahau, eb, kan

a   b

9 12 9 8 9 4 9 13 9 9 7 3

Dresden, ţolkin 27

prudent and polite, and affable, with those who understand them; also extremely generous. They cannot keep a secret; and they are not as clean and proper in their persons and affairs as they should be, in spite of their washing like the ermines.

They were very devout and pious, rendering many devotions to their idols, burning incense before them, offering gifts of cotton, food and drink; it was also their charge to prepare the offerings of food and drink to be made during the ceremonies; but they did not share the custom of drawing blood for the evil spirits, and never did so. Neither were they allowed to come to the temples at times of the sacrifices, except in a certain festival where certain old women were admitted to take part therein. At the time of accouchement they went to their sorceresses, who made them believe all sorts of lies, and also put under their couch the image of an evil spirit called **Ixchel,** whom they called the goddess of childbirth.

When the children were born, they bathed them at once, and then when the pain of pressing the foreheads and heads was over, they took them to the priest that he might cast their fate, declare the office the child was to fill, and give him the name he was to retain during his childhood; because they were accustomed to call the children by different names until they were baptised or somewhat grown up; afterwards they dropped these and called themselves after their fathers until they were married. Then they took the names of both father and mother.

SEC. XXXIII. FUNERALS. BURIALS OF THE PRIESTS. STATUES TO
    PRESERVE THE ASHES OF THE CHIEFS, AND THE HONORS THEY
    PAID TO THEM. THEIR BELIEF REGARDING A FUTURE LIFE,
    WITH REWARDS AND PUNISHMENTS.

This people had a great and excessive fear of death, and this they showed in that in all their services they rendered to their gods were for no other end than that they should give them health and life and their subsistence. But when it came the time to die, it was a thing to see what were the grief and lamentations they displayed for their deceased, and the sadness they felt. They wept during the day in silence, and during the nights with loud and mournful cries that were grievous to hear. For many days they went about

The text figures are from the Dresden codex, and probably show the goddess Ixchel, in the first as goddess of childbirth, or Lucina; in the second she bears the signs of ' new day,' spring, renewal time. The wife of Itzamná, in the Maya pantheon she corresponded to Isis.

in deepest mourning. They kept abstinence and fasts for the deceased, especially a husband or wife. They declared it was the devil that had taken them off, because they thought all ills came from him, especially death.

At death they shrouded the body, filled the mouth with ground maize and a drink they call **koyem,** and with this certain stones they used for money, that food might not be lacking to him in the other life. They buried them in their houses or the vicinity, throwing some of their idols into the grave; if he was a priest they threw in some of his books; if a sorcerer his divining stones and other instruments of his office. They commonly abandoned the house after the funeral, except where many people were living there, in whose company they would lose some of their fear of death.

On the death of a chief or man of position they cremated the bodies and put the ashes in large urns, and built temples over them, as is seen to have been done in the old times in the cases there have been found at Izamal. Today it is found that they put the ashes of great chiefs in hollow clay statues.

The others of the upper classes made statues of wood, left hollow in the occiput, for their fathers; then they burned part of the body and put part of the ashes therein, and stoppered it; then they removed the skin from the occiput and fastened it there, burying the remainder in the usual fashion. These images they kept with much reverence, among their idols. Among the ancient lords of the house of the Cocoms they cut off the heads after death, boiled them so as to remove the flesh; then they sawed away the back part of the skull, leaving the front with the cheeks and teeth, supplying in these half sections of the head the removed flesh by a sort of bitumen, and gave them almost the perfection of what they had been in life. These they kept together with the images, and the ashes, all in the oratorios of their houses among their idols, with great reverence and affection. On all festivals and feast days they put before them offerings of food, that nothing might fail them in the other life, where they believed the souls rested and received their gifts.

These people have always believed in the immortality of the soul, in greater degree than many other nations, even though they were not so civilized; they believed that after death there was another life better than this, which the soul enjoyed after leaving the body. This future life they said was divided into good and evil, into pains and delights. The evil life of suffering they said was for the vicious, and the good and delectable for those whose mode of life had been good. The delights they said they would come into if they had been of good conduct, were by entering a place where nothing would give pain, where there would be abundance of food and delicious drinks, and a refreshing and shady tree they called **Yaxché,** the Ceiba tree, beneath whose branches and shade they might rest and be in peace forever.

The torments of the evil life which they said awaited the wicked, lay in going to an evil place below the other, and which they called **Mitnal,** meaning hell, where they were tormented by demons, by great pains of cold and hunger and weariness and sadness. They said there was in this place a chief demon whom all the rest obeyed and whom in their language they called **Hunhau;** also they said that these good and evil after-lives had no end, because the soul itself had none. They also said, and held as quite certain, that those who had hung themselves went to this paradise; and there 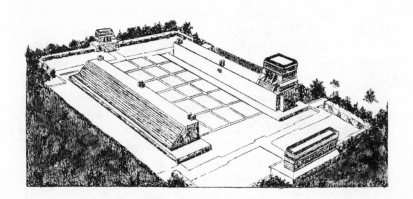 were many who in times of lesser troubles, labors or sickness, hung themselves to escape and go to that paradise, to which they were thought to be carried by the goddess of the scaffold whom they called **Ixtab.** They had no knowledge of the resurrection of the body; neither could they give account of whence had come to them these beliefs in this, their paradise and their hell.

THE BALL COURT
FROM A MODEL BY GEORGE OAKLEY TOTTEN, JR.

YUCATAN

SEC. XXXIV. COUNT OF THE YUCATECAN YEAR. CHARACTERS
OF THE DAYS. THE FOUR BACABS AND THEIR NAMES. GODS
OF THE 'UNLUCKY' DAYS.

The sun does not sink or go away far enough in this land of Yucatan for
the nights to become longer than the days; thus in their full maximum, from
San Andrés to Santa Lucía [Nov. 30 to Dec. 13] they are equal, and then
they begin to lengthen. To know the hour of the night the natives governed
themselves by the planet Venus, the Pleiades and the Twins. During the
day they had terms for midday, and for different sections from sunrise to
sunset, according to which they recognized and regulated their hours for
work.

They had their perfect year like ours, of 365 days and 6 hours, which they
divided into months in two ways. In the first the months were of 30 days
and were called U, which signifies the moon, and they counted from the
rising of the new moon until it disappeared.

In the other method the months had 20 days, and were called **uinal
hunekeh;** of these it took eighteen to complete the year, plus five days and
six hours. Out of these six hours they made a day every four years, so that
they had a 366-day year every fourth time.*

For these 360 days they had 20 letters or characters by which to designate
them, without assigning names to the five supplementary days,* as being

* We now know that the Mayas knew the *exact* length of the true solar year as 365.2420
days, that is with a minus error of 0.0002, while our present Gregorian calendar has it as
365.2425, or a plus error of 0.0003. Also that they knew and recorded it on their monuments more than a thousand years before the Spaniards came, and while Europe still had the
yet more incorrect method used in Landa's time, of an even day added each four years.

Every kind of guess has been made as to how the Aztecs and Mayas handled the leap-year
correction, until very recent researches have proved beyond doubt that the Mayas, at least,
solved it by first establishing a purely mathematical 'time unit' of 360 days, without frac-
tions, and then adjusted not only the various lunar and planetary risings and periods, but also
the solar year itself, with its seasons.

We also know that they knew the moon's period accurately, as 29.5209 days, but we find
no evidence on the monuments or in the Maya records of any use of a 30-day month, in the
ordinary sense.

This is incorrect; the five last days of the year bore their names regularly, as shown elsewhere by Landa himself in describing the common 52-year cycle used for mundane matters

sinister and unlucky.   The letters are as follows, each with its name above
to understand their correlation with ours.

I have already related that the Indian method of counting was from five
to five, and four fives making 20; thus then from these 20 characters they
take the first of each set of five, so that each of these serves for a year as do
our Dominical letters, being the initials days of the various 20-day months
(or **uinals**).   Thus:

Among the multitude of gods worshipped by these people were four whom
they called by the name **Bacab**.   These were, they say, four brothers placed
by God when he created the world, at its four corners to sustain the heavens
lest they fall.   They also say that these **Bacabs** escaped when the world was
destroyed by the deluge.   To each of these they give other names, and they
mark the four points of the world where God placed them holding up the
sky, and also assigned one of the four Dominical letters to each, and to the

by both Mayas and Aztecs, or 52 x 365 days, the 2nd, 3rd and 4th years of each 4-year
'lustrum' beginning with the 6th, 11th and 16th in order of the twenty.   Had the last five
days been actually *nameless*, every year would have begun on the same day of the twenty.
This also would have thrown their Long Count, or chronological order of days, completely
out of order.

Throughout the following pages we have substituted the standard type forms' of the characters for the days and months or **uinals**, for the shapes found in the Landa manuscript,
there being no question of their identity.   See the present writer's *Outline Dictionary of Maya
Glyphs*.

place he occupies; also they signalize the misfortunes or blessings which are to happen in the year belonging to each of these, and the accompanying letters.

The evil one, who has in this as in many other cases deceived them, fixed for them the services and offerings that had to be made in order to evade these misfortunes. Thus if they failed to occur, they said it was because of the ceremonies performed; but if they did come to pass, the priests made the people believe that it was because of some error or fault in the ceremonies,

The first of these Dominical letters, then, is **Kan**. The year served by this letter had as augury that Bacab who was otherwise called **Hobnil, Kanal-bacab, Kan-pauahtun, Kan-xibchac**. To him belonged the South.

The second letter, or **Muluc**, marked the East, and this year had as its augury the Bacab called **Can-sicnal, Chacal-bacab, Chac-pauahtun, Chac-xibchac**.

The third letter is **Ix**, and the augury for this year was the Bacab called **Sac-sini, Sacal-bacab, Sac-pauahtun, Sac-xibchac**, marking the North.

The fourth letter is **Cauac**, its augury for that year being the Bacab called **Hosan-ek, Ekel-bacab, Ek-pauahtun, Ek-xibchac**; this one marked the West.

In whatever ceremony or solemnity these people celebrated for their gods, they always began by driving away the evil spirit, in order the better to perform it. This exorcism was at times by prayers and benedictions they had for this purpose, and at other times by services, offerings and sacrifices which they performed for that end. In order to celebrate the solemnity of the New Year with the greatest rejoicing and dignity, these people, with their false ideas, made use of the five supplementary days, which they regarded as ' unlucky,' and which preceded the first day of their new year, in order to put on a great fiesta for the above Bacabs and the evil one, to whom they gave four other names, as they had done to the Bacabs; these names were: **Kan-uvayeyab, Chac-uvayeyab, Sac-uvayeyab, Ek-uvayeyab**.* These ceremonies and fetes being over, and the evil one driven away, as we shall see, they began their new year.

---

* In the above names the words *chac, sac, ek, kan* mean respectively red, white, black and yellow, the four colors assigned in this order to the East, North, West and South. It is delightful to note Landa's naïve persistence that they always exorcised the evil one in order to worship him. Uvayeyab simply means ' the couch of the year.'

SEC. XXXV. FESTIVALS OF THE 'UNLUCKY' DAYS. SACRIFICES FOR THE BEGINNING OF THE NEW YEAR KAN.

In all the towns of Yucatan it was the custom to have at each of the four entrances to the town two heaps of stones, one in front of the other; that is, at the east, west, north and south; and here they celebrated the two festivals of the 'unlucky' days, in the following manner.

For the year whose Dominical letter was **Kan,** the augury was **Hobnil,** and they say that both of these ruled the South. In this year, then, they made an image or clay figure of the demon they called **Kan-uvayeyab** and carried it to the piles of stone they had erected at the South. They chose a leading man of the town, at whose house was celebrated this fiesta on these days, and then they made a statue of a demon whom they called **Bolon-tz'acab,** which they set at the house of the principal, erected in a public spot to which all might come.

This being done, the chiefs, the priest and the men of the town, assembled and having the road clean and prepared, with arches and green branches, as far as the two heaps of stone where the statue was, there they gathered most devoutly; on arriving there the priest incensed the statue with forty-nine grains of ground maize, mixed with incense; then the nobles put their incense into the brazier of the idol, and incensed it. The ground maize alone was called **sacah,** and that of the lords **chahalté.**

Thus incensing the image, they cut off the head of a fowl, and presented it as an offering. When all had done this, they placed the image on a wooden standard called **kanté,** placing on his shoulders an angel as a sign of water and of a good year, and these angels they painted so as to make them frightful in appearance. Then they carried it with much rejoicing and dancing to the house of the principal, where there was the other statue of **Bolon-tz'acab.**

The illustration is a page of the Dresden codex, showing the **Kan-uvayeyab** ceremonies at the East.

From the house of this principal they brought out to the road, for the chiefs and the priest, a drink made of 415 grains of toasted maize (which they call **picula kakla,** of which all drank. On arrival at the house they set the image they were carrying in front of the statue of the demon they had there, and then made many offerings of food and drink, of meat and fish; these offerings were given to whatever strangers there were there; and to the priest they gave a leg of venison.

Others drew blood by cutting their ears and anointing therewith a stone image they had there, of the demon **Kanal-acantun.** They molded a heart of bread and another of calabash seeds, and offered those to the image of the demon **Kan-uvayeyab.** They kept this statue and image through those fateful days, and perfumed them with their incense, and with the ground maize and incense. They believed that if they did not perform these ceremonies, certain sicknesses would come on them in the ensuing year. When these fatal days were over they took the statue of **Bolon-tz'acab** to the temple, and the image to the eastern entrance where the next year they would go for it; there they left it and went to their houses to do what was their part in celebrating the new year.

These ceremonies over, and the evil spirit exorcised according to their deluded beliefs, they looked on the coming year as a good one, because it was ruled by the character **Kan** and the bacab **Hobnil;** and of him they said that in him there was no sin as in his brothers, and because of that no evils would come upon them. But since they often did so come, the evil one provided ceremonies therefor, so that when they happened they might throw the blame on the ceremonies or celebrants; and thus they continued always deluded and blind.

It was then commanded to make an idol called **Itzamná-kauil,** and place it in the temple. Then in the temple court they burned three balls of a milk or resin they called **kik** (rubber), while sacrificing a dog or a man; this they did keeping the same procedure I have described in chapter 100 (Sec. xxvii), except that in this case the method of the sacrifice differed. In the temple court they erected a great pile of stones, and then placed the dog or the man to be sacrificed on something much higher, from which they threw him, tied, upon the pile below; there the attendants seized him and with great swiftness drew out his heart, raised it to the new idol, and offered it between two plates. They offered other gifts of food, and in this festival there danced old women of the town, chosen therefor, clothed in certain vestures. They say that an angel descended and received this sacrifice.

SEC. XXXVI. SACRIFICES FOR THE NEW YEAR OF THE CHAR-
ACTER MULUC. DANCES OF THE STILT-WALKERS. DANCE
OF THE OLD WOMEN WITH TERRACOTTA DOGS.

In the year whose dominical letter was **Muluc** the augury was **Cansicnal.**
On this occasion the chiefs and the priest selected a president to care for the
festival, after which election they made an image of the demon as they had
done in the previous year, and which they called **Chac-uvayeyab,** and carried
this to the piles of stone at the East, where they had left the other
one the year before. They also made a statue of the idol called
Kinchahau, and placed it in the house of the president in a convenient place; from there, with the road all cleaned and dressed,
they all proceeded together for their accustomed devotions before
the god **Chac-uvayeyab.**

On arriving the priest perfumed it with 53 grains of the ground
maize, with the incense, which they call **sacah.** The priest gave
this to the chiefs, who put in the brazier more incense, of the kind
called **chahalté;** then they cut off a fowl's head, as before, and taking the
image on a wooden standard called **chacté,** they carried it very devoutly,
while dancing certain war-dances they call **holcan-okot, batel-okot.** During this they brought to the road for the chiefs and principal men their drink
made from 380 grains of maize, toasted as before.

When they had arrived at the house of the president they put this image
in front of the statue of **Kinch-ahau,** and made all their offerings to it,
which were then distributed like the rest. They offered to the image bread
formed like the yolks of eggs, others like deer's hearts, and another made of
dissolved peppers. Many of them drew blood from their ears, and with it
anointed the stone they had there, of the god **Chac-acantun.** They took
boys and forcibly drew blood from their ears, by blows. They kept this
statue and the image until the fatal days were passed, meanwhile burning their
incense. When the days were over, they took the image to the part of the
North, where next year they had to go to seek it; the other they took to the
temple, and then went to their houses to care for the works of the new year.
If they did not do all these things, they feared the coming especially of eye
troubles.

The dominical letter of this year being **Muluc,** the Bacab **Can-sicnal** ruled,
whence they held it a favorable year, for they said he was the best and greatest
of these Bacab gods; for this they put him first in their prayers. Yet for all
this the evil one caused them to make an idol called **Yaxcoc-ahmut,** which
they placed in the temple and took away the old images; then they erected in
the temple court a stone block on which they burned their incense, and a ball

of the resin or milk **kik,** with a prayer there to the idol, asking relief for the ills they feared for the coming year; these were a scarcity of water, buds (*hijos*) on the maize, and the like. To gain this protection the evil one ordained offerings of squirrels and an unembroidered cloth, which was to be woven by old women whose office it was to appease **Yaxcoc-ahmut.**

In spite of this being held a good year, they were still menaced with many other evils and bad signs, if they did not perform the sacrifices ordained. These were having dances on tall stilts, with offerings of heads of turkeys, bread and drinks made of maize. They had to offer clay dogs with bread on their backs, the old women dancing with them in their hands, and sacrificing a virgin puppy with black back. The devotees had to draw their blood and anoint the stone of **Chac-acantun** with it. This ceremony and sacrifice they regarded as acceptable to their god **Yaxcoc-ahmut.**

SEC. XXXVII. SACRIFICES FOR THE NEW YEAR WITH THE SIGN IX. SINISTER PROGNOSTICS, AND MANNER OF CONJURING THEIR EFFECTS.

In the year whose dominical letter was **Ix** and the augury **Sac-sini,** after the election of the president for the celebration of the festival, they made an image of the demon called **Sac-uvayeyab,** and carried it to the piles of stone at the North, where they had left the other one the year before. They then made a statue of the god **Itzamná** and set that in the president's house, then all together, with the roadway prepared, they went devoutly to the image of **Sac-uvayeyab.** On arrival they offered incense in the usual way, cut off the head of a fowl, and placed the image on a wooden stand called **Sac-hia,** and then carried it ceremoniously and with dances they called **alcab-tan kam-ahau.*** They brought to the road the usual drinks, and on arriving at the house they set this image before the statue of **Itzamná,** and there made their offerings, and distributed them; to the statue of **Sac-uvayeyab** they offered the head of a turkey, patés of quail with other things, and their drink.

Others drew blood and with it anointed the stone of the demon **Sac-acantun,** and they then kept the idols as they had done the year before, offering them incense until the last day. Then they carried **Itzamná** to the temple and **Sac-uvayeyab** to the place of the West, to leave him there to be gotten the next year.

The evils the Indians feared for the ensuing year if they were negligent in these ceremonies were loss of strength, fainting and ailments of the eyes; it

---

* This may be rendered: " Hasten to receive the Lord."

was held a bad year for bread and a good one for cotton. And this year bearing the dominical **Ix,** and which the Bacab **Sac-sini** ruled, they held as ill-omened, with many evils destined to occur; for they said there would be great shortage of water, many hot spells that would wither the maize fields, from which would follow great hunger, and from the hunger thefts, and from the thefts slavery for those who had incurred that penalty therefor. From this would come great discords, among themselves or with other towns. They also said that this year would bring changes in the rule of the chiefs or the priests, because of the wars and discords.

Another prognostic was that some men who should seek to become chiefs would fail in their aim. They also said that the locusts would come, and depopulate many of their towns through famine. What the evil one ordained that they should do to avert these ills, some or all of which were due to fall on them, was to make an idol of **Kinch-ahau Itzamná,** which they should put in the temple, where they should burn incense and make many offerings and prayers to the god, together with the drawing of their blood for the anointing of the stone of the demon **Sac-acantun.** They danced much, and the old women danced as was their custom; in this festival they also built a new oratorio for the demon, or else renewed the old, and gathered there for sacrifices and offerings to him, all going through a solemn revel; for this festival was general and obligatory. There were some very devout persons who of their own volition made another idol like the above, and placed it in other temples, where they made offerings and revels. These revels and sacrifices were held to be very acceptable to the idols, and as remedial for freeing them from the ills indicated as to come.

SEC. XXXVIII. SACRIFICES OF THE NEW YEAR OF THE LETTER CAUAC. THE EVILS PROPHESIED AND THEIR REMEDY IN THE DANCE OF THE FIRE.

In the year whose dominical was **Cauac** and the augury **Hosan-ek,** after the election of the one to serve as president had been made, they made an image of the demon named **Ek-uvayeyab,** and carried this to the piles of stone on the West, where they had left the other the year before. They also made a statue of a demon called **Vacmitun-ahau,** which they put in the president's house in a convenient place, and from there went all together to where the image of **Vacmitun-ahau** stood, having the road thither all properly prepared. On arriving the priest and the chiefs offered incense, as they were accustomed, and cut off the head of a fowl. After this they took the image on a standard called **yax-ek,** placing on the back of the image a skull and a corpse, and on top a carnivorous bird called **kuch** ['vulture'], as a sign of great mortality, since they regarded this as a very evil year.

They then carried it thus with their sentiment and devotion, dancing various dances, among which was one like the *cazcarientas*, which they thus called the **xibalba-okot,** meaning the dance of the devil. The cup-bearers brought to the road the drink of the chiefs, which they drank and came to the place of the statue **Vacmitun-ahau,** and then they placed before it the image they brought. Thereupon commenced the offerings, the incense, and the prayers, while many drew blood from many parts of the body, to anoint the stone of the demon called **Ekel-acantun;** thus the fatal days passed, after which they carried **Vacmitun-ahau** to the temple, and **Ek-uvayeyab** to the place of the South, to receive it the next year.

This year whose sign is **Cauac** and which was ruled by the bacab **Hosan-ek,** they held as one of mortality and very bad, according to the omens; for they said that many hot spells would kill the maize fields, while the multitudes of the ants and the birds would eat up the seeds that had been sown; but since this would not happen in all parts, in some places they would lack food, and in others have it, though with heavy labor. To avoid this the evil one caused them to make four demons called **Chichac-chob, Ekbalam-chac, Ahcanuol-cab, Ahbuluc-balam,** and set them in the temple where they should offer incense, and burn two balls of the milk or resin called **kik,** together with some iguanas, and bread, a miter, a bunch of flowers, and one of their precious stones. After this, to celebrate the festival, they made a great vault of wood, filling it aloft and on the sides with firewood, leaving doors to enter and go out. Then the most of the men took each two bundles of rods, very dry and long, tied together, and a singer standing on top of the firewood sang and made sound with one of their drums, while those below danced in complete unison and devotion, entering and leaving the doors of that wooden vault; dancing thus until the evening, each left there his bundle, and they then went home to rest and eat.

When the night came on they returned, and with them came a great crowd, because this ceremony was held in great regard. Each then took his bundle of rods, lit it, and each for himself put fire to the firewood, which burned high and quickly. When only the coals were left, they smoothed and spread them out; then those who had danced having come together, some of them began to walk unshod and naked from one side to the other across the hot coals; some of these came off with no lesions whatever, some came burned or half burned. In this way they believed to lie the remedy against the ills and bad auguries, and that this was the service most acceptable to their gods. After this they went off to drink and get intoxicated, for this was called for by the customs of the festival, and by the heat of the fire.

SEC. XXXIX. THE AUTHOR'S EXPLANATION AS TO VARIOUS
THINGS IN THE CALENDAR. HIS PURPOSE IN GIVING THESE
THINGS NOTICE.

Together with the characters of the Indians shown above in our chapter
100 (Sec. XXXIV), they gave names to the days of their months, and from all
the months together they made up a kind of calendar, by which they regulated
their festivals, their counting and contracts as business, as we do ours; save
that the first day of their calendar was not the first day of their year, but
came much later; this being the result of the difficulty with which they
counted the days of the months all together, as will be seen in the Calendar
itself we shall give herein later. The reason is that although the signs and
names of the days of their months are twenty, they were used to count them
from 1 to 13; after the 13 they return to 1 again, thus dividing the days of
the year into twenty-seven thirteens or triadecads, plus nine days, without
the supplementary ones.

With these periodical returns and the complicated count, it is a marvel to
see the freedom with which they know how to count and understand things.
It is notable that the dominical always falls on the first day of their year,
without fail or error, no other of the twenty ever taking that position. They
also used this way of counting to bring out by the aid of these characters a
certain other count they had for their ages; also other matters which,
although they were important for them, do not concern us much here. We
shall therefore be content with saying that the character or letter with
which they began their count of the days or Calendar is called **Hun Imix**
(One **Imix**), which is this: and which has no fixed day on which
it must fall. For each modifies its own count, and with all this
the dominical letter as they have it never fails to fall on the first day of the
following year.

Among these people the first day of the year always fell upon our 16th
of July, and was the first of their month **Popp.** Nor is it to be wondered
at that this people, however simple as we have found them in many ways,
also had ability in these matters and ideas such as other nations; for in the
gloss on Ezekiel we find that according to the Romans January began the
year, according to the Hebrews April, according to the Greeks March, and
according to the Orientals October. But, although they began their year in
July, I put their calendar here in the order of ours, and parallel, so that our
letters and theirs will come noted, our months and theirs, together with their
above-mentioned count of the thirteens, placed in the order of their progression.*

* In the pages following, the manuscript sets out in full each of the successive 365 days,

And since there is no need for putting the calendar in one place and the festivals in another, I shall place in each of the months its festivals and the observances and ceremonies with which they celebrated it. Thus I shall do as I before promised, giving their calendar and with it telling of their fasts and ceremonies wherewith they made their idols of wood, and other things; all of these things and what else I have told of these people serving no other purpose than to praise the divine goodness which so has permitted and has seen well to remedy in our times. This in order that, in recording them, with Christian entrails we pray Him for their preservation and progress in true Christianity; and that those whose charge this is may promote and aid this end, so that neither to this people for their sins, nor to ourselves, may there be lacking help; nor may they fail in what has been begun and so return to their misery and vomitings of errors, thus falling into worse case than before, returning the evil ones we have been able to drive out of their souls, out of which with so laborious care we have been able to drive them, cleansing them and sweeping out their vices and evil customs of the past. And this is not a vain hope, when we see the perdition which after so many years is to be seen in great and very Christian Asia, in the good, Catholic and very august Africa, and the miseries and calamities which today our Europe suffers, and where in our nation and houses we might say that the evangelical prophecies over Jerusalem have been fulfilled, where her enemies encircle her and crowd her almost to the earth. All of this God already had permitted for us, as we stand, were it not that his Church cannot pass, neither that which is said concerning her: *Nisi Dominus reliquisset semen, sicut Sodoma fuissemus.*

with the names and character together; with each it gives the day of the European month, and also the succession of the Church dominical letters, A b c d e f g. To July 16th, **12 Kan**, the 1st of **Pop'**, he assigns the church dominical A, fixing his calendar as computed for the year 1553, when July 16th fell on Sunday, and the only year between 1525 and 1581 when it did so fall. The present abbreviated transcript of Landa's work, made in 1566, was thus written thirteen years after the computation was made.

In the manuscript the series of days begins not with the Maya **Pop'** the 1st, but with our Jan. 1st; then when it reaches July 15th, with **12 Lamat**, it skips a day, to begin the year, incorrectly, with **12 Kan**. A year beginning with **12 Kan** must end with **12 Lamat**, with the next year beginning with **13 Muluc**. It therefore seems most probable that the later copyist simply transposed the two halves of the Maya year so as to start with our January, and hence the obvious error. For now that our calendar correlation is definitely established, we know that July 16th, Sunday, 1553, was **12 Kan**, the 1st of **Pop'**, and the **12 Lamat** then came on July 15th, 1554, to be followed regularly by **13 Muluc** on the 16th. And this completely disposes of any idea that an extra bissextile day was inserted every four years.

In addition to repeating the glyphs for the days, the manuscript inserts those for the successive **uinals** or 'months,' as they come. We shall do the same here, using the standard type forms as we have for the day-signs, also showing the forms in the manuscript. We shall also arrange the calendar in Maya form, beginning with the month **Pop'**.

SEC. XL. MONTHS AND FESTIVALS OF THE YUCATECAN CALENDAR.

POP'

A   July 16:   12 **Kan**

The first day of **Popp.** which is the first month of the Indians, was its
New Year, a festival much celebrated among them, because it was general,
and of all; thus the whole people together celebrated the festival for all their
idols.   To do this with the greater solemnity, on this day they renewed all
the service things they used, as plates, vases, benches, mats and old garments,
and the mantles around the idols.   They swept their houses, and threw the
sweepings and all these old utensils outside the city on the rubbish heap,
where no one dared touch them, whatever his need.

For this festival the chiefs, the priest and the leading men, and those who
wished to show their devoutness, began to fast and stay away from their
wives for as long time before as seemed well to them.   Thus some began three
months before, some two, and others as they wished, but none for less than
thirteen days.   In these thirteen days then, to continence they added the
further giving up of salt or pepper in their food; this was considered a grave
penitential act among them.   In this period they chose the **chacs,** the officials
for helping the priest; on the small plaques which the priests had for the
purpose, they prepared a great number of pellets of fresh incense for those
in abstinence and fasting to burn to their idols.   Those who began these
fasts, did not dare to break them, for they believed it would bring evil upon
them or their houses.

When the New Year came, all the men gathered, alone, in the court of the
temple, since none of the women were present at any of the temple ceremonies,
except the old women who performed the dances.   The women were admitted
to the festivals held in other places.   Here all clean and gay with their red-
colored ointments, but cleansed of the black soot they put on while fasting,
they came.   When all were congregated, with the many presents of food and
drink they had brought, and much wine they had made, the priest purified

the temple, seated in pontifical garments in the
middle of the court, at his side a brazier and the
tablets of incense.   The chacs seated themselves
in the four corners, and stretched from one to
the other a new rope, inside of which all who
had fasted had to enter, in order to drive out the
evil spirit, as I related in chapter 96 (Sec. XXVI).
When the evil one had been driven out, all
began their devout prayers, and the chacs made

new fire and lit the brazier; because in the festivals celebrated by the whole community new fire was made wherewith to light the brazier. The priest began to throw in incense, and all came in their order, commencing with the chiefs, to receive incense from the hands of the priest, which he gave them with as much gravity as if he were giving them relics; then they threw it a little at a time into the brazier, waiting until it ceased to burn.

After this burning of the incense, all ate the gifts and presents, and the wine went about until they became very drunk. Such was the festival of the New Year, a ceremony very acceptable to their idols. Afterwards there were others who celebrated this festival, in this month **Pop'**, among their friends, and with the chiefs and the priests, these latter being always first in their banquets and drinking.

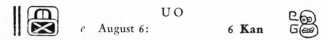

UO

c August 6:   6 **Kan**

In the month **Uo** the priests, and the physicians and sorcerers (who were one) began, with fasting and the rest, to prepare to celebrate another festival. The hunters and fishermen began to celebrate on the 7th of **Sip**, each celebrating for himself on his own day. First the priests celebrated their fete, which was called **Pocam** ['the washing']; gathered in their regalia in the house of the chief, they first cast out the evil spirit as was their custom; after that they brought out their books and spread them upon the fresh leaves they had prepared to receive them. Then with many prayers and very devoutly they invoked an idol they called **Kinch-ahau Itzamná**, who they said was the first priest, offered him their gifts and burned the pellets of incense upon new fire; meanwhile they dissolved in a vase a little verdigris and virgin water which they say was brought from the forests where no woman had been, and anointed with it the tablets of the books for their purification. After this had been done, the most learned of the priests opened a book, and observed the predictions for that year, declared them to those present, preached to them a little enjoining the necessary observances, and then assigning this festival for the coming year to the priest or chief who should then perform it; if he should die within the year his sons were under obligation to carry it for the deceased. After this they ate the gifts and food that had been brought, and drank until they were filled; thus they ended this festival, in which at times they gave the dance **okot-uil**.

SIP

f August 25:   13 **Kan**

On the following day the physicians and sorcerers gathered in the house
of one of them, with their wives. The priest exorcised the evil spirit. After
that they opened the wrappings of their medicines, in which they had brought

foolish things, including (each of them) small idols of the goddess
of medicine whom they called **Ixchel**, from whom this festival
was called **Ihcil-Ixchel**, as well as certain little stones called **am**,
and with which it was their custom to cast the lots. Then with
great devotion they invoked the gods of medicine by their prayers,
these being called **Itzamná**, **Cit-bolontun** and **Ahau-chamahes**,
the priests offering the incense burned in braziers with new fire;
meanwhile the chacs **covered** the idols and the small stones with
a blue bitumen like that of the books of the priests.

After this each one wrapped up the implements of his office,
and taking the pouch on his back all danced a dance they called
Chantuniah. After the dance the men sat by themselves, and
the women by themselves; and after putting over the festival
until the next year, they ate the presents, and became drunk without regard;
except the priests, who as they say refrained from the wine, to drink it when
alone and at their pleasure.

The next day the hunters gathered in the house of one of them, bringing

their wives, like the others; the priests came and
exorcised the evil spirit in their manner. Then
they placed in the center the materials prepared
for the sacrifice of the incense and the new fire,
and the blue bitumen. Then with worship the
hunters invoked the gods of the chase, **Acanum**,
Suhuy-sib, **Sipitabai**, and others; they dis-
tributed the incense, which they then threw in the brazier; while it burned
each one took an arrow and the skull of a deer, which the **chacs** anointed
with the blue pitch; some then danced with these, as anointed, in their hands,

while others pierced their ears and others
their tongues, and passed seven leaves of a
broadish plant called **ac,** through the holes.
When this was done, the priest first and then
the officers of the festival at once made their
offerings, and thus dancing they served the
wine and became drunk.

The first two figures on this page are from the Dresden Codex, showing **Ixchel** as goddess

Immediately on the following day the fishermen celebrated their festival in the same order as the others, except that what was anointed was the fishing tackle, and they did not pierce the ears but tore them on the sides; they danced a dance called **chohom,** and when all this was done they blessed a tall thick tree trunk and set it up erect. After this festival had been celebrated in the towns, it was the custom for the chiefs to go with many of the people to the coast, where they had great fishing and sport, having taken with them a great quantity of drag-nets, hooks and other fishing equipment. The gods who were the patrons of this festival were: **Ahkakne-xoi, Ahpua, Ahcitz-amalcum.**

S O T Z

e September 14: 7 **Kan**

In the month **Sotz** the proprietors of the bee-hives prepared themselves to celebrate their festival in **Tzec,** and although the chief preparation here was fasting, there was no obligation save on the priest and the officers who assisted therein, and it was voluntary on the part of the rest.

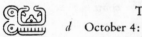
T Z E C

d October 4: 1 **Kan**

When the day of the festival had come, they all gathered in the appointed house, and did as in the others, except that there was no drawing of blood, since the patrons were the Bacabs, and especially **Hobnil.** They made many offerings, and especially to the four **chacs** they gave four platters with balls of incense in the middle of each, and painted on the rims with figures of honey, to bring abundance of which was the purpose of the ceremony. They ended it with wine as usual, in plenty, the hive owners giving honey for it in abundance.

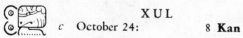
X U L

c October 24: 8 **Kan**

In the twelfth chapter (Sec. VI) was related the departure of Kukulcán

of medicine; of the rest, from the Madrid codex, in one the god **Ekchuah** traps the deer; next a vulture or **kuch** preys on the slain deer, and a hunter strikes a rattlesnake as it bites him; in the next a peccary, **citám,** is caught in a spring trap, and in the next an aspersarium, previously described, is being used in what is known as the ' chapter of the bees.' A little further on, under the month **Xul,** is shown one of the very handsome handled incense burners, of which a number of specimens have been found.

from Yucatan, after which some of the Indians said he had departed to heaven with the gods, wherefore they regarded him as a god and appointed a time when they should celebrate a festival for him as such; this the whole country did until the destruction of Mayapán. After that destruction only

the province of Maní kept this up, while the other provinces in recognition of what they owed to Kukulcán made presents, one each year, turn and turn about, of four or sometimes five magnificent banners of feathers, sent to Maní; with which they kept this festival in that manner, and not in the former ways.

On the 16th of **Xul** all the chiefs and priests assembled at Maní, and with them a great multitude from the towns, all of them after preparing themselves by their fasts and abstinences. On the evening of that day they set out in a great procession, with many comedians, from the house of the chief where they had gathered, and marched slowly to the temple of Kukulcán, all duly decorated. On arriving, and offering their prayers, they set the banners

INCENSE BURNER

on the top of the temple, and below in the court set each of them his idols on leaves of trees brought for this purpose; then making the new fire they began to burn their incense at many points, and to make offerings of viands cooked without salt or pepper, and drinks made from their beans and calabash seeds. There the chiefs and those who had fasted stayed for five days and nights, always burning copal and making their offerings, without returning to their homes, but continuing in prayers and certain sacred dances. Until the first day of **Yaxkin** these comedians frequented the principal houses, giving their plays and receiving the presents bestowed on them, and then taking all to the temple. Finally, when the five days were passed, they divided the gifts among the chiefs, priests and dancers, collected the banners and idols, returning them to the house of the chief, and thence each one to his home. They said and believed that Kukulcán descended on the last of those days from heaven and received their sacrifices, penances and offerings. This festival they called **Chicc-kaban.***

We probably have here a survival from an earlier adjustment of the calendar, as shown both by the month-names and the ceremonies. **Xul** means 'end, termination.' and on the 16th they created new fire, and continued offerings and other ceremonies for the last five days of the month, paralleling those later carried on before the New Year beginning the 1st of **Pop'. Kin** means 'sun, day, time,' so that **Yaxkin** means 'new time.' And so even in the later changed arrangement they kept the month **Yaxkin** for the renewal of all utensils

YAXKIN

b   November 13:   2 **Kan**

In this month of **Yaxkin** they began to get ready, as usual, for the general festival they would celebrate in **Mol,** on the day appointed by the priest for all the gods; they called it **Olob-sab-kamyax.** After they were gathered in the temple and the same ceremonies and incense burning as in the previous festivals had been gone through with, they anointed with the blue pitch all the instruments of all the various occupations, from that of the priest to the spindles of the women, and even the posts of their houses. For this festival they assembled all the boys and girls, and in place of the painting and the ceremonies they gave to each nine little blows on the knuckles of their hands, outside; for the girls this was done by an old woman, vestured in a robe of feathers, who brought them there; from this she was called **Ixmol,** meaning the bringer together. These blows they gave them that they might grow up expert craftsmen in their fathers' and mothers' occupations. The conclusion was a fine drinking affair, with eating of the offerings, except that we must not believe that the devout old woman was allowed to become so drunk as to lose the feathers of her robe on the road.

---

with preparation for the very sacred ceremonial carving of the new images in the following month **Mol,** and carried through into **Ch'en.** In the accompanying figures, taken from the Madrid codex, the makers are ceremonially garbed in the habiliments of the gods, and are using what must have been the hardened copper tools elsewhere referred to by Landa, and such as have been actually recovered from the sacred cenote. Then in the months **Ch'en** or **Yax** followed the **Oc-na** ('house-entering' ceremony) or renovation of the temples, in honor of the gods of the fields.

In Landa's time the 16th of **Xul** fell on Nov. 8th, **Yaxkin** beginning Nov. 13th, and **Mol** ending just at the winter solstice, Dec. 22nd. Owing to our ignorance still as to just how the natural seasons and the months were kept adjusted without our quadrennial leap year method, we have not yet solved the question of the varying New Year dates found through all Middle America; but it is most interesting that this **Xul-Yaxkin** incidence should be tied in so closely with Quetzalcóatl, in whom we have the most tangled problem in the whole field. Nevertheless, while such specific seasonal ceremonies as planting, harvesting, hunting, etc., must somehow have been kept lined up to their regular month associations, still such a purely historical religious ceremony as this could remain fixed in the months once allotted, regardless of seasonal questions.

What we can say with certainty is that, some thousand years before Landa wrote, the Mayas knew that 1507 true solar years of 365.2422 days equalled 1508 'vague' years of 365 days; so that New Year's or any other fixed date would keep falling behind not quite a quarter day every year, to come back in place again only after 1507 revolutions. So that we have here a case where clearly 'New Year' ceremonies were celebrated far out of their current place at Landa's time, and in a secondary 'survival' form, attached to the transitory presence of Quetzalcóatl in Yucatan (according to the traditions), while the greater and fuller sin-cleansing five-day ceremonies fell in July.

MOL

A   December 3:   9 **Kan**

In this month the bee-keepers held another festival like they did in the month **Tzec,** to the end that the gods might provide flowers for the bees.

One of the most arduous and difficult things these poor people had to do was the making of images of wood, which they called the gods.   Thus they had a particular month designated for this work,
and this was the month **Mol,** or some other if
the priest said it was right.   Those then who
wished to make them first consulted the priest,
and after taking his counsel went to the
artisans; they say that the artisans always excused themselves, believing that either they or some one of their household would die or would suffer heart attacks or strokes; when however they had accepted, the **chacs** whom they had chosen to serve in the matter, together with the priest and the artisan, began their fasts.   While they were fasting, he who was to have the idols went himself or else sent to the woods for the material, which was always cedar.   When the wood arrived they built a small fenced-in hut of thatch, in which they put the wood and a large urn into which to put the idols, and
 to keep them covered up while they were working.   They put incense to be burned to the four deities called the **Acantuns,** which they brought and placed at the four cardinal points. They also brought the instruments with which to scarify themselves or draw blood from their ears; and also the tools for carving their black gods.   When all these were ready in the hut, the priest, the **chacs** and the artisan shut themselves in the hut, and they began their making the gods, from time to time cutting their ears and anointing the statues herewith, and burning the incense.   Thus they worked until they were finished, their families bringing to them their food and needs; during the period they were not to consort with their wives, even in thought; nor could any one enter that place where they worked.

CH'EN

ʒ   December 23:   3 **Kan**

They worked in much reverence and fear, as they say, making the gods. When they were finished and the idols perfected, the owner made them the finest present he was able, of birds, game and their money, to pay for the labor of those who had made them.   Then they removed them from the hut and set them in another enclosure of branches prepared for them in the court, where the priest blessed them with great solemnity, and an abundance of devout prayers; but first the priest and the artisans removed the soot with which they had covered themselves during their fasting. Then having exorcised the evil one and burned the sanctified incense, they put the images wrapped in a cloth in a chest and delivered them to their owner, who very devotedly received them. Afterwards the good priest preached a little on the excellence of the artisans' profession, or making new images of the gods, and on the ills that would have attended them had they not been faithful to the precepts of abstinence and fasting. After that they ate much and drank more.

YAX
e January 12:   10 **Kan**

In whichever of the months **Ch'en** or **Yax** were designated by the priest, and on the day set by him, they celebrated a festival they called **Oc-na,** meaning the ' renovation of the temple,' in honor of the **Chacs**, regarded as the gods of the maize fields. In this festival they consulted the predictions of the Bacabs, as we have told at more length in chapters 111 to 116 (Secs. XXXV to XXXVIII), and in conformity with the order there given. Each year they celebrated this festival and renewed the idols of terra cotta, and their braziers, since it was the custom for each idol to have his own little brazier for burning his incense; and if it was necessary they built a new house, or repaired the old one, placing on the wall the record of these things, with their characters.

A: January 29: **1 Imix.** Here begins the calendar of the Indians, saying in their language, **Hun Imix.***

SAC
d February 1:   4 **Kan**

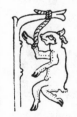
The hunters, who had celebrated one festival in the month **Sip,** now celebrated another in the month **Sac,** on a day set by the priest, doing this to appease the anger of the gods against them and their fields because of the blood they shed in their hunting; for they regarded with abhorrence any shedding of blood except in their sacrifices. For this reason, whenever they went to the hunt, they invoked the god and burned incense to him; and if possible later they anointed the faces with blood from the heart of the game.

* The ' book of divination,' of lucky and unlucky days, called **tzolkin,** meaning ' day-count ' in Maya, **ch'olkih** in Quiché, and **tonalamatl** in Aztec, was a period of **260 days,** revolving continuously without regard to the calendar. It began with the day **1 Imix** and ended with **13 Ahau,** successively combining the thirteen numerals with the twenty day-names.

f: **February 17: 7 Ahau.** On whatever day of the year **7 Ahau** fell they celebrated a very great festival with incense and offerings, and restrained drinking; and since this was a movable feast it was in the care of the priests to publish it in sufficient time ahead, that they might fast in due manner.

                                CEH
                        c   February 21:   11 **Kan**

                                M A C
                        b   March 13:   5 **Kan**

On some one of the days of this month **Mac** the oldest people celebrated a festival to the **Chacs,** the gods of sustenance, and **Itzamná.** One or two days ahead of this they performed the following ceremony, which they called **tupp-kak** (' fire-quenching '). They hunted for as many animals and crea-

 tures of the fields as they could, and as there were in the country. With these they gathered in the temple court, where the **chacs** and the priest placed themselves in the corners to exorcise the evil spirit according to custom, and each with a jar of water, as brought there to him. In the middle they placed, set up erect, a large bundle of dry sticks, tied together; then first burning the incense in the braziers they set fire to the sticks, and as they burned they drew out the hearts of the birds and animals, liberally, and threw them into the flames. If they had been unable to get any of the larger animals, such as tigers, lions or caimans, they made hearts out of incense instead. If they had killed any, they brought their hearts for the fire. Then when the hearts were all consumed, the **chacs** extinguished the fire with their jars of water.

This and the coming festival were to obtain the needed rains for their maize crops in the ensuing year; they thereupon celebrated the fiesta.

This was done in a different manner from the others, since for this they did not fast, except that the provider of the festival did his fast. When the time arrived, all the townsfolk, the priest and the officials assembled in the temple court, where they had a pyramid of stones, with stairways, all clean and dressed with green branches. The priest then gave the prepared incense to the one providing, and he burned it in the brazier, whereby they said the evil spirit was exorcised. This being done with their accustomed reverence, they spread the lower step of the pyramid with mud from the well, and the other steps with blue pitch.

They used much incense and invoked **Itzamná** and the **Chacs** with prayers and rituals, and made their offerings. When this had been done they took their comfort in eating and drinking what had been offered, confident that their service and invocations would bring a prosperous new year.

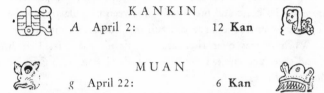

KANKIN

A April 2:   12 **Kan**

MUAN

g April 22:   6 **Kan**

During the month **Muan** the owners of cacao plantations made a festival for the gods **Ekchuah, Chac** and **Hobnil,** who were their protectors. To do this they went to the property of one of them, where they sacrificed a dog spotted with the colors of the cacao, burned incense to their idols, and offered up iguanas of the blue sort, with certain bird's feathers, and other game; then they gave to each one of the officers a branch of the cacao fruit. After the sacrifice and the prayers they ate the gifts and drank, but (as they tell) no more than three draughts of the wine, no more than this having been brought. After this they went to the house of him who had provided the fiesta, for various diversions.

PAX

f May 12:   13 **Kan**

In this month of **Pax** they celebrated a festival called **Pacum-chac,** for which the priests and chiefs of the smaller villages gathered at the larger towns, where they all watched for five nights in the temple of **Cit-chac-coh,** with prayers, offerings and incense, as has been related of the festival to Kukulcán in the month **Xul,** in November. Before these days were passed, they all went to the house of their war general, the **Nacon** (of whom we spoke in chapter 101) (See. xxx), and with great pomp they conducted him to the temple, offering incense to him as to an idol, and then seating and incensing him as if he were a god; there he and they stayed through the five days, during which they ate and drank of the gifts that had been brought to the temple, and performed a great dance in the style of war manoeuvers, called in their language **Holcan-okot,** or the dance of the warriors. After these five days they went on to the fiesta which, since it was for matters of war and victory over their enemies, was very solemn.

First they went through the ceremony and sacrifices of the Fire, as I told under the month **Mac;** then in the usual manner they drove out the evil spirit with great solemnity. After this came prayers and the offering of gifts and incense, and while they were doing this the chiefs and those who had before assisted in this, again carried the **Nacon** on their shoulders around the temple, with incense. When they returned with him, the priests sacrificed a dog, drew out its heart and presented it between two platters to the demon, while the **chacs** each broke large jars full of liquor, and with this ended the festival. When it was over they ate and drank the gifts that had been brought, and then reconducted the **Nacon** to his home, with great ceremony, but without perfumes.

There they held a great fiesta in which the lords and the priests and leading men drank to intoxication, and the rest of the people went to their towns; but the **Nacon** did not join in the intoxication. On the next day, when the effects of the wine had passed off, all the lords and priests of the towns who had remained at the chief's house and taken part in this last act, received from him a great quantity of incense prepared for the purpose, which had been blessed by the holy priests. He then joined them and gave a long discourse in which with much emphasis he enjoined on them the festivals they should, in their own towns, celebrate for the gods, that the coming year might yield many things for their support. After the address, all departed with much expression of affection and noise, each going to his town and home.

There they busied themselves with the fiestas, which according to the circumstances, continued until the month **Pop',** and which they called **Sabacilthan,** and performed as follows. They looked through the town for the richest men able to afford the costs of the fiesta, and set a day, to provide the most entertainment during the remaining three months before the new year. They gathered at the house of the feast maker, went through the ceremonies of driving away the evil spirit, burning copal, with offerings and dances, and making themselves such wine kegs, and such was the excess in these fiestas for these three months that it was painful to see them; for they went about scratched and bruised and red-eyed with the drink, all for this love of the wine for which they had destroyed themselves.

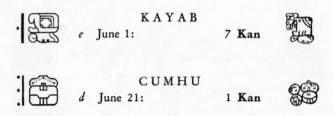

KAYAB

e June 1:   7 **Kan**

CUMHU

d June 21:   1 **Kan**

VAYEB Xma-kaba kin
  c July 11:   **Kan**

It has been told in the preceding chapters how the Indians began their year
following these ' nameless days,' preparing there as with vigils for the celebration of the New Year festival; in the same interval they celebrated the festival
of the **Uvayeyab** demon, for which they left their houses, which otherwise
they left as little as possible; they offered besides gifts for the general festival,
and counters for their gods and those of the temples. These counters they
thus offered they never took for their own use, nor anything that was given
to the god, but with them bought incense for burning. During these days
they neither combed nor washed, nor otherwise cared for themselves, neither
men nor women; neither did they perform any servile or heavy work, fearing lest evil fall on them.

SEC. XLI. CYCLE OF THE MAYAS. THEIR WRITINGS.

Not only did the Indians have a count for the year and months, as has been
before set out, but they also had a certain method of counting time and
their matters by ages, which they counted by 20-year periods, counting
thirteen twenties, with one of the twenty signs in their months, which they
call **Ahau**, not in order, but going backwards as appears in the following

circular design. In their language they
call these periods **katuns,** with these
making a calculation of ages that is marvelous; thus it was easy for the old man
of whom I spoke in the first chapter to
recall events which he said had taken
place 300 years before. Had I not
known of this calculation I should not
have believed it possible to recall after
such a period.*

As to who it was that arranged this
count of katuns, if it was the evil one
it was so done as to serve in his honor;
if it was a man, he must have been a great idolater, for to these **katuns** he
added all the deceptions, auguries and impostures by which these people
walked in their misery, completely blinded in error. Thus this was the
science to which they gave most credit, held in highest regard, and of which

* The center of the wheel reads: They call this count in their language **vazlazon katun,**
which means the ' revolution of the katuns.'

not even all the priests knew the whole. The way they had for counting their affairs by this count, was that they had in the temple two idols dedicated to two of these characters. To the first, beginning the count with the cross above the circular design, they offered worship, with services and sacrifices to secure freedom from ills during the twenty years; but after ten years of the first twenty had passed, they did no more than burn incense and do it reverence. When the twenty years of the first had passed, they began to follow the fates of the second, making their sacrifices; and then having taken away that first idol, they set up another for veneration during the next ten years.

Verbi gratia. The Indians say that the Spaniards finally reached the city of Mérida in the year of Our Lord's birth 1541, which was exactly at the first year of the era of **Buluc** (11) **Ahau,** which is in that block where the cross stands; also that they arrived in the month **Pop',** which is the first month of their year. If the Spaniards had not arrived, they would have worshipped the image of **Buluc Ahau** until the year '51, that is for ten years, and then would have set up another idol for **Bolon** (9) **Ahau** up to the year '61, when they would remove it from the temple and replace it with the idol for **Vuc Ahau,** then following the predictions of **Bolon Ahau** for another ten years, thus doing with all in their turn. Thus they venerated each **katun** for twenty years, and during ten years they governed themselves by their superstitions and deceits, all of which were so many and such as to hold in error these simple people, that one would have to marvel over it who did not know the things of Nature and the experience the devil possesses in dealing with them.

These people also used certain characters or letters, with which they wrote in their books about the antiquities and their sciences; with these, and with figures, and certain signs in the figures, they understood their matters, made them known, and taught them. We found a great number of books in these letters, and since they contained nothing but superstitions and falsehoods of the devil we burned them all, which they took most grievously, and which gave them great pain.

Of their letters we give here an *a, b, c,* their cumbersomeness not permitting more, because for all the aspirations of the letters they use one character, and then for uniting the parts another, going on in this way *ad infinitum,* as in the following example. **Le** means a lasso, and to hunt with one; to write it with their letters, they wrote them with three, at the aspiration of the **l** the vowel **e,** put before it; in this they are not at fault, although they use the **e** if they wish to do so for definiteness. Example: **e l e lé;** afterwards they put the syllable joined:

Há means water; because the sound of the letter *aitch* is composed of a, h, before it, they put it at the beginning with **a**, and **a ha** at the end in this fashion:

They also wrote in syllables, but in one and the other style: I only put it here in order to give a complete account of the matters of this people. **Ma in kati** means 'I do not wish,' and they write it in syllables in this manner:

Here begins their *a, b, c*:

de las partes otro, y assi viene a hazer in infinitum como
se podra ver en el siguiente exemplo. Le, quiere dezir lazo
y caçar con el, para escrivirle con sus caraçores, aviendo
les nosotros hecho entender que son dos letras lo escrivian
ellos con tres puniendo a la aspiracion de la ʒ, la vocal, o,
que antes de si trae, y y en esto no yerran aunq vsen de si
quisieren ellos de su curiosidad. Exemplo.
despues al cabo le pegan la parte junta. Ha. que quiere dezir
agua porq la b dho tiene a. h. ante de si lo ponen ellos al
principio con a. y al cabo desta manera   ha   Tambie
lo escriven a partes, pero de la vna y otra vna   manera, y
no pusiera aqui ni tratara dello sino por dar cuenta entera
de las cosas desta gente   Mainkati   quiere dezir no quiero, ellos
lo escriven a partes desta manera   ma   in   kati   ti

Syguese su a, b, c.

    c   t   e   h   i   ca   h   l   l

    m   n   o   o   p   cu   ku   Xp   x   u   p

    u   3   De las letras que aqui faltan carece esta lengua.
        y tiene otras añadidas de la nuestra, para otras
cosas q las ha menester, y ya no vsan para nada dellos
sus caratteres especialmente la gente moça q an aprendido
los nros

The letters that do not appear are wanting in this language; and they have others in addition to ours, for other things where they are needed. But they no longer use any of the characters, especially the young people who have learned ours.

PARIS CODEX, PAGE 6

SEC. XLII.   MULTITUDE OF BUILDINGS IN YUCATAN.   THOSE OF IZAMAL, OF MERIDA, AND OF CHICHEN ITZA.

If the number, grandeur and beauty of its buildings were to count toward the attainment of renown and reputation in the same way as gold, silver and riches have done for other parts of the Indies, Yucatan would have become as famous as Peru and New Spain have become, so many, in so many places, and so well built of stone are they, it is a marvel; the buildings themselves, and their number, are the most outstanding thing that has been discovered in the Indies.

Because this country, a good land as it is, is not today as it seems to have been in the time of prosperity when so many great edifices were erected with no native supply of metals for the work, I shall put here the reasons I have heard given by those who have seen these works.   These are that they must have been the subjects of princes who wished to keep them occupied and therefore set them to these tasks; or else that they were so devoted to their idols that these temples were built by community work; or else that since the settlements were changed and thus new temples and sanctuaries were needed, as well as houses for the use of their lords, these being always constructed of wood and thatch; or again, the reason lay in the ample supply in the land of stone, lime and a certain white earth excellent for building use, so that it would seem an imaginary tale, save to those who have seen them.

It may be that this country holds a secret that up to the present has not been revealed, or which the natives of today cannot tell.   To say that other nations compelled these people to such building, is not the answer, because of the evidences that they were built by the Indians themselves; this is bared to view in one out of the many and great buildings that exist, where on the walls of the bastions there still remain figures of men naked save for the long girdles over the loins called in their language **ex**, together with other apparel the Indians of today still wear, worked in very hard cement.

While I was living there, in a building we were demolishing there was found a large jar with three handles, adorned with figures applied on the outside; within, among the ashes of a cremated body, we found three counters of fine stone, such as the Indians today use as money, all showing the people were Indians.   It is clear that if such they were, they were of higher grade than those of today, and greater in bodies and strength.   This shows more clearly here in Izamal than elsewhere, there being here, as I say, today on the bastions figures in semi-relief, made of cement, and of men of great height.   The same is true of the extremities of the arms and legs of the man whose ashes we found in the jar I have referred to; these also were very

thick, and their burning a marvel. We see the same thing on the steps of
the buildings, here only in Izamal and Mérida, of a good two palms in height.

Here in Izamal is a building, among the others, of a startling height and
beauty, as is seen in this sketch and its explanation.* It has twenty steps,
each more than two palms in height and in
breadth, and being over a hundred feet in
length. These steps are of very large carved
stones, although now much worn and damaged
by time and water. Around them, as is shown
by the curved line, is a very strong dressed
stone wall; at one and a half times the height
of a man there is a cornice of beautiful stone
going all the way around, from which the work
continues to the height of the first stairway,
and the plaza in the sketch.

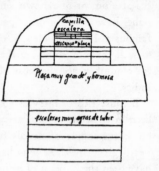

From this plaza there rises another stairway like the first, but not so long
nor with so many steps, again with an encircling wall. Above these steps
there is another fine small platform, on which, close to the surrounding wall,
is a very high mound with steps facing the south like the other great stairs,
and on top of this a beautiful finely worked chapel of stone. I went to the
top of this chapel, and Yucatan being a flat country I could see as far as the
eye could reach, an amazing distance, as far as the sea. There were eleven
or twelve of these buildings at Izamal, this being the largest, and all near
together. There is no memory of the builders, who seem to have been the
first inhabitants. It is eight leagues from the sea, in a beautiful site, good
country and district, and so in 1549, with some importunity, we had the
Indians build a house for St. Anthony on one of these structures. There and
all around great benefit has come in its Christianity; so that two good communities have been established in this place, distinct from each other.

The second of the chief ancient structures, such that there is no record
of their builders, are those at Tiho, thirteen leagues from those at Izamal,
and like them eight leagues from the sea; and there are traces of there having
been a fine paved road from one to the other. The Spaniards established a
city here, and called it Mérida, from the strangeness and grandeur of the
buildings; the chief one of which I shall show here as well as I can, as I did
that at Izamal, that it may be seen what it was like.

This is the sketch I have drawn; to understand it, it must be noted that
it is a squared site of great size, more than two runs of a horse.* On the east

---

* In front, " steps very hard to climb."   Then a very large and beautiful plaza;   another
plaza, and then steps with a chapel on top.

front the stairway begins at the ground level, with seven steps as high as
those at Izamal; on the other three sides, the south, west and north, there
runs a very broad strong wall. On top of this first mass, all squared and
of dry stone, and flat, there starts again on the east side another stairway, 28
to 30 feet further in than the other stairway, as I judge, and with steps
equally large. On the north and south, but not on the west, it is again set
back the same distance, with two strong walls reaching the height of the
stairway, and continuing until they meet those of the west face, forming a
great mass of dry stone in the center, built by hand, of an amazing height
and greatness.

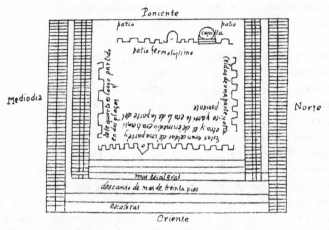

On the East, stairway, platform of more than 30 feet; then more stairs. At the South, a
long apartment, divided; at the North, another, same. At the West another range broken
by an arcade, and with a chapel, and patios in front and behind. In the center a great patio,
between the two ranges, each made up of rooms, broken by arcades.

On the level top are buildings in the following manner: six feet back of
the stairway is a long range not reaching to the ends, of very fine stonework,
made up of cells on each side, twelve feet long by eight wide; the doors of
these have no sign of facings or hinges for closing, but are flat and of stone
elaborately worked, the whole marvelously built, and the tops of the doorways
formed of single large stones. In the middle is a passageway like the arch
of a bridge; above the doors of the cells there projected a relief of worked
stone the whole length of the structure. Above this was a line of small
pillars, half inset in the wall with the outer part rounded, and reaching to
the level of the cell roofs. Above these there was another relief extending
the whole length of the range; and then came the terrace, finished with a very
hard stucco made with the water from the bark of a certain tree.

* An early distance reckoning for as far as a horse will run without taking breath; roughly
1,200 feet.

On the north was another range with cells, the same as the above, but the whole only half the length.   On the west was another line of the cells, pierced at the fourth or fifth by an arcade going clear through the whole, like the one in the east front; then a round, rather tall building; then another arcade, and the rest cells like the others.   This range crosses the whole court not quite in the center, thus making two courts, one to the back at the west, the other on the east, surrounded by four ranges as described.   The last of these ranges however, to the south, is quite different.   This consists of two sections, arched along the front like the rest, the front being a corridor of very thick pillars topped by very beautifully worked single stones.   In the middle is a wall against which comes the arch of the two rooms, with two passageways from one to the other; the whole is thus enclosed above and serves as a retreat.

About two good stone-throws distant from this edifice is another very high and beautiful court, containing three finely ornamented pyramids, on top of them chapels, arched in the fashion they were used to employ.   Quite a distance away was a pyramid, so large and beautiful that even after it had been used to build a large part of the city they founded around it, I cannot say that it shows any signs of coming to an end.

The first of the above structures, with the four ranges, was given to us by the admiral Montejo, all covered with heavy trees; we cleared it, and there built us a proper monastery all of stone, and a fine church which we called after the Mother of God.   There was so much stone that after leaving the southern range, and part of the others, we gave much stone to the Spaniards for their houses, particularly for their doors and windows; such was the abundance.

The buildings at Tikoch are not so many nor so sumptuous as many of these others, although they were good and noteworthy; I only mention them here on account of the great population there must have been, as I have before had to relate; thus I leave this here.   These buildings are three leagues from Izamal toward the east, and seven leagues from Chichén Itzá.

Chichén Itzá, then, is a fine site, ten leagues from Izamal and eleven from Valladolid.   Here as the old men of the Indians say, there reigned three lords, brothers who (as they recall to have been told them by their ancestors) came from the land to the west, and gathered in these places a great settlement of communities and people whom they ruled for some years in great peace, and with justice.   They greatly honored their god, and thus erected many magnificent buildings; especially one, the greatest, whose design I shall give here as I sketched it by standing on it, the better to explain it.

They say that these lords lived as celibates and with great propriety, being highly esteemed and obeyed by all while they so lived. In the course of time one of them failed, so that he died; although the Indians say that he went away by the port of Bacalar, out of the country. However that was, his absence resulted in such a lowering among those who ruled after him that partisan dissensions entered the realm; they lived dissolutely and without restraint, to such a degree that the people came to hate them so greatly that they killed them, overthrew the régime, and abandoned the site. The buildings and the sites, both beautiful, and only ten leagues from the sea, with fertile fields and districts all about, were deserted. The following is the plan of the principal edifice:

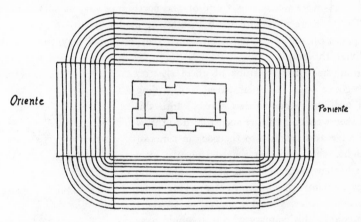

This structure has four stairways looking to the four directions of the world, and 33 feet wide, with 91 steps to each that are killing to climb. The steps have the same rise and width as we give to ours. Each stairway has two low ramps level with the steps, two feet broad and of fine stonework, like all the rest of the structure. The structure is without corners, because starting from the base it narrows in, as shown, away from the ramps of the stairs, with round blocks rising by stages in a very graceful manner.

When I saw it there was at the foot of each side of the stairways the fierce mouth of a serpent, curiously worked from a single stone. When the stairways thus reach the summit, there is a small flat top, on which was a building with four rooms, each having a door in the middle, and arched above. The

---

* So much is available on Chichén Itzá, thanks to the work of the Mexican government under its local director, Señor Eduardo Martínez, and of the Carnegie Institution of Washington, that we have only attempted to confirm Landa's statements by a few instances of the things he refers to. For those things illustrated on the next page, from among the objects dredged from the cenote, we owe the courtesy of Mr. Willard; they show a repoussé gold plate, and three copper cutting tools.

one at the north is by itself, with a corridor of thick pillars. In the center is a sort of interior room, following the lines of the outside of the building, with a door opening into the corridor at the north, closed in the top by wooden beams; this served for burning the incense. At the entrance of this doorway or of the corridor, there is a sort of arms sculptured on a stone, which I could not well understand.

Around this structure there were, and still today are, many others, well built and large; all the ground about them was paved, traces being still visible, so strong was the cement of which they were made. In front of the north stairway, at some distance, there were two small theatres of masonry, with four staircases, and paved on top with stones, on which they presented plays and comedies to divert the people.

From the court in front of these theatres there goes a beautiful broad paved way, leading to a well two stone-throws across. Into this well they were and still are accustomed to throw men alive as a sacrifice to the gods in times of drought; they held that they did not die, even though they were not seen again. They also threw in many other offerings of precious stones and things they valued greatly; so if there were gold in this country, this well would have received most of it, so devout were the Indians in this.

This well is seven long fathoms deep to the surface of the water, more than a hundred feet wide, round, of natural rock marvelously smooth down to the water. The water looks green, caused as I think by the trees that surround it; it is very deep. At the top, near the mouth, is a small building where I found idols made in honor of all the principal buildings in the land, like the Pantheon at Rome. I do not know whether this is an ancient invention, or one of the modern ones, that in coming with offerings to the well, they might come into the presence of their idols. I found sculptured lions, vases and other things, so that I do not understand how anyone can say that these people had no tools. I also found two immense statues of men, carved of a single stone, nude save for the waist-covering the Indians use. The heads were peculiar, with rings such as the Indians use in their ears, and a collar that rested in a depression made in the chest to receive it, and wherewith the figure was complete.

SEC. XLIII. FOR WHAT OTHER THINGS THE INDIANS MADE SACRIFICES.

The calendar festivals of this people that have been described above, show us what and how many they were, and wherefor and how they were celebrated. But because their festivals were only to secure the goodwill or favor of their gods, or else holding them angry, they made neither more nor bloodier ones. They believed them angry whenever they were molested by pestilences, dissensions, or droughts or the like ills, and then they did not undertake to appease the demons by sacrificing animals, nor making offerings only of their food and drink, or their own blood and self-afflictions of vigils, fasts and continence; instead, forgetful of all natural piety and all law of reason they made sacrifices of human beings as easily as they did of birds, and as often as their accursed priests or the **chilánes** said it was necessary, or as it was the whim or will of their chiefs. And since there is not here the great population there is in Mexico, nor were they after the fall of Mayapán ruled by one head but by many, there were no such mass killings of men; nevertheless they still died miserably, since each town had the authority to sacrifice whomever the priests, or the **chilán,** or the chief saw fit; and to do this they had in their temples their public places as if it were the one thing of most importance in the world for the preservation of the state. In addition to this slaughter in their towns, they had those accursed sanctuaries of Chichén Itzá and Cozumel whither they sent an infinite number of poor creatures for sacrifice, one thrown from a height, another to have his heart torn out. From all such miseries may the merciful Lord see fit to free us forever, He who saw fit to sacrifice himself to the Father, on the cross for all men.

O Lord my God, light, being and life of my soul, holy guide and safe road for my customs, consolation of my griefs, inner joy of my sadnesses, refreshment and rest of my toils: Why, O Lord, dost thou command me tasks that I cannot perform, rather than rest? What dost thou lay on me that I cannot carry through? Lord, dost thou not know the measure of my cup and the extent of my members and the quality of my forces? Dost thou perchance fail me, Lord, in my labors? Art thou not the loving Father of whom the holy prophet spoke in the psalm, I will be with him in tribulation and labors, and I will liberate him and glorify him? Lord, if thou art, and thou art He of whom the prophet spoke when full of thy holy spirit, that makest of thy command a burden, and thus it is, Lord, that those who have not enjoyed the sweetness of thy service and the performance of thy precepts, find a burden in them; but Lord, it is a pretended burden, a burden feared, a burden to the pusillanimous, and they fear it who never put the hand to the plow to finish; but those who give themselves to thy services find them sweet, they seek after the odor of their unctions,* their sweetness refreshes them at every step; many more pleasures do they find daily that the others cannot know, as in the other kingdom of Saba.

Thus do I implore thee, Lord, that thou give me grace in thy example to leave the house of my sensuality and the kingdom of my vices and sins, making of all the occasion to serve thee and keep thy commandments, in order that in those things the experience of thy service can most instruct me, so that reading only those and working with them I may find the good of thy grace for my soul; and thus as I believe thy yoke to be pleasant and light, I may render thee thanks that I find myself under thy protection, and free from that wherein thou seest that so many multitudes of people walk and have walked, traveling toward hell. So grave is the suffering that I know none whose heart it would not break, seeing the mortal weight and intolerable burden wherewith the demon has always led, and leads the idolaters to hell. And if this on the demon's part, which he procures and does, is a great cruelty, it is justly permitted, on God's part, in order that, since men will not let themselves be ruled by the light of the reason he has given them, they may commence to be tormented in this life and to endure part of the hell they deserve for the toilsome services they continuously render to the demon, with long fasts, and vigils, and abstinences, with unbelievable offerings and presents of their effects and property, constant pourings out of their own blood, severe pains and wounds in their bodies, and what is worse and graver, with the lives of their neighbors and brothers. Yet with all this the demon is never filled or satisfied by their torments and toils, nor with carrying them off to hell where he torments them eternally. Certain it is that God is more appeased and with less of torments and deaths; for did he not cry unto the great patriarch Abraham and bid him to stay his hand from taking the life of his son, because his Majesty was determined to send his own into the world and let him lose his life in fact upon the cross, that men might see that for the son of the eternal God the command of the Father is heavy, and yet very sweet is it to him, and for men only a pretended burden.

Wherefore may men cease the lukewarmness of their hearts, and the fear of a burden in this blessed law of God; for the burden is unreal, and turns soon into sweetness in soul and body; beyond all which it is worthy that God be well served, and this we owe to him as a just debt and payment; it is all for our benefit, not only eternal but temporal also. Therefore let all us Christians and especially the priests behold what shame and confusion there

* Such as the tortures at Maní and the burned towns in the east.

is in this world, and yet more in that to come, to see the demon find those who serve him with unbelievable labors to be paid for by going to hell, and that God can hardly find one who by keeping his so sweet commandments serves him faithfully that he may go to eternal glory.

Wherefore do you, priest of God, tell me if you have taken note of the office of these unhappy priests of the demon, and of all those who, as we read in the divine writings, there have been in times past, how much more burdensome were their fasts than yours, and how long and many; how much longer were their vigils and their miserable prayers than you give, how much more serious and careful they were of the affairs of their office than you are of yours; with how much more zeal than you they understood how to teach their pestiferous doctrines. If thereby you find yourself in any fault, correct it, and see that you are a priest of the Lord above, who solely by your office obliges you to seek to live in cleanness and prudently, the cleanness of an angel rather than of a man.

Sec. XLIV.   The soil and its products.

Yucatan is a land of less soil than any I know, being all live flat stones with very little earth, so that there are few places where one can dig down a fathom without meeting great banks of large rocks. The stone is not very good for fine carving, is hard and coarse; but such as it is it has served to produce the great number of buildings in the country. The country is excellent for lime, of which there is much; it is a marvel how much fertility exists in the soil on or between the stones, where is to be found all there is, more among the stones than there is elsewhere; since on the earthy ground where it is to be found, no trees grow, but only grass. But where they sow over the stony parts they secure crops, and all the trees grow, some of them marvelously large and beautiful. The cause I think is that more moisture is preserved among the stones than in the earth.

In seeking to illustrate the objects of use referred to by Landa we are helped by the known extent of their trading relations, from Honduras as far as the Mizteca region. Cortés needing to cast brass cannon sought and found the needed source of tin, and that this hardened copper was a part of the Tabasco trade we know. Landa also speaks in his last chapter of fire-hardened spears, a weapon hard to find still surviving as a specimen. The same with their ancient bows and arrows. Even the marginal figure here referred to in the text has been left out in the transcribed copy of Landa's manuscript; all however without leaving us wholly without pictured reproductions. Of the illustrations on these pages the collection of implements is taken from the manuscript of Fuentes y Guzmán's history of Guatemala, as also are the interesting human figures representing native bowmen, and also an " Indio noble " holding what is clearly a spear of hardened wood. Of the three small figures in the margin above we have a copper axe from an original Mexican codex, a copper bell from the

In this country there has so far been found no kind of local metal; it is astonishing that without it they have erected so many buildings, since the Indians can tell nothing as to what tools were used. But since they lack metals, God gave them a flint ridge near where the sierra we first spoke of crosses the country; of this they made points for the war spears, and also the knives used in sacrifice (of which the priests have a great store); they also served and still do as arrow tips, thus taking the place of metal. They had a certain soft brass which, when founded with 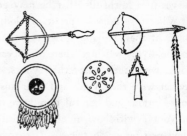 a light mixture of gold yielded them hatchets and the little rattles they used in their dances, as well as a certain sort of chisels which they used in making the idols and boring out the blowpipes, as in this figure in the margin; they use the blowpipe a great deal, and shoot well with it. This brass and other placques or sheets, of greater hardness, is part of their traffic in Tabasco for their idols. They had among them no other kind of metal.*

According to the wise, one of the things most needed by man is water, without which the earth cannot produce its fruits or man live. Yucatan lacks the abundance of rivers to be found in the neighboring countries, having only two; one of these is the Rio de Lagartos, which enters the sea next to a headland, and the other is that of Champotón; both being salty and of bad water, God provided many choice water sources, some natural and others brought out by industry. In this respect nature has acted differently in this country from the rest of the world, where the rivers and springs flow above the ground,

Indio Salvaje   Indio plebeyo

cenote at Chichén Itzá, and an illustration of the use of one of the very copper chisels to carve the 'idols,' from the Madrid codex. A chipped flint sacrificial knife, also from the cenote, has been shown previously.

whereas here all run in secret channels underground. As we have been told, the entire coast is full of springs of sweet water, rising in the sea, and from many of which one can get water, as I myself have done, when the ebb tide has left the shore dry.

Indio Noble

Inland God has provided various breaks in the natural rock, which the Indians call cenotes, cut and reaching down to the water; at times there are below furious currents so as to carry off cattle that fall into them; all these go out into the sea, and from them the above springs come. These cenotes contain fine water and are a great sight, for some of them are of cut natural rock clear down to the water; others have mouths that God created, or were caused by the accidents of thunderbolts (such as often fall), or in other ways. Inside we find handsome arches of the living rock, while on the top are trees, so that above is forest and under-neath the cenotes; in some a boat may be taken and used; with others larger or smaller. The people who got to these cenotes drank of them, having no wells, or very poor ones due to their lack of tools. Now however we have given them work at making good wells, as very excellent pumping wells whence the water can be taken as from a spring. There are also found lagoons, but all of these are of brackish water, bad to drink, and without the currents found in the cenotes.

THE UNDERGROUND CAVE OF LOLTUN

There is one thing in this country, in all this marvellous matter of the wells, which is that wherever we find them there comes out fine spring water, and some so beautiful that a lance goes down into them; and also that in all places where they have dug there has been found at half a man's height above the water a bench of seashells and caracols of many different kinds and colors, large and small, like those found on the seashore, with the sand already converted into hard white rock. At Maní, the royal town, we dug a great pumping well for the use of the Indians, and after having dug seven to eight fathoms in the living rock we found a grave a good seven feet long, filled with very fresh red earth and with human bones, which when removed were found to be almost converted into stone. This was still two to three fathoms from the water, before reaching which we came to a hollow arch, made by God, in such fashion as that the grave was set within the rock, and one could walk underneath to where it was. We could not understand how this could have been, unless we might say that the grave was opened there on the inside, and afterwards by the moisture of the cave, and the lapse of time, the rock hardened and grew to close it up.

Besides the two rivers which we have said are in the country, there is a spring three leagues from the sea near Campeche that is brackish; and in the whole land there is no other, nor other waters. The Indians living toward the sierra, needing to have their wells very deep, are accustomed to gather the rain water for their homes in that season, in great cavities in the rocks; because very heavy rains come then, with much thunder and lightning at times. All the wells, especially those near the sea, rise and fall every day at the hours of high and low tides, showing clearly that the underground rivers run into the sea.

SEC. XLV. THE WATERS AND THE FISHES FOUND IN THEM.

There is a marsh in Yucatan worthy of mentioning, since it is seventy leagues in length, and entirely saline. It begins near the coast of **Ekab,** which is near the Isla de Mugeres, and continues, very close to the seacoast, between the coast and the bushy woodland, on to near Campeche. It is not deep for lack of soil, but it is bad to cross going from the towns to the coast, or coming thence, because of the trees and much mud. This marsh is saline, created by God with the finest salt I have seen in my life; when ground it is white, and a half peck of it salts further than a peck from other places. Our Lord created the salt in this marsh from the rain water and not from the sea, for this does not enter because of a strip of land the whole distance, between the marsh and the sea.

In the rainy season these waters become swollen, and the salt coagulates in large and small lumps that look like nothing other than sugar candy. Four or five months after the rains have ceased and the lagoon somewhat dried, the Indians in the early times had the custom of going to gather the salt, taking the lumps from the water and carrying them off to dry. For this purpose they had places marked in the lagoon where the salt was richest and there was less water and mud. It was the custom not to harvest this salt without the license of the chiefs near by, who had thereby control; to these all that came to gather salt gave some tribute, either of the salt itself or of things from their own region. Inasmuch as a leading man named Francisco

Euan, a native of the town of Caucel, made proof of this, and showed that his ancestors on the coast had received from the administration of Mayapán the charge of this matter and of the distribution of the salt, the Audiencia of Guatemala commanded him to give the same today to those who went to this district for the purpose. Still today a great deal is gathered to carry to Mexico, and to Honduras and Havana. This marsh at some places breeds very fine fish, of good taste although they are not large.

There are fish not only in the lagoon but also along the coast in such abundance that the Indians care little for those of the lagoon, except those of them who have no nets; these capture many in the shallows with their arrows, while the others others carry on their extensive fisheries both for their eating

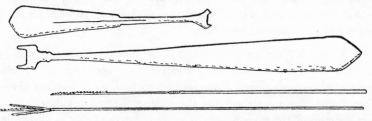

and to sell throughout the whole country. It is their way to salt and cook them, and then to dry them in the sun without salt, having their reckoning of what is here needed by each kind of fish. Those that are cooked they keep for days, and carry twenty to thirty leagues to sell; for eating they then season and dress them, so as to be both savory and wholesome.

The fish they kill there are skates (*lizas*), very fat and good; trout no more or less in color, speckles and taste, yet fatter and savory to eat, which they call **izcay**; very fine bream (*róbalos*), and sardines; also flounders, saw-fish, horse-mackerel, mojarras, and an infinite variety of other small fish. On the Campeche coast there are very good cuttle-fish, three or four kinds of pike (*sollos*) that are good and wholesome, especially one kind with a different head from the others; these have a round head, remarkably flat, with the mouth inside and the eyes on the sides of the circle; these they call **alipechpol**. They capture some very large fish that look like mantles, which they slice and salt; it dies around the edges, and is very excellent; I do not know whether it is a ray-fish.

There are many manatí on the coast between Campe(che) and La Desconocida, which apart from the amount of flesh they give also yield a great deal of oil useful for preparing the food. These manatí they regard as marvels; the author of the Natural History of the Indies relates that an Indian chief in the Isla Española raised one in a lake that was so tame that it came to the shore when called by the name he had given to it, which was

Figure of manatí
from the Fuentes y Guzmán ms.

matu. What I can say about them is that they are so large as to provide much more meat than a large calf, and much oil. They beget their young like the animals, having their male and female parts; they have two at a birth, and never more; they do not lay eggs as do other fish. They have two fins like strong arms for swimming; the face is much like that of an ox, and they thrust it out of the water to eat the herbage on the shore. The bats bite them on a round flat snout they have, turning up on the face, and this kills them, for they are very full of blood and bleed to death in the water from a cut. The flesh is good, especially when fresh, when with mustard it tastes like good beef.

The Indians kill them with harpoons in the following manner; they hunt for them in the streams and low places (for it is not a fish that swims in deep water), carrying their harpoons tied to lines with floats on the end. When found they spear them and then release the line and floats; the fish from the pain of the wounds seek to escape this way or that in the shallows, never going into the depths of the sea; being so large they stir up the mud and leave a trail of blood, which the Indians then follow in their boats until they capture them with the line and float. It is a fish of great value and much appreciated, since it is all flesh and fat.

There is another fish on this coast which they call **ba,** broad and round, and good to eat, but risky to kill or to come against. It also does not go into deep water, but swims in the shoals, where the Indians hunt it with bow and arrow; but if they are careless in their walking, or step on it in the water, it comes up at once with its long narrow tail, and gives such a wound with a saw it carries that it cannot be removed without greatly enlarging the cut, the teeth being set backwards as in the sketch here given. These small saws the Indians use to cut themselves with in their sacrifices to the evil one, and it was the office of the priest to have them. Thus they had many very fine ones, for the bone is white and curiously shaped like a saw, so sharp and pointed that it cuts like a knife.

There is a small fish that is so poisonous that no one who eats it escapes death, very quickly swelling all up. Although it is known, yet at times it deceives people through its being slow to die out of the water; the whole body swells greatly. There are also very fine oysters in the Champotón river; also there are many sharks along the coast.

Beside the fishes that live in the water, there are other creatures they also use, living both in the water and on the land; such as the number of iguanas, which are like the lizards of Spain in shape and size, and also in color save in their not being as green. These lay many eggs, and always keep near the sea or where there is water, staying in either element; thus the Spaniards eat them in the fast periods, finding them a special and wholesome food. There are so many of them that they supply everybody during Lent. The Indians catch them with lassos as they lie on the trees or in their holes, and it is incredible how long they can go without food, even for twenty or thirty days after they are captured without eating a mouthful, and still not getting lean. I have also heard as a fact, that if their stomachs are floated with sand, they fatten up. Their excrement is an admirable medicine for curing clouds over the eyes, applied to them while fresh.

There are turtles of great size, much larger than immense shields, of excellent eating, and satisfying. They lay eggs as large as a hen's, in number up to fifty or a hundred, or even two hundred; for these they scoop out a great hole in the sand wherein to lay them, then covering them up and leaving them until they hatch out. There are other kinds of turtles on the land, in the dry forests and in the lagoons. One fish I saw several times on the coast, which being completely in a shell I left to put here. It is of the size of a small turtle, covered above with a delicate round shell of beautiful shape and a very bright green; it has a tail covered in the same way with a shell, very slender like a gimlet, and some six inches long. Underneath it has many feet, and is filled with eggs, which are the only edible part; these the Indians eat much of, calling it in their language mex.

There are many fierce alligators which, although they live in the water, come out and stay much on the land; they eat while on the land, or with the head out of the water, since they lack glands and cannot chew in the water. It is a heavy animal, and does not go far from the water, moving furiously in attack, or in flight. It will swallow any kind of strange thing; to my own knowledge one killed one of our monastery Indians while he was bathing in a lake. Then one of the friars quickly went with some Indians to kill it; to do this they took a small dog, running a pointed hard stake through the body from mouth to tail, then fastening a very strong rope to it inside they threw it in the lake; at once the alligator came out and seized it with its teeth, and swallowed it. Then the people that came with the friar pulled hard, while the stake turned crosswise in its body; and then on opening the belly they found inside the half of the man, with the dog.

These alligators beget their young like the animals, and lay eggs; these to the number of three hundred, and larger than birds' eggs; they lay them in a large hole in the sand very near the water, where they leave them until the time when nature has taught them they are to hatch; then they come and wait until the young are out. These are the size of the palm of the hand, and they wait for a wave of the sea striking close to them, whereupon they leap from where they are into the water, and all that do not reach it stay dead on the sand, hot as it is from the sun; they being so tender that they burn up and die at once. Those that reach the water begin all to swim immediately until they meet their parents and follow them. In this way very few escape, in spite of the number of eggs that are laid, by the favor of the divine providence that looks out more for those things that are beneficial to us than for those that injure us, and could do harm as would these beasts if all of them came to life.

SEC. XLVI. HOW THERE ARE SERPENTS AND OTHER POISONOUS ANIMALS.

The diversity of snakes or serpents is great, of many colors and not harmful, except for two kinds of very poisonous ones, much larger than those we have here in Spain; one of which they call **taxinchan.** There are also others very large and very poisonous, with rattles in their tails. Others there are so large that they will swallow a hare, or two, but are not harmful; it is to be related that some of the Indians take hold of both kinds, without being harmed.

There is a kind of lizard, larger than ours here, of which it is surprising the great fear the Indians have of them, for they say that for them merely to touch a person causes a sweat that is a deadly poison. There are many scorpions among the rocks, but they are not as poisonous as those here in Spain.

There is a kind of large ants whose bite is very bad, and which pains and suppurates more than that of the scorpions, and lasts twice as long, as I know by experience. There are two kinds of spiders, one small and very pestiferous, and the other very large and all covered with very fine black spines that look like down, and which hold the poison; thus the Indians are most careful not to touch them. There are many other reptiles that are not poisonous. There is a small red worm of which they make a yellow ointment that is excellent for swellings and sores, and needing no more than to crush and apply them; it also serves as oil for painting vases and strengthening the paint.

Sec. XLVII. Of the bees and their honey and wax.

There are two kinds of bees, both being much smaller than ours; the larger of these are raised in very small hives, and do not form a comb as do ours, but instead certain small sacs like wax-nuts, all close together and full of honey. To get this it is only necessary to open the hive and break the sacs for the honey to run out, and then remove the wax as convenient.

The others live in the woods, in the hollows of trees and rocks, where one must hunt the wax. With this and the honey the country abounds, the honey being most excellent save for the fact that it is somewhat watery on account of the fertility of the food of the bees; it is therefore necessary to heat it at the fire, which makes it very good and very hard. The wax is fine, except for being smoky, the reason for which I have not been able to discover; in some provinces it is much yellower on account of the flowers. These bees do not sting, even when the honey is gathered.

Sec. XLVIII. Of the plants, flowers and trees; of the fruits and other edibles.

Great and notable is the diversity of plants and flowers that adorn Yucatan in their seasons, as well among the trees as the plants, many of them being marvelously fine and beautiful, of many colors, and odorous; outside also of the beauty with which they dress the woods and fields, these plants afford the greatest abundance of supply for the bees for honey and wax. Among these I shall give here a number, both for their exquisite smell and beauty, and for the benefits derived from them by those who dwell in that land.

There are sages much fresher and more odorous than those here, and with longer and slenderer leaves; these the Indians cultivate for their odor, and for their pleasure. I have noted that they increase their beauty by putting ashes around the base.

There is one plant with broad leaves and tall, thick branches, of a singular freshness and fertility, growing as they do in profusion from cuttings, the same as do osiers, although not like these in any way; rubbing the leaf a little between the hands it has a real odor of clover, although it loses this when dry; it is good for freshening the temples at fiestas, and for this it is used.

There is also sweet basil found in the woods and fields, which in some parts are full of it; growing in those rocks it is very fresh, beautiful and odorous, though not comparable with what is grown in the gardens, imported from here, and which grows and spreads in a notable fashion.

There is a flower they call **tixzula,** of the most delicate odor I have ever known, much more so than the jessamine; it is white, or light purplish in some cases, and could be brought here to Spain, since it sprouts from a thick bulb. These bulbs put forth tall, thick and very fresh spires that last the year around, and once a year bear in the center a green stem as broad as three fingers and as long as the spires; at the end of these come the flowers in a bunch, each being some six inches long with its stem; when open they have five long leaflets, open and connected at the base by a delicate white membrane, with pellicles in the center, white and yellow and wonderfully beautiful. When this stalk is cut and put in a jar of water, it holds the soft odor for many days, the joined flowers only opening a little at a time.

There are certain small lilies that are very white and odorous, which last long in water and would be easy to bring here, since they also grow from bulbs and are quite like our lilies, except that the odor is more delicate and does not give headaches; also it lacks the yellow center of our lilies.

There is a rose they call **ixlaul,** which they tell me is of much beauty, and odorous.

There is also a kind of tree they call **nicte,** that bears many white roses, and others half yellow, and yet others half purplish; these are fresh and odorous, and of them they fashion handsome garlands, and lectuaries when they so desire.

There is a flower they call **kom,** that is very odorous and gives a burning heat when smelled; it could easily be brought here. Its leaves are broad and wonderfully fresh.

Besides these flowers and odorous plants there are many others most beneficial and medicinal, among them two varieties of the *yerbamora* or nightshade, fresh and very handsome. There is much *doradilla* or ceterach, and also maiden's hair; also a plant whose leaves boiled are a wonderful remedy for swollen feet and legs.

There is another especially good for the cure of sores, which they call **yaxpahalché.** Another has the odor of fennel; this is both eaten raw or boiled, and so applied for the cure of sores. At Bayhalar there is also found *zarzaparilla*.

They have a certain plant that grows in the pools and other places, three-cornered like the sedge, but much thicker, out of which they make their baskets, staining them beautifully with colors.

Also they have a plant that grows both wild and cultivated near their houses (this being the best), and which is a kind of hemp (*cáñamo*), which they employ for an infinity of useful things.

Again on certain trees there grows without cultivation a plant that bears fruit like small cucumbers, out of which they make glue for sticking things together, when needed.

The seeds they have for human sustenance are very good *maize,* of many different kinds and colors; of this they gather much and keep in a granary or silo for poor years.   There are two kinds of small beans, one black and the other of different colors; others small and white that have been brought over from Spain.

Their peppers have many different pods;   the seeds of some of these are used for seasoning.   Others are for eating baked or boiled, and still others for cups for household use.   They have fine melons, and also Spanish cala-bashes.   They have millet, which yields excellently and is good food.

They have a yellow fruit that is fresh and tasteful;   this they sow, and the root, growing like the turnip, short, fat and round, is the fruit;   this they eat raw with salt.

There is another root that grows under the earth, being sown, and is great as food;   of this there are many kinds, purplish, yellow and white, which they eat boiled or roasted;   they are good eating, and taste somewhat like chestnuts;   they also serve roasted for a drink.   [? the peanut]

There are two other kinds of good roots they use as food;   also others that grow wild and have a salty flavor, of which I have before spoken and which serve them in seasons of famine;   otherwise they do not use them.

They have a small tree with soft branches containing much sap, whose leaves they eat as a salad, tasting like cabbage and good with plenty of fat bacon.   The Indians plant it wherever they make their homes, and then have the leaves for gathering the whole year.   There is much fresh chicory grown in the gardens, but they do not eat it.

It is a matter for praise to be given to God, with the prophet who has said " Admirable, O Lord, is thy name in all lands," because of the great number of trees thy Majesty has created in this land, and all so unlike ours, so unlike what I have seen elsewhere (I speak of Yucatan), and of all both the Indians and the Spaniards have great use and benefit.

One there is with a fruit like round gourds, out of which the Indians make their vessels (*jicaras*);   they are very handsome, and they paint them elabor-ately and beautifully.

There is also another of the same species, only smaller and very hard, of which they make small cups for ointments and other purposes.

There is another kind that bears a fruit like filberts, of whose kernels they make fine beads, and whose bark is used for washing clothes the same as soap, making a fine lather.

They cut the incense tree a great deal, for the demons;   this they extract cutting the bark with a stone for the sap to run out.   This tree is fresh, tall, and with fine leafage and shade, but its flower turns the wax black when it is present.

There is a very handsome tree that grows by the wells, tall and with fresh leaves; this spreads its branches in a marvelous manner, growing in a very orderly fashion from the trunk, in threes or more, around the tree, and continuing to extend and the shoots to grow.

There are also cedars, but not of the finer kind.

There is a sort of yellowish tree, veined like an oak, marvelously strong and hard, and so stout that we have seen it used as doorposts in the houses at Izamal, and supporting the entire weight above.

There is another of the hardest kind, of a tawny color, of which they make bows and lances.

There is another of the color of an orange, of which they make staffs, very strong. I think it is called *brazil*.

There are many trees which they say are good for the affliction of pustules, which they call **zon**.

There is a tree whose sap causes sores when touched, and even its shade is noxious, if one sleeps under it.

There is another with double thorns, long and very hard and thick, on which the birds never rest; these thorns are all hollowed inside, and always filled with ants.

There is another tree of great height and size, which bears a fruit like carob beans, filled with certain black seed-nuts that they eat in time of famine; from the roots of this tree they make buckets for drawing water from the wells.

There are others from whose bark the Indians make small cups for taking water; also others from which they make ropes; also yet others whose crushed bark they use for polishing plastered walls and hardening them.

There are beautiful mulberry trees, of fine wood; also so many other useful and beautiful trees as to astonish one.

In the woods and fields there are many kinds of long osiers or willows (not the kind of which they make baskets), which they use for tying in erecting their houses, or whatever else they have need for; the use they make of these is very great indeed.

Another tree gives a sap that is fine to strengthen the gums.

Another bears a certain large fruit that is filled with a wool that for pillows is superior to tow.

Fearing to offend the fruit or their trees, I have felt best to put them to themselves; and I will speak first of the wine that the Indians esteem so highly, and therefore plant them in all their enclosures or around their houses. It is an ugly tree, producing nothing but its roots, and its wine by using honey and water.

In the country there are certain wild vines bearing edible grapes; we find many of these on the Cupul coast. There are plums of many kinds, some of them very tasteful and wholesome; they are very different from ours, having but little meat and a large stone, contrary to what is found with those we have here; this tree puts forth its fruit before the leaves, and without flower.

There are many bananas, these having been brought by the Spaniards, since previously they did not have them.

There is a very large tree that bears a large, longish fruit, and fat with a red meat, very fine to eat; it does not produce a flower, but only the fruit, at first very small and growing by degrees.

There is another very leafy and beautiful tree, whose leaves never fall; this also bears no flowers, but a fruit much sweeter than the one above, small, dainty, well tasting and very delicate; some of these are better than others, and the best would be much in favor if they were brought over here; they call them **ya** in their language.

Another fresh and beautiful tree also holds its leaves without their falling, and bears a small fig they call **ox.**

Another, exceedingly beautiful and fresh, bears a fruit like large eggs; the Indians gather it green and ripen it in the ashes; when ripe it lasts well, is sweet and tastes like the yolk of an egg [*papaya*].

Another tree bears also a yellow fruit, not so large as the one above, but softer and sweeter; this when eaten leaves a kernel like a soft prickly body, curious to see.

Another fresh and beautiful tree bears a fruit like hazelnuts, with its husk, inside are fruit like *guindas*, with a large kernel. The Indians call these **vayam,** and the Spaniards *guayas*.

There is another good and wholesome fruit the Spaniards brought, which they call *guayavas*.

In the sierras there are two kinds of trees, one bearing fruit as large as a good pear, very green, with a thick skin; these they ripen by beating them on a stone, whereupon they have a special flavor. The other bears fruit like pineapples, good to eat, juicy and acid; this has many small kernels, but these are not wholesome.

There is another tree that grows only in open places, alone and never among other trees; its bark is good for tanning hides, serving like sumac; it bears a small tasty yellow fruit, which is much eaten by the women.

There is a very large and fresh tree that the Indians call **on;** it bears a fruit like largish small calabashes, soft and tasting like butter; it is fatty and of much substance and nourishment. It has a large kernel, a thin skin, and is eaten cut in slices like a melon, and with salt.

There are artichokes (*cardos*) that are very spiny and ugly, growing always on stems attached to other trees and growing from them; the fruit of these is red-skinned, shaped like an artichoke (*alcachofa*), soft to open, and without spines. The flesh inside is white, with many small black seeds; it is sweet, most delicious, watery and melting in the mouth, being eaten like an orange in sections around, and with salt; the Spaniards eat as many as the Indians bring in from the woods.

There is a spongy tree, ugly but large, that bears a sort of large fruit full of very savory yellow meat, with pits like hemp seeds but larger; these are good for the urine. They make an excellent conserve from this fruit; the tree puts out its leaves after the fruit has gone.

There is a small, rather spiny tree bearing a fruit shaped like a slender cucumber, somewhat long; it is like the artichoke (*cardo*) in taste, and is eaten in the same fashion, with salt, and in slices; the seeds are like those of the small cucumbers, many and tender. If by some chance a hole is made in the fruit while still on the tree, a gum collects in it smelling like fine civet. The fruit is also an excellent remedy for women's periodic troubles.

There is another tree whose flower is full of a soft odor, and whose fruit is like what we here in Spain call blanc mange; there are many different sorts, with fruit of different quality.

There is a tree that the Indians raise near their houses, bearing spiny pods like chestnuts, but not so large nor so rough; they open when ripe and contain small seeds which both Spaniards and Indians use to color their condiments, as one does with saffron; the color is marked, and stains a great deal [*achiote*].

I am sure that there remain yet other fruits, but I shall however speak of those of the palms, of which there are two kinds. One kind [*huano*] serves for thatching the houses, and is very tall and slender; these bear great bunches of a black fruit like pulse, of which the Indians are very fond.

The other kind is a low, very spiny palm whose leaves are very short and thin, and serve no purpose; these bear great bunches of a round green fruit, of the size of pigeons' eggs. When the husk is removed there remains a very hard kernel, inside of which is a pit the size of a hazelnut, of good taste and useful in times of poor harvests; they make of it a hot food which they take in the mornings, and on occasions use the milk for flavoring as one does almonds.

They gather a very great amount of cotton, which grows in all parts of the country, there being two sorts. One is sown each year and does not last over, and the tree of this is small; the tree of the other kind lasts five or six years. The fruit of both is in the forms of pods like nuts, with a green husk that opens when ripe, showing the cotton within.

They are accustomed to gather the cochineal, which is said to be the finest in the Indies, as growing on dry soil; the Indians gather some little here and there.

There are colors of many kinds made from the juices of certain trees and of flowers, but because the Indians have not known how to perfect them by gums to temper them in prevention, they fade. But those who gather the silk have already discovered the remedies, and say that they give as perfect results as anywhere found.

SEC. XLIX. OF THE BIRDS.

This country possesses an immense number of birds, of so great variety that He who gave them as a blessing is greatly to be praised. They have domestic fowls which they raise at their homes, and cocks in great number, although they are troublesome to raise. They have taken to raising Spanish fowls, in great numbers, so that all the year they have chickens from them. They raise tame pigeons like ours, which multiply much. They breed a certain kind of large white ducks for their plumage, coming I think from Peru; thus they pluck their breasts often, and are fond of using their feathers for embroidering their garments.

There are many kinds of birds, and many very handsome ones, among these two kinds of fine turtle doves, one being quite small and tame about the houses. There is a little bird like the nightingale, and sweet singing, which they call **ixyalchamil,** which stays on the walls of houses that have gardens, or in their trees. There is another large and very beautiful bird, of very dark green plumage, and with only two long feathers in the tail, and no others, but with down on them at the ends; it lives in the buildings and does not go out except in the mornings.

There are other birds like the magpies both in their bodies and conduct, always crying at the passers-by, and not letting them pass quietly. There are many martins or swallows, though I think they are martins since they do not breed in dwellings as do the swallows.

There is another large one, of many colors and much beauty, with a large strong beak; it always goes about the dry trees, holding to the bark by its claws and hammering so loud with the beak that it can be heard a good distance off, extracting from the decayed wood the worms they live on. These birds carry on this boring to such an extent that trees harboring the worms are riddled from top to bottom.

There are many field birds of excellent eating, among them three kinds of handsome little pigeons. There are birds like Spanish partridges in every way except that their legs are long, although red; they are very poor eating, but very tame if raised by the house.

There are many fine quail, somewhat larger than ours, and fine for eating; they fly but little, and the Indians catch them climbing in the trees, with dogs, and by lassos they throw over the breasts, in quite delightful hunting.

There are many grayish brown pheasants, and also spotted, of a fair size, but not so good to eat as those of Italy. There is one very large bird as big as the turkey-hens, which they call the **kambul,** very beautiful and very courageous, and good to eat. Another they call **cox,** equally large, with a furious way of walking and stirring about; the males are all black as jet, with a handsome crest of little curled feathers, and yellow eyelids, fine to look at.

There are many turkeys, which while not of as fine plumage as those here in Spain, are still very gallant and handsome; they are as large as the Indian cocks, and as good eating. There are many other birds that I have seen, but do not remember. All the large ones are hunted in the trees with arrows by the Indians; they steal their eggs and take away the hens, which they raise quite domesticated. There are three or four kinds of large and small parrots, in such crowds that they do much harm to the plantations.

There are other nocturnal birds like the owls, the red owl or *mochuelo,* and blind fowl because of which it is diverting to travel at night with great stretches of the road filled with them flying in front. They irritate the Indians greatly, for they take them as birds of omen, the same as with certain others.

There are carnivorous birds that the Spaniards call *auras,* and the Indians **kuch;** these are black, with head and breast like the native hens, and a long hooked beak. They are very filthy, since they always go among the stables and privies eating and hunting dead meats. It is a known fact that so far it is unknown where they nest or how they breed; thus some say they live two hundred years or more, and others believe them to be in fact crows. The dead meat smells so that when the Indians have shot a deer and it gets away wounded, the one way to find it is by climbing a tree and looking where these birds are gathering; there they are sure to find the game. There is a great variety of birds of rapine; there are small eagles, very handsome goshawks, large hunting birds, and also very fine sparrowhawks, larger than the Spanish kind. There are lanners, and falcons, and others whose names I do not remember since I am not a hunter. On the sea the variety, diversity and multitude of birds is infinite, as is also the beauty of each one of the species. There are great birds as large as brown ostriches, and with larger beaks. They move on the water hunting the fish, and when one is seen they rise in the air and launch themselves with great force upon the

fish; they never make a mis-stroke, and on making the dive continue swimming and swallowing the fish without preparation of any kind.

There are certain large lean birds that fly a great deal, and fly high, with
the tail divided in two ends, and whose fat is an excellent remedy for scars,
and for numbness caused from cuts.

There are large ducks that stay under water a long time hunting fish to
eat; they are very quick, and have a hook on the beak that they use for the
fish. There are other small ducks, raised at the house and very tame, and
staying at home; these they call **maxix.**

There are many kinds of large and small herons, some white and others
brown, in the Laguna de Términos. Many are of a very bright red, like
powdered cochineal; and so many sorts of small birds, as well as large, that
their numbers and variety are causes for wonderment; and still more is the
seeing them so busy hunting their food on the shore, some entering the
incoming breakers only to break away from them, others hunting food on
the beaches or hurrying away; but most of it all is seeing how God has
provided for it all.

SEC. L.   OF THE LARGER ANIMALS, AND OF THE SMALLER ONES.

The Indians are wanting in the possession of many animals, especially those
most necessary for the service of man; they have others, most of which
they make useful for their support, none however being domestic except the
dogs; these do not bark or do harm either to people or to the game, though
they aid in trapping the quail and other birds, and join in the hunting of
the deer, some of them being fine trackers. They are small, and the Indians
eat them at fiestas, though I understand they are ashamed of it, and have
poor regard for it. They say that they have a good flavor.

There are tapirs among the dogwood trees only in the country beyond the
Campeche hills, where there are many to be found. The Indians have told
me that they are of many colors, gray, dappled, bays and chestnuts; others
quite white, and also black. They go more in this part of the country than
in any other, for it is an animal very fond of the water, and there are many
lakes among those woods and sierras. They are of the size of ordinary mules,
very light-footed, with cloven hoofs like cattle, and a trunk in which they
hold water. The Indians hold it a great achievement to kill them, and
preserve the skins even for their great-grandchildren, as I have seen. They
call them **tzimin,** and from that they have given this name to horses.

There are small lions and tigers, which the Indians kill with the bow as
they lie on the trees. There is also a certain kind of bear, or *quierque,* very

fond of robbing the hives; it is brown with black spots, long bodied, with short legs and a round head. There is a kind of wild goats, small and very fleet, and dark colored.

There are certain small pigs, very different from ours, for they have the navel on the loin, and stink badly. There are a great number of small deer, the meat of which is excellent. There is an infinite number of hares, like ours in all respects save that the nose is long and not at all flat like that of cattle; they are large and good eating.

There is a small animal of sad nature, which goes about in caverns and dark places, or at night; it is similar to the hare, moving by leaps and drawn together, and the Indians hunt it by setting a kind of trap in which it is caught. The front teeth are very long and thin; the tail is still shorter than that of the hare, and it is of a dark greenish color. It is exceedingly tame and friendly, and is called **sub** [the agouti].

There is another little animal like a newborn pig with its paws and snout, and a great rooter, but all covered with graceful shells so that it looks just like a blanketed horse, with only the ears and feet sticking out, and even its breast and head covered with the shells. It is tender and very good to eat.

There are other animals like little dogs, with a head shaped like a pig's, and a long tail; they are a smoky color, and so sluggish that one often catches them by the tail. They are quite greedy and go about the houses at night, so that no fowl gets away from their slow approach. The female brings forth fourteen to eighteen little ones at a birth, completely hairless and very torpid; but God has provided the mother with a strange sort of pocket in the belly for their protection, the skin over the pocket growing the entire length of the belly, and covering the nipples, concealing them when it is closed. When the mother wishes it so, it opens so that each of the little ones can get a teat into its mouth; when they are all inside she brings the flanks or the skin up and closes it so tightly that none of them can fall out. Then thus laden she goes about in search of her food. She cares for them in this way until they have hair and can walk.

There are foxes in every way like ours, except that they are smaller and without the long tail.

There is an animal the Indians call **chic** [badger, *pisote*], which is very mischievous, as large as a small dog, and with a snout like a new pig. The Indian women raise them, and there is not a thing they do not get into and turn upside down; it is a sight to see how fond they are of playing with the women, and how they hunt for fleas; but they will not look at the men for their lives. There are many of these, and they always go about in troops, in a line with the snout of one under the tail of the other, and doing much damage in the fields as they go through.

There is a small animal like a white squirrel, with dark yellow stripes about the body, which they call **pay**; this defends itself against those who follow it or hurt it by letting loose its urine, which has such a horrible smell that nobody can tolerate it, nor can anything it touches be taken hold of. They tell me that it is not actually the urine, but a kind of sweat they carry at the back in a bag; be that as it may, its armor defends it so well that only as by a miracle do the Indians ever kill one.

There are many very beautiful squirrels, moles and weasels; and many rats like those of Spain, except that their snouts are longer.

The Indians have not lost, but have gained much with the coming of the Spaniards, even in smaller matters; but there has been much increase in many of the things that come on with the passage of time, at first by force, but which they are now beginning to enjoy and use. There are many and fine horses, and mules and machos. Asses do not do well, and I think their introduction has not been good, for it is without doubt a hard-tempered beast. There are many and fine cows, boars, sheep, ewes, goats, and such of our dogs as suit their needs, and which have come to be regarded as beneficial in the Indies. Cats are very useful and necessary, and the Indians are fond of them.

Hens, pigeons, oranges, limes, citrons, grapes, pomegranates, figs, guavas, dates and bananas, melons and the other legumes; of these only the melons and calabashes grow from their own seeds; for the rest one must bring fresh seeds from Mexico. Silk is now produced, and it is very good. They have received tools, and the use of mechanical devices, and these go well. There is also the use of money and many other things that have come to them from Spain; and although they had gone, and could have gone on without them, yet they live beyond question more as men by having them and their aid in their corporeal activities, and the raising of them; as, by the opinion of the philosopher, art aids nature.

SEC. LI. THE AUTHOR'S CONCLUSION AND APPEAL.

God has not only given through our Spanish nation all this increase of these things, so necessary for man's service, that for these alone what they give or will give to the Spaniards is no payment, but there has come to them without payment that which can neither be bought or deserved, which is justice and Christianity, and the peace in which they live. For these they owe more to Spain and the Spaniards, and chiefly to their very Catholic sovereigns, who with such continuous care and such great Christianity have provided and do provide them with these two things, than they do to their first founders, evil parents who begat them in sin and as sons of wrath, while Christianity gives them birth in grace and for the enjoyment of life eternal.   Their first founders did not know what order to give them that they might evade the so many and so great errors in which they have lived.   Justice has taken them out from that through the preaching, and it must keep them from returning; or if they revert, it must pull them out.

It is with reason then, that Spain can glorify God in that he elected her among the nations for the remedy for so many peoples, and for which they owe her much more than they do to their founders or progenitors.   For as the blessed St. Gregory said, it had been of little good to us to be born had we not come to being redeemed through Christ.   We can say too with Anselm, that being redeemed is of no value to us if we do not attain the fruit of redemption, which is our salvation.   And thus they err who say that because the Indians have received aggravations, vexations and bad examples from the Spaniards, it had been better for them not to have been discovered; because those were still greater vexations and aggravations which they perpetually inflicted on each other, killing, enslaving, and sacrificing themselves to the demons.   As to the bad example, if they have had such, or today have it from some, the King has remedied it, and daily does remedy it by his Justices, and by the constant preaching and persevering opposition of the men of religion * to those who set such examples, or have set them; for the teaching is evangelical, and scandals and bad examples are necessary things.   So I believe it has been among these people, that they might understand, separating the gold from the clay and the grain from the chaff, how to esteem virtue as they have done; seeing with the philosopher how the virtues shine amidst the vices, and the virtuous among the vicious; bad examples and scandals were terrible afflictions indeed, were they not squared by what is good.

And so do thou, dearest reader, on thy part pray God therefore, and receive my small effort with a pardon for its defects, remembering when you meet them that not only do I not defend them (as St. Augustine said of Tullius that he declared he had never spoken a word he desired to revoke, which the saint disapproved because it is human to err); but first, before you come to them, you will meet them revoked or confessed in my introductions or prologues.   Thus you will judge, in company with the blessed Augustine in his letter to Marcella, the difference between him who confesses his error or fault and him who defends it; and you will pardon mine as the prophet says God does both mine and yours, saying: " Lord, I said I will confess my ill deeds and injustice, and thou dost quickly give pardon."

* Los religiosos was used specifically for the members of the monastic orders, in distinction from the regular clergy, whose heads were the Bishops, in whom alone rested inquisitorial rights.

SEC. LII. CRITICISM AND CORRECTION OF CERTAIN STATEMENTS.

The historian of the Indies, to whom much is due for his labor and the light he gave, in speaking of the things of Yucatan, says that they used slings in war, and spears hardened by fire; I have told in chapter 101 of the things they used in war, and I am not surprised that Francisco Hernández de Córdova and Juan de Grijalva thought that the stones thrown at them by the Indians at Champotón were discharged from slings, since they retreated. But they neither throw from a sling nor knew them, though they throw a stone very sure and hard, aiming when they throw with the left arm and index finger as they do it.

He also says that the Indians are circumcised, and how this is will be found in chapter 49. He says that there are hares, and about that you will find in the fifteenth paragraph of the last chapter. He says that there are partridges, and of what kinds, and about that you will find in the thirteenth paragraph of the last chapter.

Our historian further says that at Cape Cotoch they found crosses among the dead and the idols, and he does not believe it, because if they were spoil taken from the Spaniards who perished, they would perforce have been found elsewhere first, in many places. This reasoning does not convince me, because no other places are known where it could have happened, where they could have come before they did to Yucatan, whether they did arrive or not, nor as in these parts of Yucatan. Why I do not believe it, is because when Francisco Hernández and Grijalva arrived at Cotoch, they did not go about digging up dead people, but hunting gold among the living. I also believe so much in the virtue of the cross and the malice of the evil one, that he could not endure seeing a cross amongst the idols, because of the fear that some day miraculously its virtue would break them, and confound him as the ark of the covenant did with Dagon, although not sanctified by the blood of the son of God and dignified by his divine members, as was the holy cross.

Besides all this, I will say what was told me by a lord among the Indians, a man of fine understanding and much reputation among them. Talking with him on this matter one day, and having asked of him whether he had at any time heard reports of Christ our Lord, or of the Cross, he answered that he had never heard from his ancestors anything about either Christ or the Cross, except that once while tearing down a small building on a certain part of the coast, they had found in some graves, on the bodies and bones of the dead, some small metal crosses. That they had not seen anything of the cross until today when they became Christians and saw it venerated and worshipped; they believed it must have been those dead men that had been buried there. If that was so, it is possible that some small party had come from Spain and quickly disappeared, with no memory left.

FINIS.

Letter in Maya to the King

An exact duplicate of the above, in wording and handwriting, and accompanied by a Spanish translation, both the Maya and Spanish versions signed as by eight caciques of Calkini, Numkini and other towns, the signatures being all in the same writing as the body of the letter, was published, with facsimile of the Maya version, in the great *Cartas de Indias*, in 1877.

Its value as a real expression of Maya sentiment is considerably invalidated by the fact, only shown by the recent discovery of the above duplicate, in the same writing, and signed by another set of caciques, as one of *several more like letters*, dated all together within a few days. The one in the *Cartas de Indias* is dated February 11th, and this February 12th. In short, they are as stated in the following letter from Montejo Xiu, the Lord of Maní, concocted by the friars to influence the king. Readers of the single one published have been impressed by this ' spontaneous ' affection, but one may doubt whether Philip II was impressed by— shall we say? — the duplicity of affection. Anyhow, politics before the Council of the Indies, or before the United States Senate, seems quite alike.

Translation of the Letter shown in Facsimile.

Because we, your majesty's vassals, all understand the desire your majesty has that we shall be saved, and to provide sufficient ministers in your majesty's dominions to enlighten, instruct and teach those who are ignorant, and that although far from those realms of Castile, your majesty has the same care for us as if we were near, and that it is your pleasure and care that we be told what is most truly needed, according to our inferiority and capacity, and our poverty in temporal goods; Wherefore we make known before your majesty that from the beginning of our conversion to Christianity we have been taught the doctrine by the Franciscan friars, and they have preached and in their poverty do preach and teach us the law of God. We love them as true fathers, and they love us as true sons, and because of sufferings and infirmities and persecutions of the demon, they have been very few in this country, and since no others arrive, as it is so far from that land of Castile.

For this cause we beg that you will have compassion on our souls, and will send us Franciscan friars who will guide us and teach us the way of God; and especially those of them who have been in this country, and went back from here to Castile, those who know well our language in which to preach and teach us; they are called fray Diego de Landa, fray Pedro Gumiel of the province of Toledo, and especially fray Diego de Landa for he is great, sufficient, worthy and good in the eyes of our Father God, who calls on us much to be Christians; Miguel de la Puebla and the other padres, as many as you see good to send. And because we understand that jointly and quickly we may do service whereby your majesty with Christian heart desires us all good, and so we trust that we may be quickly aided by your majesty, whom may God shine on and ever increase your vision in his service.

Here in Yucatan on the twelfth day of February of the year 1567.

We are subjects of your majesty's realm and kiss your majesty's sacred hands.

Signed as for MELCHIOR PECH, governor of Samahil province; JUAN PECH; JUAN EK, town governor of Suma, PEDRO PECH, town governor of Kini, LUIS PECH, town governor of Moxop'ip'.

Letter of Francisco de Montejo Xiu.

Governor of Maní, and other prominent town governors,
To the King, April 12, 1567.

Sacred Catholic Majesty:

After we learned the good, in knowing God our Lord as the only true god, leaving our blindness and idolatries, and your majesty as temporal lord, before we could well open our eyes to the one and the other, there came upon us a persecution of the worst that can be imagined; and it was in the year '62, on the part of the Franciscan religious, who had taken us to teach the doctrine, instead of which they began to torment us, hanging us by the hands and whipping us cruelly, hanging weights of stone on our feet, torturing many of us on a windlass, giving the torture of the water, from which many died or were maimed.

Being in these tribulations and burdens, trusting in your majesty's Justice to hear and defend us, there came the Dr. Quijada to aid our tormentors, saying that we were idolaters and sacrificers of men, and many other things against all truth, which we never committed during our time of blindness and infidelity. And as we see ourselves maimed by cruel tortures, many dead of them, robbed of our property, and yet more, seeing disinterred the bones of our baptised ones, who had died as Christians, we came to despair.

Not content with this, the religious (i. e. the friars) and thy royal Justice, held at Maní a solemn auto of inquisition, where they seized many statues, disinterred many dead and burned them there in public; made slaves of many to serve Spaniards for from eight to ten years, and placed the sambenitos. The one and the other gave us great wonder and fear, because we did not know what it all was, having been recently baptised, and not informed; and when we returned to our people and told them to hear and guard justice, they seized us, put us in prison and chains, like slaves, in the monastery at Mérida, where many of us died; and they told us we would be burned, without our knowing the why.

At this came the bishop whom your majesty sent, who, although he took us from prison and relieved us from death and the sambenitos, has not relieved us from the shame of the charges that were made against us, that we were idolaters, human sacrificers, and had slain many men; because, at the last, he is of the habit of San Francisco and does for them. He has consoled us by his words, saying that your majesty would render justice.

A receptor came from Mexico, and made inquiry, and we believe it went to the Audiencia, and nothing has been done.

Then came as governor don Luís de Céspedes, and instead of relieving us he has increased our burdens, taking away our daughters and wives to serve the Spaniards, against their will and ours; which we feel so greatly that the common people say that not in the time of our infidelity were we so vexed or maltreated, because our ancestors never took from one his children, nor from husbands their wives to make use of them, as today does your majesty's Justice, even to the service of the negros and mulattos.

And with all our afflictions and labors, we have loved the fathers and supplied their necessities, have built many monasteries for them, provided with ornaments and bells, all at our cost and that of our vassals and fellows; although in payment of our services they have made of us their vassals, have deprived us of the signories we inherited from our ancestors, a thing we never suffered in the time of our infidelity. And we obey your majesty's justice, hoping that you will send us remedy.

One thing that has greatly dismayed and stirred us up, is the letters written by fray Diego de Landa, chief author of all these ills and burdens, saying that your majesty has approved the killings, robberies, tortures, slaveries and other cruelties inflicted on us; to which we wonder that such things should be said of so Catholic and upright a king as is your majesty. If it is told that we have sacrificed men after that we received baptism, it is a great and false witness invented by them to gild their cruelties.

And if there have been or are idols among us, they are but those we have gathered to send to the religious as they required of us, saying that we had confessed to their possession under the torture; but all know that we went many leagues to gather them from places where we knew that they had been kept by those before us, and which we had abandoned when we were baptised; and in good conscience they should not punish us as they have done.

If your majesty wishes to learn of all, send a person to search the truth, to learn of our innocence and the great cruelty of the padres; and had not the bishop come, we should all have been brought to an end. And though we cherish well Fray Diego and the other padres who torment us, only to hear them named causes our entrails to revolt. Therefore, your majesty, send us other ministers to teach us and preach to us the law of God, for we much desire our salvation.

The religious of San Francisco of this province have written certain letters to your majesty and to the general of the order, in praise of fray Diego de Landa and his other companions, who were those who tortured, killed and put us to scandal; and they gave certain letters written in the Castilian language to certain Indians of their familiars, and thus they signed them and sent them to your majesty. May your majesty understand that they are not ours, we who are chiefs of this land, and who did not have to write lies nor falsehoods nor contradictions. May fray Diego de Landa and his companions suffer the penance for the evils they have done to us, and may our descendants to the fourth generation be recompensed the great persecution that came on us.

May God guard your majesty for many years in his sacred service and for our good and protection. From Yucatan, the 12 of April, 1567.

Your majesty's humble vassals kiss your royal hands and feet.

(signed by)

don FRANCISCO DE MONTEJO XIU, govr. of Maní
JUAN PACAB, govr. of Muna
JORGE XIU, govr. of Panabá
FRANCISCO PACAB, govr. of Te-Xul.

Letter of Diego Rodríguez Bibanco.

By royal appointment Defender of the Indians of Yucatan,

To the King, March 8, 1563.

Diego Rodríguez Bibanco, citizen of Mérida in Yucatan, Defender of the Indians of this province, named by your majesty as granted in your royal Audiencia of the Confines, whereby it is my obligation to report to your majesty on their needs and grievances, herein give the harm that has been done them by wounds, deaths, losses and disturbances.

What happens is that the friars of the order of San Francisco in this province used the ecclesiastical jurisdiction before the bishop's arrival, saying they had the power by apostolic bulls to do this in places where there are no bishops; and in this title, good or bad, using the said Bulls, which it is understood did not give them the right to do what they have done, they gave orders to proceed against the Indians of all these provinces, generally, *por via de inquisición*, the Provincial constituting himself Inquisitor, and accompanied by the subordinate friars who also served as inquisitors; and together or singly they have inflicted irregularities and punishments on these Indians never heard of in all the Indies, under color of and saying that they were idolaters.

And in order to have more power and force than they had, they called for aid from the alcalde mayor of the province, doctor Diego Quijada, whom your majesty sent here two years ago more or less; he inconsiderately, being a weak man of little judgment or prudence, gave them lay judges who carried out all that the friars directed; this without any process, nor fault in the Indians, whereby the royal aid was given solely on the information of the idiot friars, some of whom do not even know how to read.

And so, with the power they claimed as ecclesiastical judges, and that which your Justice gave them, they set about the business with great rigor and atrocity, putting the Indians to great tortures, of ropes and water, hanging them by pulleys with stones of 50 or 75 pounds to their feet, and so suspended gave them many lashes until the blood ran to the ground from their shoulders and legs; besides this they tarred them with boiling fat as was the custom to do to negro slaves, with the melted wax of lit candles dropped on their bare parts; all this without preceding information, or seeking first for the facts. This seemed to them the way to learn them.

The poor Indians, weak and miserable, afflicted and maltreated, in fear of the torture, while under the torture confessed irregularities they have neither committed nor thought of, saying they were idolaters, and had quantities of idols, and had even sacrificed human beings and done other great cruelties; all being false and stated in fear and for the pain they suffered.

Thus they brought in a great quantity of idols they had had in ancient buildings and the woods and caves, already left and forgotten, and said that they now had and used them; on which confessions, without listening to the Indians or their Defender, or making any verification beyond what came by the tortures, they sheared them, beat and punished them, usually every one in the pueblos they visited. Some individuals, leading caciques and persons, they condemned to ten years slavery, more or less; put on them the penitential sambenito garments of the Inquisition, banished them from their signories and towns, and made them slaves, and so treated them. From all they also exacted fines of two, three or more ducats, and from the common people two or four reales, by which they collected great sums of money; and in this way they did with most of the Indians where the Inquisition and punishment were instituted. They made two Autos of Inquisition, erecting high tablets and banners with insignia, such as your majesty's inquisitors use, putting great numbers of Indians in the province in the corozas [shame headdresses] and sambenitos, and declared it was necessary in the case.

From all which, and much more I cannot tell your majesty for the prolixity, great harm to the Indians resulted; for seeing the things, they fled many to the forests, others hung themselves in despair, many others were left wounded, without hands or feet, and many others died of the tortures inflicted. Thus the whole country was afflicted, aroused, oppressed and maltreated, until last August the bishop, don fray Francisco de Toral arrived, named by your majesty as prelate and pastor for this province; who took on himself the matter and the state of things he found, and before whom I, in the name of the Indians, asked relief.

This I could not do before, because the friars laid public excommunication upon any person who opposed them, saying this was improper, and interfered with the Holy Office of the Inquisition, because it was the royal Justice who gave the chief favor to the friars. Thus I could not use my office, for they deprived me of liberty; only by letter could I admonish them, but these did no good. Before the bishop, who heard the charges without passion and with Christian zeal, I laid the charges and showed the Indians molested without fault; thus a great number held in prison were freed, the sambenitos were taken off, they were taken from the slavery imposed, and wherein they were, and the land was quieted, when it was without doubt at the stage of dissolution.

All this put the friars to great pain, knowing the wrong they had done, without order or justice; and thus they tried in every way to find faults in the Indians, to show that it had all been necessary. To this end I am advised that they secured proofs by rewards. The alcalde mayor presented witnesses to testify that he was a good governor, speaking in his defense and that of the friars, and declaring that the punishments had not been severe, and the like. Desiring to excuse themselves before your majesty, and knowing that it would be necessary to lay the facts before your majesty, they took pains to get statements in their favor, saying that it was all in the service of God our Lord and your majesty, and that they were not guilty, seeking to do you wrong, that you might not give remedy.

So it would be useless unless your majesty should provide a judge who would hear all, as I tell your majesty and have proven to the bishop, and will prove when called upon, and should relieve these poor people of the wrongs inflicted with no fault done by them: attacks, killings, loss and destruction of their houses and property, banishment. I in the name of these poor ones in my charge, and of the other Indians of these provinces, complain before your majesty as I can, as is my duty, and beg with all the proper respect that you grant the needed remedy and justice to these Indians; and against the alcalde mayor, who has done so great harm; and against the ministers and friars who have done it, that they be punished either by your prelates or those who should do this, and remove them from this land, in which they ever hold hatred against the Indians, since they cannot go on with that they have done; the same the alcalde mayor who seeks all kinds of vexations to prevent their speaking or complaining of what has happened, so that they are put in fear and afraid, wherein I fear rebellion and destruction.

Thus I humbly implore your majesty that you order it remedied, in the service of God our Lord and the good of these poor ones and the service of your majesty. I am not sending the processes of what took place and was done before the bishop, for they are long and costly. Your majesty will understand the truth from what the bishop will inform you, and what he shall say in justice as a servant of Our Lord and zealous in his and your majesty's service, and for these poor ones. May Our Lord guard the sacred Catholic and royal person of your majesty for many years, with increase of lands and dominions.

That your majesty may be advised, I ask the royal secretary of the council of this city to attach the certificate that I am such Defender of the Indians.

Sacred Catholic royal majesty, I kiss your royal feet.

Your humble vassal,

DIEGO RODRIGUEZ BIBANCO.

I, Hernando Dorado, royal and public Secretary here in Merida, certify that the sender hereof, Diego Rodríguez Bibanco, is here Defender of the Indians by your royal order through the Audiencia of the Confines, and signed his petition before me.

HERNANDO DORADO,
Your majesty's Secretary.

The Xiu Family Papers

These form a volume of 160 pages of signed and dated documents, running continuously from 1608 to the end of the Spanish rule, 1817. In the middle of the volume are four items of outstanding importance for our knowledge of the history of western Yucatan, and which should particularly be included here in detail, in connection with the preceding translation of Bishop Landa's work. That we may treat them separately, they may be numbered as follows:

1: A genealogical tree showing the members of the Xiu family, from the Tutul Xiu, born about 1380, who led the family from Uxmal to Maní after the destruction of Mayapán in 1420, down to Juan Xiu, who became head of the family in 1640, and died about 1690.

2: Two pages of text in Maya, dated 1557, relating the gathering of various representatives at Maní, for the settlement of boundaries of their lands and towns, and those of their neighbors, the Cocomes, the Canules, those of Calotmul, Maxcanú, etc.

3: A map, here reproduced as drawn from the original, on a double-page sheet, to go with the preceding, certified, text.

4: A single page, signed by Juan Xiu in 1685, and stating that it was taken by him from a record in " *carácteres.*" This page gives a number of events, with attached dates from 1533 (the year after Montejo's departure for Mexico after his first, unsuccessful, attempt at the conquest of Yucatan) down to 1545, and set out in terms of both the Maya and our European chronology. This page, after being for many years known, ignored, studied, criticised and rejected as a base for a correlation of Maya and European dates, has at last through the work and researches of J. Eric Thompson and the late Dr. John E. Teeple, been accepted as our one confirmed and authoritative base point; it has been so acknowledged by, we believe, every American writer save one, and also the leading Yucatecan scholar, Señor Juan Martínez H., of Mérida.

This volume of papers was sent to me over twenty years ago to photograph for my own use, and as an addition to my collection of original material, but nothing of it has heretofore been published save Item 4, as to be noted later below. The volume thus brings before us, brought out within the scope of their family history from 1380 to the present time, a stretch of 450 documented years, the five chief outstanding figures therein: the Tutul Xiu of Uxmal; that Ahpulhá Napot Xiu who led the dramatic and ill-fated pilgrimage in 1536 to invoke divine aid for a cessation of the drought that coincided with the end of the first Spanish attempt; the Kukum Xiu, Lord of Maní, who voluntarily came to join himself as feudatory to the Spanish as a result of the breach between the East and West that began with the destruction of Mayapán and came to its climax at Otzmal in 1536, one of its first results having been the re-erection of the Itzá state at Tayasal on Lake Petén (lasting as the one remaining independent native state until 1695, just ten years after Juan Xiu wrote our Item 4); Naxiu Chi, a Xiu on his mother's side, who having married the great-great-granddaughter of Tutul Xiu of Uxmal, was baptised Gaspar Antonio, and became one of Landa's chief informants in the Relation we have herein translated; finally the most important later member, the Juan of 1685.

For clearer reading the names written on the several ' blossoms' are replaced by numbers, and the names corresponding are given below, by their generations, the better to show the kinships:

1: Tutul Xiu.
2a: Ah-tz'un Xiu; 2b: Ah-uitz Xiu.
3a: Ah-op Xiu; 3b: Ah-cetz Xiu; 3c: Ah-uitz; 3d: Ah-kauil Xiu; 3e: Ah-cuat Xiu; 3f: Ah-uitz Xiu.
4a: Nap'ol Xiu; 4b: Ah-kukil Xiu; 4c: Ah-tzam Xiu; 4d: Ah-lol Xiu; 4e: Ah-atira Xiu; 4f: Ah-uitz Xiu.
5a: Ah-ziyah Xiu, Yacman; 5b: don Diego Xiu, Tikit; 5c: don Juan Xiu; 5d: Ah-tz'ulub Xiu, grandfather of don Francisco Pacab, Ox-kutzcab; 5e: Ah-uitz Xiu; 5f: Ah-mochan Xiu; 5g: Nabatun Xiu; 5h: Ah-chac Xiu, Panabá.
6a: Melchor Xiu; 6b: Montexo Xiu, go^r Maní, husband of doña Maria Xiu; 6c: Ah-tzam Xiu; 6d: Ah-op Xiu; 6e: doña Maria Xiu; Calotmul, wife of Montexo Xiu; 6f: Ixkaual Xiu, wife of Gaspar Antonio; 6g: Ixkaual Xiu; 6h: Ah . . . . ; 6i: Ah-pitz Xiu; 6j: Ah-tz'un Xiu; 6k: Nacahun Xiu; 6l: Ah-ziyah Xiu; 6m: Ah-kukil Xiu; 6n: Ah-cuate Xiu; 6o: don Alonso Xiu, Tikit; 6p: Nanachan Xiu.
7a: don Francisco Xiu, son of don Melchor; 7b: Nabtu (?) Xiu; 7c: don . . . . Xiu.
8:   Pedro Xiu, son of Francisco, gov^r Oxkutzcab.
9a: don . . . . o Xiu; 9b: . . . . o;
10: don Juan Xiu, son of Alonso Xiu.

In tabular form it reads:

TUTUL XIU

Ah-tз'un						Ah-uitз	
Ah-op	Ah-cetз	Ah-uitз	Ah-kauil			Ah-cuat	Ah-uitз
Nap'ol	Ah-kukil	Ah-tзam	Ah-lol			Ah-atira	Ah-uitз
Ah-ziyah	Diego	Juan	Ah-tз'ulub	Ah-uitз	Ah-mochan	Nabatun	Ah-chac
Melchor / Ah-op / Ah-tзam / Montejo	Maria, w.f. of Montejo	Ah-piв / Ah-. . . / Ixkaual / Ixkaual	Ah-tзun	Ah-cuate / Ah-kukil / Ah-ziyah / Nacahun	Alonso	Nanachan . . .
Francisco			Nabtu				
Pedro			. . .				
Alonso							
Juan							

The last five names, from Francisco to Juan, are in darker ink, and the calix of the flowers differently drawn. The Tree was clearly made in the time of Melchor and Montejo, probably in 1548, and then completed by Juan, as shown by the pointing hand. While the tear in the leaf has taken nearly all of the circle for Alonso, the entries as above are not only clear, but are positively confirmed in the first of the coming documents; the two names between Francisco and Juan must be those of Pedro and Alonso; also the separate circle at the extreme left must have sprung from Pedro, representing a brother of Alonso, not otherwise mentioned.

No Spanish baptismal names occur before the fifth generation, of people old at the time of the Conquest; here we find Diego of Tekit, and Juan the father of Maria of Calotmul, the wife of (Kukum) Montejo. Probably these four were all baptised at once, in 1548.

The only Spanish names we find in the sixth generation are those of Maria, Montejo and Melchor, the ancestor of the whole following line to which these Papers belong. But here we also find Ixkaual, wife to Gaspar Antonio, and her first cousin, one **Ah-tz'un**, who is probably the famous **Ahpulhá** who died at Otzmal in 1536.

The 1685 page by Juan Xiu, while describing the Otzmal event and those killed there, does not name the leader as ' Napot Xiu,' as he is elsewhere called; it only reads:

" The day 8 Cauac, the 1st of Pop, when there died the rain-bringers (**ah-pulháob**) at Otzmal, namely Ah-tz'un Tutul Xiu and Ah-ziyah Napuc Chi," etc.

Ah-tz'un simply meaning ' leader,' these probably refer to the same person.

The direct line, arranged in order of primogeniture, then reads:

Tutul Xiu.
Ah-tz'un.
Napot Chuvat; probably the water-bringer, ah-pulhá, killed at Otzmal in 1536.
Ah-ziyah Yacman; perhaps a companion of Napot.
Kukum, baptized in 1548 at Maní, as Francisco de Montejo Xiu.
Melchor, brother of Kukum.
Ixkaual, wife of Gaspar Antonio Chi, the interpreter.
Francisco, son of Melchor; governor of Oxkutzcab in 1608.
Alonso, son of Pedro; succeeds him at Yaxa in 1624.
Catalina Cimé of Pencuyut, granted exemptions in 1632.
Juan (born about 1620), and his sister Maria and Petrona.

The births of the sixth generation must have fallen about 1500; Kukum must have been he who surrendered to Montejo on his arrival at Tiho, was baptised in 1548 as Francisco de Montejo Xiu, and was thereafter governor of Maní, the **halach-vinic** at whose house took place the gathering in 1557, to be later described. In 1608 Francisco, then governor of Oxkutzcab, signed the oldest document surviving in our volume, confirming his " son Pedro " as cacique of Yaxa Cumché, in the Oxkutzcab district.

Alonso, " son of Pedro," succeeds him at Yaxa in 1624, and in 1632 Catalina Cimé of Pencuyut is granted exemptions as " widow of Alonso "; his rights are also referred to in papers dated 1657, 1660. Then Juan, with his sisters Maria and Petrona, are certified in 1640 as " children of Alonso and grandchildren of Pedro"; and again so mentioned in a paper dated at Tekax in 1641.

This is the Juan Xiu to whom we owe the famous page above mentioned, establishing the correlation of the chronologies — our Item 4. His long and prominent record includes:

> Signed paper, in Maya, no date.
> Two others same, apparently about 1660.
> Confirmed as head of line, 1662; also right to bear arms.
> Made Captain for Oxkutzcab, 1664.
> Given command of 40 archers, 1667.
> Governor of Oxkutzcab, 1667.
> Succeeds the governor of Maxcanú, removed for misconduct, 1667.
> Certificate, 1678, as to his son Roque by his first wife Francisca Chulim; born 1646; this Roque apparently died unmarried.
> Writes above page of chronology, 1685.
> Mentioned, 1689, as having a " very valuable book " from which names or data had been copied by one Diego Chi, secretary of the cofradía at Maní.
> Probably died about 1690.

The Tree thus gives us eleven names in the direct line, from the Tutul Xiu from whose loins spring all the others, down to Juan, or about 26 years to a generation from the birth of the first to that of Juan's successor, in 1661. To follow the lineage beyond the Tree and Juan Xiu, we must turn to the body of documents in the volume, where we get an overlapping of the data on the Tree (Pedro, Alonso and Juan appearing in each), and then six successors to Juan, down to Antonio, who is shown as the family head in the last paper, 1817, as follows:

> Juan Antonio, son of Juan, by his second wife Maria Beltrán, born in 1661.
> Salvador, son of Juan Antonio and Pasquala Ku; born 1697, and still living as one of the ' elder men,' in 1759.
> Lorenzo, " the old man," heads list of Xiu names in 1764, and is still mentioned among them in 1771.
> Pablo; heads five successive lists from 1779 to 1793.
> Pedro; heads the lists from 1801 to 1812.
> Antonio; heads the last list, of 1817.

Here our documents cease, but nevertheless leaving us at the very bottom of the last list the names of Andres, born in 1788, and Bentura, born in 1814, and thus again overlapping, by these two names, the oral information gotten over a hundred years after the papers ceased, from very old surviving descendants, who remembered Andres and Bentura as the grandfather and father of Bernabe, born in 1839 and dying in 1911. This volume of family papers, after passing through the hands of all these family heads for over 300 years, from at least 1608 down to Bernabe, was still intact in his possession a couple of years before his death, when (as stated in a letter from Sylvanus Morley to me in 1920) it " was stolen, bought or received from Bernabe Xiu." *

The final links were then made when given to me on a visit to Oxkutzcab in the autumn of 1917, by old Doña Felipa, daughter of Bernabe and mother of young Nicomedes Xiu, 1896- — ; and further confirmed the next Spring by Morley in Ticul in the little three-year old Dionisio, the last Xiu XXIII, in the direct male line, as below:

Andres, born 1788.
Bentura, his son, born 1814.
Bernabe, his son, 1839-1911.
Ildefonso, his son, 1861-1911.
Nemensio, his son, born about 1887.
Dionisio, his son, born 1915. And further
 Felipa, daughter of Bernabe, born 18
 Nicomedes, her son, born 1896.

The Tree itself as it stands is thus wholly such as might have been drawn up in England about the year 1160 to show the descendants of Sir So-and-So, who had led his troop with William of Normandy; and then with additions made another hundred years later by the then head of the family, to bring the line down to himself; and then supplemented by a continued documentary register to the present day.

* In confirmation of this I can add the following, from my own visit of 1917. Having already, as stated above, made a full photographic copy of the Xiu volume, and later translating it, I spoke of this to Doña Felipa and others of the family. At once they said: " Oh señor, cannot you get back for us these papers? They belong to us; they are the records of our ancestors that have been in our possession from back of the time that we can remember. But a few years ago Don Bernabe loaned them to (as we thought) our ' good friend ' Don Eduardo Thompson, and we have never been able to get him to return them. Cannot you get them for us? "

But, soon after the ' borrowing,' Don Eduardo had sold them in the United States, where they still remain, in the ' keeping ' of a certain institution. One feels quite permitted to ask, what would a Mayflower or Virginia descendant feel if *his* family papers, records not half as ancient, and not even of royal caste, had been borrowed by a Xiu, and sold as just interesting historical records — to the local Museum in Mérida?

We must here picture the Yucatan states as consisting of the **halach-vinic,** or ' true man,' at the head, then the **almehenob** (a compound meaning ' sons of a mother and father,' and exactly corresponding to the Spanish *hidalgo,* or ' son of somebody '), and finally the **vinicob** or common folk. As confirmed by what we find in our Item 2 and the other documents in the volume, this patent of nobility must have been drawn in the time of Francisco de Montejo Xiu on the occasion of his baptism and recognition as feudatory to the Spanish Crown, in 1548.

At the bottom we see reclining the Tutul Xiu who first established the capital at Maní; then his descendants as seen in the table, ending with our Juan Xiu of Item 4, with a hand pointing to his own name, as the extreme left. In the lower left we see remaining the letters —n .tzil chac ume . . . **ob Tutul Xiu.** **Mehenob** denoting descendants in the male line, this makes a sort of title: " The growth of the descendants of Tutul Xiu." And then just below this we find at the torn edge of the paper a clearly distinguishable part of the Maya sign for the day **Ahau,** over a black dot (the right-hand one of an original three), and the words, —au katun loe. That can *only* stand for " this, the katun 3 **Ahau,**" meaning in the usual style of the Chronicles, an event that happened in the katun or 20-year period ending on a day 3 **Ahau,** a date that only recurs once in 260 years.

Now as finally established, thanks to our Item 4, the katun 3 **Ahau** ended in 1382, which fixes the ' root of the tree,' as that ruler or ' leader of the Xius to their new capital, as stated by Landa and confirmed by the entries in the Maya Chronicles themselves, about 120 to 125 years before the coming of the Spaniards to Mérida.

The entire volume, outside of the four special items noted, consists of documents in both Maya and Spanish, attesting the succession in headship, births, and membership in the Xiu family. The first three attest the legitimacy, recognized headship and privileges of Pedro in 1608, Alonso " son of Pedro " in 1624, Juan and his sisters " children of Alonzo and grandchildren of Pedro " in 1640.

In these Spain followed the universal custom of conquering or expanding empires, allowing to the local chieftains or rulers as full a measure of their former headship and privileges as possible, subject to, and in proportion to their degree of recognition of political suzerainty, the *right* to economic exploitation and support, and as necessary incident, the social recognition of the new masters as ' superior beings.' Thus did in succession the Romans, the British, the Dutch, and others, the degree and nature of the resulting dominance over the acquired ' subjects ' depending on the nature or character, plus the real or professed purposes of the ' occupation.'

Ancient Rome, Holland, Britain sought the spread of empire and trade, and leaving the essentials of life, religion and local customs, as nearly untouched as possible; giving in return protection. The occupied lands, in most cases the field of destructive internecine wars such as would be the case in India today save for the handful of Indian regiments protecting both the *raj* and the people, lost superior suzerainty (actually non-existent in the country) in exchange for the order of a firm administration. To the common man one far distant Emperor is the same as another, so long as the currents of local life go along and the customs and ' gods of our fathers ' are respected—whether the ryot, the fellahin or the masehual be in Ceylon, Egypt or Mexico. The emperor may then be Akbar in Delhi, Edward in London, or Charles in Spain; the only further thing asked is that he protect the defenseless people from the wanton murders, tortures, rapings and burnings of the foreign ' public enemies ' set loose among them. If this is not done, the work of the Diego de Landas and the Pedro de Alvarados will only breed revolts that must end either in total annihilation as in Cuba, or in final freedom, however late.

To these demands Spain however added that of enforced conversions to Christianity and the " blessings of European civilization " (as professed by others today in their thirst for conquest), all " by the divine command" that justifies all ' necessary ' means to save men from the eternal hell ordained by God for those who cannot recognize his image of peace and love in the autos de fé and the hangings — escapable however by humbleness and gold.

Yet these people even in the later days, of the Sixteenth Century, were higher in polity, science and all that really makes civilization, than the invaders — who only had gunpowder, horses, lusts, and (heaven save the mark) the Cross. In these words lies the whole story of the lands south of us, where now in these last ten years *only*, is the long debt to the Indian race beginning to be paid by seeking to make him once more a free working citizen of his own country, educated in the things that lead to economic prosperity for the individual, the local community, and the State. For Mexico *is* today making the Indian again a ' man ' — while we in this country manufacture and offer him roseate white-man's plans for his anthropological welfare instead of liberty; keep him against his helpless will the slave of the most generations-long intrenched bureaucracy in our whole log-rolling system, that wastes, and worse, his property, while we decimate him by our imported immoralities, and exploitations.

Returning to our documents. These form an interesting and informative picture of the course of events in Yucatan from the surrender of Kukum Xiu, the Lord of Maní, in 1541. Through that century and the next, down to and including Juan Xiu, the papers are in the form first above referred to. They constituted the official investiture of the local head of his own district and people, who thus continued to look to him as " their immediate **halach-vinic**," with things going fairly peacefully and thus of easier administration, save for the constant troubles caused by Landa and his Franciscans, and army bandits like Pacheco on the east coast. That the population of the districts decreased at a rate almost as great as that of the Missions in California (roughly 100% each ten years so long as yet more Indians remained in the unconverted back country to be brought in to receive the blessings of working for the whites for their ' welfare '), as testified to, and *complained* of by many of the original company of Montejo's soldiers, among whom the lands of the whole state were divided. (See the documents at the end of this volume, for 1549, 1579 and 1581.) The causes were regularly: sickness by change of their old ways, forcible concentration into single town centers where church instruction was more convenient, and flight into the back forests to escape the constant individual cases of oppression, etc. Nevertheless the political system of recognizing as part of the local state government the members of the old ruling caste, of ' hidalgo ' standing, persisted (as it still does in the heavily Indian highland regions of Guatemala today) until the death of Juan Xiu about 1690, after a practical headship of his family for over fifty years, from the death of his father in 1632.

At this time a very definite change in the character of the Spanish occupation began, to pave the way for the first great uprising of the Mayas for freedom at Cisteil in 1731, to which hidden references are undoubtedly to be found in the veiled language of the Chumayel manuscript. A marked surge of Hispanic activity springs up in many lines, both literary and physical.

As one goes today through Yucatan one meets at every town of any size a tremendous dominating ' Rhine castle ' of stone, taken from the ancient palaces and temples by Indian labor, to erect towering churches. Many of these have dated lintels, which run from about 1690 to 1720, when Yucatan ceased to be merely ' occupied ' by the *encomendero* families under the Montejo grants to his seventy odd soldiers, and the full weight of the new order settled in place.

At this same time there began a definite literary change: the voluminous histories came on to be written, by Cogolludo for Yucatan, Villagutierre on the final conquest of the last Itzá kingdom at Lake Petén, Torquemada's *Monarquía Indiana* for Mexico, Fuentes y Guzmán for Guatemala. In 1710 Padre Ximénez found, copied and translated the *Popol Vuh*, the magnificent

Quiché story of cosmogony, mythology and history; at the same time writing his long history, trilingual dictionary and grammars, and his treatise on the natural history.

The first students of the native languages, in the 16th century, set down the native languages as they found them, and did it marvelously well; what was done in that time and up to about 1650, is worth everything we have of later date, even up to now in our own boasted era of sciolistic anthropologism. In the 17th century amplified studies and grammars were written, departing little from the spirit of the languages as they still stood, nearly untouched save that they were no longer the languages of an active native culture, but relegated to the submerged class.   Then in the 18th century after the passing of its first generation, a conscious *Hispanization* began on every side, in every way.

This affected the form of our documents of *hidalguía,* and resulted in more or less vagueness in the details, only, of the Xiu primogeniture.   Roque Xiu passes out of our picture, and his step-brother Juan Antonio must have succeeded to headship on Juan's death, but we have no specific confirming document.   Up to and including Juan, each new document was a confirmation of the *rights* and position of the succeeding heir, " legitimate son of " his predecessor; but beginning with Salvador we have only papers confirming the leading elders and those of their family name, as hidalgos, and entitled to the privileges of such quality: that is, services and contributions from their own people, but probably no part in the governmental set-up.   Also, from 1727 on the papers do not tell us who is the son of whom, and we thus have to deduce the direct line by the prominence given to the successor, at the head of those named as recognized Xius.   That Salvador was in fact the " son of Juan Antonio Xiu and Pasquala Ku " we only know from his baptismal certificate, in 1697; in 1759 he was still alive, among those named;   then Lorenzo, " the old man," heads the list in 1764, and is still among them in 1771.

At this time, as the spirit of liberty was stirring in the United States and in France, we have still another change in the style of our papers;   most fortunately for our present purpose, as it resulted in our final bridge to the present.   This final, very condensed form, then lasted until 1817, when colonial (but not Maya) freedom was ushered in.   This form undertakes to give a list of all living Xius, men, women, and *boys* of any age, the actual age of the youngest being added.   From 1779 to 1793 Pablo Xiu heads the list, then Pedro from 1801 to 1812, and Antonio in 1817.   And then almost all baptismal records through the State having perished in the war of 1847, when the Mayas nearly regained the peninsula, we are without direct evidence of the parentage of these last.   But, as told above, from the first Pedro in

1608, and the Tree, these are the continuous family records of the Xius of Maní and Oxkutzcab, from the time Mayapán was destroyed and they abandoned Uxmal; and also they did remain undisturbed in the possession of the succeeding heads in Oxkutzcab, until about 1910.

For here comes our last piece of good fortune; since just as the first Pedro appears both on the Tree and in the documents, so in the last Pedro's lists we are told that Andres was a boy " 1 year old " in 1788, and again " 4 years old in 1793." And then finally, in the last paper of all, we are told that Bentura was 3 years old in 1817.

Now Bentura's son Bernabe Xiu, who loaned the papers to Consul Thompson, died in 1911, but his younger sister Felipa still lived when the present writer visited the town in 1917; also other elder Xius when Morley followed in 1918, as related in his letters of that time. As told above, these old people remembered back to Andres and Bentura, and from them this final gap was filled, to be completed by the gathering then by Morley and myself, separately, of the later data, and the present names of the living: a complete record from **Katun 3 Ahau** to *Century XX*.

Here also seems the place for the duties laid upon Juan Xiu in 1665, incident to his appointment by Francisco de Esquivel, royal councillor and Governor and Captain General of Yucatan, to serve for one year, as the local governor of Oxkutzcab.

In this office, he shall exalt the royal justice in said town and its confines, shall care for all matters pertaining to said office, administering and doing justice in conformity with the royal ordinances, defending the widows, common people and the poor from the powerful, or from other persons also who may unjustly oppress them, remitting to us all such matters as we should be advised of.

Item: He shall take great care to see that the Indians attend to hear mass on Sundays and the other prescribed days, and to the preaching of the Holy Christian Gospel (punishing those who without cause fail in this); and that they respect its ministers as their spiritual fathers.

Item: That each family shall live in a separate house, even when near relations; that they keep it clean and in good repair, with a Cross or image of Our Lord and his Holy Mother; with rosaries, couches, mats, hens, cocks, and the other things required by the Ordinances.

Item: That he take care that order and the Spanish way of government be observed; that the streets lead properly to the church, and that the houses and wells of the town be kept repaired.

Item: That inasmuch as the milpa to be cultivated for the town in commonalty is essential and necessary, I command that he take great care that it be properly sown, harvested and stored, and not consumed except in accordance with the royal decrees.

Item: That care is taken that the Indians of the town stay in it without permitting them to live away on ranches, milpas or work-places; that no Indians of other towns be allowed unless already married in their own town; that he make a list of all returning Indians and of these who go off into the bush, in conformity with the dispatches and orders I have remitted, rendering account of this within four months, as commanded by the decrees.

Item: That he take care that the Indians of his town shall work each in his calling, shall care for the milpas, sowing 60 mecates of corn, as well as beans, chile, squash, yuccas, cotton and cacao, as they have them; that in the patios and gardens of their houses they shall plant chayas, bananas and other fruit-trees, with such other things as the earth produces; that each have near his house a granary for storage of said edibles, and they go on supporting themselves therewith, and their wives and children; failing in which they shall be punished in proportion to the fault.

Item: It is commanded that he cause the Indians to work in the spinning and weaving of articles for the tribute, together with the maize and the chickens called for by the tax regulations; that payment in money is prohibited except in the specified cases, in order that laziness be avoided, and that prices do not go down in the pursuit of money.

Item: The said governor shall not procure the cultivation of milpas of maize, beans, cotton or other products, nor the distribution of money or other payments for the things the Indians gather or make for the Encomendero or other persons, under pain of deprivation of his office for four years.   He shall see to it that the tribute is paid punctually to the Encomendero, in the mantles, maize and chickens prescribed.

Item: Inasmuch as it is prohibited the local governors of this province to negotiate, contract or procure assignments of Indians for different people; also prohibited the judges any aggressions on the milpas with the consequent injury to the Indians and harm to the province thereby; it is ordered that the said governors and judges accept no money or other thing for making such assignments of the Indians, and all persons are forbidden to make such collections in their name to that end, under pain of privation of their offices, of 200 blows, and of banishment from the pueblo.

Item: I order that that he permit the Indians as to everything they produce beyond the amount of the tribute, with their gatherings of wax, honey, cochineal and fruits, a free sale by them in the town, or in the city and villages of Campeche and Valladolid, to whomever will pay them best, to the end that they may have money for their needs and the things they require for apparel.

Item: Having been informed that at times when orders go for wet-nurses solicited by different persons, it has been the custom to seize poor women lately widowed or abandoned by their husbands with their three, four or five infants, I order that none such be sent except after a half year of widowhood or with one or two infants, who shall accompany them, and not be left uncared for, that they may give breast to their own, and in the house of their nearest relative; it being further required of the judges to have them returned within a year and a half.

Item: Since it is so disposed that the governor, in order properly to discharge his duties, does not himself cultivate his milpa, but that a milpa of 70 mecates of the commonalty be farmed for him; and since I am advised that many governors have enforced the cultivation for themselves of large tracts, all which abuses and corruptions should be reformed, I order and command that no more than the above 70 mecates be so cultivated, and no more than this amount of produce be stored for them, and the weekly service thereto be observed during his term of office. The said governor shall not require any more to be done for him, even under the pretext of paying for it, under pain of loss of office for four years and banishment ten leagues away from the pueblo.

. .*Item:* Being advised that many aggravations and extortions are practised by those trading and dealing in the towns, oppressing those poor and miserable, taking them off as muleteers and in service, I order that the present governor shall not during his term of office engage in business or trade, nor molest any Indian, nor take them from their houses for the like purposes, under the same penalties.

I therefore command that the alcades, regidores and other principal Indians of the said town of **Oxkutzcab** receive as their Governor the said don Juan Xiu, that they obey, esteem and respect him, keep and cause to be kept all the honors, graces and exceptions, and the prerogatives which belong to him by said office, doing nothing in contravention thereof, under pain of the due prosecution for such disobedience; that he present himself under this title before the town Council and the Cabildo, making the proclamation thereof to all the Indians of the said pueblo, for their information of what is ordained, as in the book of communities.

DON JUAN FRANCISCO DE ESQUIVEL, (rubric)
Dated in Mérida this 12th of September, 1665.

The Map, and the Meeting at Maní.

In 1842, after Stephens and his party had finished at Uxmal, they went as the Xius had done over 400 years before, to Maní. Being there permitted to hunt in the archives for some records to throw light on the past, he found not only the drawing reproduced in Cogolludo and later in Morley's *Copan,* of what was supposed to be the massacre at Otzmal in 1536 (really a semi-prophetic **katun**-wheel), but also a map and two papers dated 1556 and 1557, all three bearing the word **Uxmal**. The full story should be read in his *Travels in Yucatan,* in volume two; but in substance the earlier paper related, in Maya, how a commission appointed by the governor, under the judge Felipe Manrique, and accompanied by the interpreter *Gaspar Antonio* (our *Chi*), arrived from Uxmal at Maní with an assemblage of the leading men, Xius and others, to delimit and fix the boundaries of Xius, Cocoms and other clans, in 1556. The other paper, also in Maya, tells of the

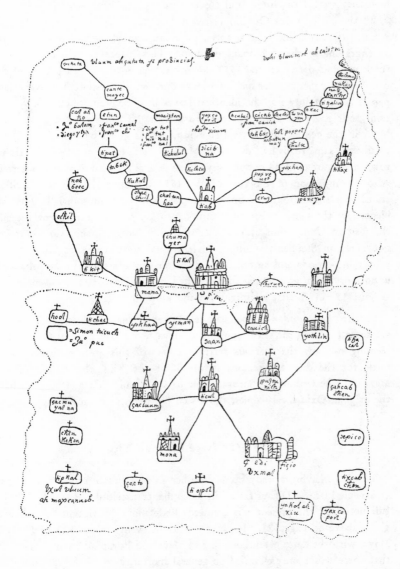

gathering at Maní in 1557 at the house of the Xiu chief man, Francisco Montejo Xiu, governor of Maní, " and of the jurisdiction of Tutul Xiu," and how they settled the limits and erected crosses, at twenty-two places.

By the aid of Cura Carrillo (later Bishop), they with much trouble got a translation, of which the essential parts are printed by Stephens; and also an engraving of the accompanying map. These papers he tells us were in a thick volume, of which the 1557 document was on the 157th page, and the other a few pages further on. To make our own story short, however, these papers are certainly not the identical leaves in our volume, but equally certainly our pages are contemporary transcripts. The map is the same, with Maní in the center, and Uxmal showing, just as given by Stephens. Practically the same roads lead out from Maní in each, but a number of outlying town names are omitted in our copy, while several personal names are inserted. Also a comparison of the text of the 1557 document here with Carrillo's translation shows that the originals must have been substantially but not identically the same. Our copy omits mention of the judge Manrique and the visit to Uxmal, but also it is considerably longer, listing various towns not given in Stephens, ending with the final statement that after all the proper inspections and agreements of the various **almehenob**, the **ubatabil cahob** or town governors, this certified ' transcript ' had been made, on August 15, 1557, that all might see and know it as true.

Furthermore, similar independent references to this assemblage and its work are to be found in the still unpublished Maya text of the Calkiní Chronicle,* seeming to show that various certified copies of this great settlement were made for the different regions involved, of the Xius, the Canuls beyond Maxcanú, the Cocoms of Sotuta, those of Calotmul, etc.; and here we have the original Oxkutzcab copies, those seen by Stephens having disappeared.

The 1685 page by Juan Xiu.

This page having already been published in Morley's *Inscriptions at Copan* (Carnegie Inst., 1921), as traced in facsimile, transcribed and translated with full notes, by the present writer, needs little more description here than as given above on page 121. It gives a series of events from 1533 to 1545, in Maya, with the dates given both in full Maya and European terms. We learn that there was a **maya-cimlal** or general mortality in 1533 (the very year that the elder Montejo retired beaten on his first attempt at conquest), the killing of the " rain-bringer " Napot Xiu at Otzmal in 1536, a hurricane in

* A photographic facsimile of the Calkiní has however been published by the Maya Society, in its Publ. No. 8.

1538, the founding of Mérida by the Spaniards in 1542, " and the beginning of the tributes, by the aid of those of Maní, on the day 5 **Ahau**, the 17th of the month **Tzec**," the battle at Tz'itz'omtun in 1543, and the coming of Christianity in 1545, with the arrival of the six Franciscan friars. " Copied on May 29th, 1685, from an ancient book, namely in characters as they are called, **anares**. I, don Juan Xiu."

Accurate as the dual dating in this paper is, it was rejected as a basis for correlation by Morley and myself, after long arguments, as being contrary to what we then believed were settled facts as to the periods of occupation and non-occupation at Chichén Itzá, and similar points.   Finally we agreed on the correlation given by him in Appendix II to his Copan book, based on a time-reckoning in vogue among the eastern Yucatecans or Itzás; owing to the elaborate system of triple checks in the Maya calendar, the variation between the Itzá and Xiu counts involved a difference of 260 years in the actually elapsed time from the zero-date of the Maya time reckoning, now finally fixed at August 13, 3113 B.C., or Julian Day 584, 259. Since then, later discoveries have corrected the errors above, and shown conclusively the complete accordance of Juan Xiu's page with the entire series of monumental and other dates, and giving us a definite check date of Nov.13, 1539, as expressible in Maya terms by **11.16.0-0-0, 13 Ahau,** the 8th of the month **Xul,** that is, 4720 ' mathematical ' 360-day years from the above zero-date of the Mayas.

So much we owe to Juan Xiu, Xiu XI, the last of the recognized Xiu local governors under the Spanish régime, at almost the end of his three score and ten years.

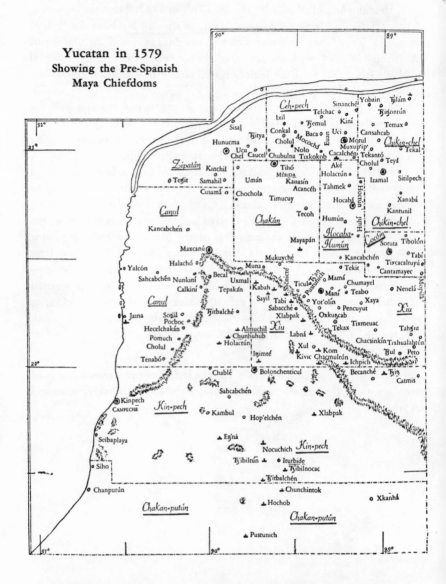

Yucatan in 1579
Showing the Pre-Spanish
Maya Chiefdoms

The above map, while actually one of northern Yucatan " as Landa left it," and to be used
particularly with the facts given in the Appendix to this volume, also shows quite clearly some
of the different historical changes in occupation and population. The Eighth Century
movement in the Sierra district, of which we knew almost nothing, appears in the concentration of ruined sites. The distinction between the East and West, involved in both the early

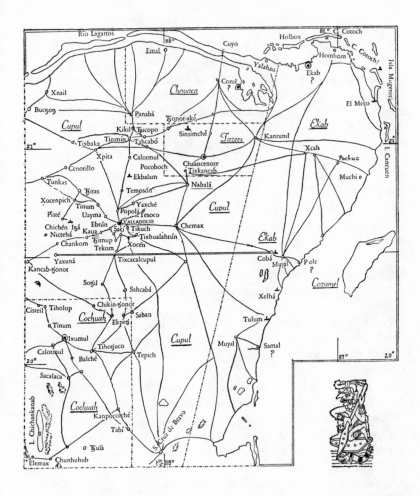

Mexicanization and later Hispanization of the West, with an outpost at Saci-Valladolid, and the Sacred Well, with its Xiu dominance, shows clearly. By 1579 the West had settled to the 'Spanish form of government,' as ordered on Juan Xiu, while in the East we have only the surviving trails, (taken from the Espinosa map), to suggest the ancient population and the seaward movement to the 'Honduras trade.' The map thus shows, just as does the present volume, that we are not at the end but only the beginning of our historical Maya or Itza research.

Yucatan in 1549 and 1579

The Tax List of 1549 and the Relaciones.

In 1517 Hernández de Córdova coasted from Ascension Bay around to Campeche; in 1518 Grijalva landed on Cozumel island and then sailed to Campeche, attempting occupation, but was driven off at Champotón. On March 4, 1519, Cortés made a peaceful stop at Cozumel, received Gerónimo de Aguilar, and continued on to Tabasco and Veracruz, for the conquest of Mexico, Montejo being one of his captains.

Montejo received from the king the capitulation authorizing his conquest of Yucatan on Dec. 8th, 1526, after his successful defense of Cortés against the pretensions of Governor Velázquez of Cuba, and then made his own landing at Cozumel in September, 1927. After his attempted settlement at Chichén Itzá, and the great battle at Aké, he was driven off from the northeast; then after abortive efforts in the west this first attempt was abandoned in 1533, save for the retention of a base in Tabasco. He was then made governor of Honduras, was forced to surrender this to the control of Alvarado, the conqueror of Guatemala, and was allowed the governorship of Chiapas.

From this point he organized a second effort against Yucatan, placing in charge his natural son Francisco (previously legitimated by royal decree), himself being then at the age of 62. From this effort came the formal establishment of Spanish rule at Tiho, renamed Mérida, on Jan. 6, 1542; and this was then only made possible by the voluntarily offered alliance of Tutul Xiu of Maní, just as the Cakchiquels had aided Alvarado in Guatemala to subdue the Quichés, to the final loss of their own independence.

Long before the Xius, themselves incomers from Mexico, had founded (perhaps re-founded) Uxmal, and later had become part of the League of Mayapán, founded by Kukulcan in the eleventh century, which governed Yucatan united under the headship of the Cocoms, an eastern family deriving from the ancient Itzá stock, for over 300 years. Then under Xiu leadership the League was broken up, Mayapan destroyed in 1420, leaving inherited rancors as bitter as those that are preparing the fall of Europe today, when 500 years after their expulsion from Spain, Moors are brought back in, by Spanish Christians to kill other Spanish Christians. To strengthen themselves against the eastern faction, the Xius gave allegiance to Montejo and Spain, surrendering their own independence. To this association was soon added the Canuls, themselves earlier incomers from Mexico, later than the Xius; also others of the western families or chiefdoms. It was Jan. 23, 1542, when the Lord Tutul Xiu came to Tiho.

Montejo at once in 1542 began the allotment of the towns as ' encomienda ' grants to his 80 soldiers, ' conquistadores.' But the news of the entry of the Spaniards and the action of Tutul Xiu had quickly spread through the peninsula, and under the leadership of Nachi Cocom, descendant of the only member of his family left after the sack of Mayapán by the Xius, an army said to have numbered 40,000, or even 60,000 men, from all the regions shown on the eastern half of our accompanying map, with those of Sotuta, attacked the Spaniards and their ᵛ ecan allies at Tiho, on June 11, 1542. Actually a combination of civil war and a drive for conquest from without, the superior arms and discipline of the compact ' foreign legion,' prevailed.

With this success behind him Montejo set out in 1543 to subdue all the eastern territory, from which he had been driven by superior valor sixteen years before. In 1544 Valladolid was established as the second city, on the site of the ancient Saci, with forty resident encomendero distributees of the population and towns; and next Salamanca at Bakhalal, with twenty, as the third capital center. Then in 1546 a great uprising took place in all the east, which after four months mercilessly exterminating warfare, and with the aid of the Xius and their neighbors, the Canuls, those of Hocabá and probably the Peches, was suppressed.

Montejo had brought with him a single priest of the regular clergy, not a friar, one Francisco Hernández, who soon returned to serve at Campeche, leaving padre Martín de Alarcón as cura at Mérida. No friars came to Yucatan until 1545, when four Franciscans came from Guatemala to Campeche under Luís de Villalpando, and four others from Mexico. Villalpando was one of the most active, as later to be noted, and seems to be the pioneer in the conversions, around Valladolid and further in Cochuah; but this was not until 1548, over a year after the uprising of 1546 was suppressed. In this same year Kukum Xiu and others of his party were baptised, and the beginnings of the later great monastery at Sisal, the suburb of Valladolid, were made. The foregoing thus brings us to the year 1549, when Landa arrived, and when the Tax-List was drawn up, as seen below.

Landa became provincial of the Franciscan order for Yucatan in 1561, was censured by Bishop Toral on his arrival in 1562; he then went to Spain to defend himself before the Council of the Indies in 1563, wrote his great work in 1566, certainly as a move to increase his own standing, while his friends back in Yucatan were carrying on the campaign for his return, and to establish their own authority over that of Bishop Toral. The latter finally went away to Mexico, where he died in 1571; Landa, appointed in 1572 to succeed him, returned as Bishop to Yucatan in 1573, and died in 1579, the same year as the Relaciones were drawn up, from which we gather our final data for the preceding thirty years in Yucatan.

We are told that the peninsula of Yucatan at the coming of Cortés and Montejo was divided into nineteen independent Chiefdoms.* It is with the purpose of giving what picture we can of it as a native Maya realm when the List was issued and Landa arrived, and then when the Reports were made, and Landa died, leaving it a Spanish colony, that the data herein are summarized. The Tax List has been known, but never yet published, to our knowledge. The *Relaciones* were published in 1898-1900, and often referred to, but are still a mine of uncoordinated material, especially for English readers.

Our knowledge of Yucatan, before and after the Conquest, rests (apart from the results of field archaeological work and our still inchoate study of the hieroglyphic Dresden and Madrid codices) on the native chronicles in the Maya language, Landa, the Xiu Papers, and these 1549 and 1579-81 documents. The Tax List we give in complete digested form; the Relations when studied and compared throw strong light on points of history, and on Landa's own story and position, far too wide to compass here, but which will be brought out later in a much fuller work on the whole Maya area and times. We are using them here for the single purpose of showing the immediate results of the invasion and conquest on the population of the country. That story is best told by a sort of commentary on the Map, as it was and is; about as we might read racial movements, animosities, wars, and history, around Dantzig and the Polish corridor, Memel, and what is left of Armenia. We shall thus seek to give a ' population picture,' of each native chiefdom * in turn, as it was when Villalpando, Landa and then the Auditor Tomás López came, and then left it, pacified in the west, unpacified in the east, but ' reduced ' in all senses of that word, in the east, north, west and south.

The Tax List in 1549 fixed the levy, to be paid by each of 175 towns in Yucatan, and 10 in Tabasco, to its encomendero, or in certain towns for the Crown. Starting in the northwestern corner, the order of listing proceeded quite closely in geographical order, a fact helping much in the many cases where the towns in time disappeared from the map, or history. The listing followed a formula of which we give a sample below, of which the rest are

---

* We are using the word ' Chiefdom ' as most nearly descriptive here. They were essentially, after the fall of Mayapán, like the independent city states of Italy, or the seigneuries of France, or again like Athens and Sparta. They were essentially also family régimes, clans, baronies or earldoms if one will; but the use of any of these terms is tinged with European political memories. Chieftainship is equally unavailable, as that implies merely the headship of a tribe, frequently a moving one, and semi-barbarous. These were civilized, settled community ' states,' with established polity, code of laws, and customs; also with far-reaching trade relationships. As a term for the *territorial* divisions so covered and ruled, the term Chiefdom thus seems best fitting.

merely duplicates save in their figures.   In many cases the population as such
is noted in the margin, but this always corresponds to the number of mantles,
mantas, to be paid in the year, each *manta* being made up of three breadths,
one to be woven and delivered each four months.   The proportions of the
other items were fairly regular, but not sharp.   Certain amounts of salt and/or
fish were to be paid by towns with access to the sea, and in Tabasco (with
which we are not here concerned) cacao and chile were also called for.   The
document thus runs as follows:

The Royal Audiencia in the City of Santiago de Guatemala.

In the City of Santiago, in the Province of Guatemala, on the second day of
February, in the year 1549 of our Lord, by the President and Justices of the
Royal Audiencia and Chancery of His Majesty the King, seated in the said city.

The town and people of Zamailco (Samahil, in Zipatán), which is in the
encomienda of Rodrigo Alvarez, a citizen of the city of Mérida, are taxed as
follows.   The people of the said town are ordered to plant each year six fanegas
(bushels) of maize and one-half fanega of beans, fencing, cultivating and
reaping in the said town.   They will also pay annually 400 mantles of the
usual kind, and of the value of two tomins (pieces of eight, or *reales*) each;
22 arrobas (quarter 100-weights) of beeswax; 2 arrobas of honey; 400 fowls,
of either the native or Spanish variety, as they prefer; 4 fanegas of salt and 3
arrobas of fish.

The above tribute they shall deliver to their encomendero in the city of
Mérida, at the rate of one-third every four months, and with pack animals or
carts which their said encomendero will supply to them they shall transport
the said tribute to him in the said City of Mérida.   They will also give him
four Indian workmen for his service.   During the period of their service the
said encomendero is required to feed the Indian workmen and have them
taught the doctrines of Christianity.   They do not have to give any other
thing, neither may the said Indians be levied upon in any manner whatever,
nor may they substitute any other thing for any part of the tribute, under
pain of the penalties in the law and ordinances laid down by his Majesty for
the good government of the Indies.

(signed) LICENCIADO CERRATO.   LICENCIADO ROGEL.

Under this order there was then levied a total of 53,285 mantles per year,
with the other above items, upon the 175 towns named as granted in the
peninsula.   Many of these towns have disappeared, 30 indeed in the chiefdom
of the Cupuls in the ensuing thirty years; but thanks to the arrangement of
the list and the fact that many of the grantees had several towns assigned, we
can separate them into their chiefdoms with little uncertainty.

A comparison of the list and the map will make clear that as an actual population index the figures must fall very short of the facts, partly because of what is to be told about the eastern half of the map, and partly because of the absence in the list of so many known towns, for reasons we do not know, in the western half. Further, to the Spanish administration, population meant only so many tax-payers, heads of households; and since the house (as well as the larger unit, the town) was itself a ' community ' organization only releasing its sons when they had so far advanced in status as new 'family heads,' we should at least multiply the taxable population by five or more, to reach what we understand as population.

Now, in comparing 1549 with 1579, we have a certain amount of definite reduction figures in the east; and in the west few of the grantees reporting through Mérida (or else Gaspar Antonio Chi, who helped most of them in their reports) seemed to consider actual figures worth mentioning, and a very large proportion said nothing even of losses, even in a vague way. But one way or another, we have continued positive evidence, confirmed by similar testimony at various places, that the reduction in the intervening thirty years ran from one-half as the smallest loss (and that in few cases only) down to a very common reduction to one-third, and frequently to one-fifth, then even to one-tenth; and over most of the eastern region, to nothing.

The '49 Tax List is then our one *definite* base from which to visualize what happened in Yucatan in the thirty years we are considering; and it only gives the number of ' man taxpayers ' reachable *and* assigned as tribute-payers *to* Montejo's captains and soldiery. Since we are also trying to remake for ourselves a native Maya map and its political and governmental set up when the Spaniards arrived, the following table should aid readers interested enough in the work of friar Landa. The figures stand for heads of households.

Cozumel	220
Ekab	165
Cochuah	300
Chauac-há	440
Tazees	2,240
Cupul	12,940
Chel	4,870
Cocom	2,740
Ceh-Pech	9,270
Hocabá	3,300
Xiu	7,290
Zipatán	3,640
Canul	1,680
Campeche	2,280
Champotón	2,110
Total	53,285

Testimony outside the Tax List indicates that the figure for Chauac-há must have been 4000 at the very least, and double that more likely. Similar testimony as to destroyed towns in the concentration calls for a like increase for the Cupul chiefdom, up to at least 18,000 in the towns we are told existed. Out of the 3365 above given for households taxed in 1549 in the first five regions in the list, 633 survived in 1579.

The Island of Cozumel.

At the coming of the Spaniards Cozumel was less a chiefdom than a sacred place of pilgrimage from over the whole peninsula and even the regions beyond, ruled by the high priest of **Ixchel,** the Isis of the Maya pantheon; he was of the **Pat** family. Stretching almost in a line to the west we had three, possibly four, other major sacred centers; the greatest Itzamal, the seat of **Itzamná,** the Great Initiator, in a way corresponding to Osiris, whither came pilgrims from all " the four roads," to worship and be healed. The sacred well at Chichén Itzá was another, and so also Cobá, whose greatness as a center we are only now beginning to learn. All these belonged to the most ancient times, of the Itzás. What place was held by Ti-ho, " at the Place of the Five," the present Mérida, we do not know.

Cortés was received in friendship at Cozumel, which is described as ' populous '; as the grant of Juan Núñez in 1549, it was taxed as for 220 ' heads of families '; by 1579 the region generally was said to have lost two-thirds its people, and Cozumel reduced to 20. The blame for this loss, along the whole east coast in the earliest period, lies first at the sweeping smallpox brought in 1520 by one negro on a Spanish ship; then from 1546 on to the merciless cruelty of the Pachecos, let loose to ' reduce ' the revolt of that year.

Ekab.

The name is an abbreviation of **ek-cab,** ' black earth,' and the province extended to an undefined southern boundary near Lake Bacalar. Of its once great population, strong enough to keep the Spaniards off until they came with Xiu backing from the west, we have little left but names. Across the 15 mile channel lies P'ole, the mainland port of Cozumel, through which passed all the pilgrimages; Juan Núñez held it, with Cozumel, in 1549, with only 17 tribute payers. Halfaway down the coast was Samal, once ' populous,' but in 1579 only taxed for 50; and today its very location is in doubt. Its description would well fit Tulum, were it not for an early statement that it lay by a creek, near a place Muyil, halfway between Cozumel and Ascension Bay. This latter is supported by the still marked trails from the interior (always a prime help in such cases, since made trails persist), and Samal was a main port on the Honduras trade. Bitanché was held in '49 taxed for 60 married men; today its location is wholly lost. Of the original capital of the chiefdom, Ekab, we know it was at the north, about as shown on the map; held as a grant in '79, its population was not reported.

And of Isla Mugeres the grantee of Ekab reported it "uninhabited" in 1579. That is all we have for Ekab chiefdom.

Cochuah.

Of Cochuah, which includes the largest inland lake left today in Yucatan, Chichen-kanab, we know somewhat more, and it also has some practically independent native population today, away from the end of the railroad at Peto. Its ancient capital, Chikin-cenote, the ' West Cenote,' held the remains of great ancient temples and buildings, and was thus taken for one of the four great convents of the Franciscans in the western half of the peninsula; the others being at Chaan-cenote, the ' Fair Cenote,' among the Tazees, and at Sisal a suburb of Valladolid, and Tizimín, both among the Cupules.

Only one town appears in the 1549 list, Chunhubub; as part of the concentrations to be told more fully when we come to the Cupuls, four towns had been destroyed and the people driven in to Chunhuhub by the Franciscans, and the tax levy in '49 for its grantee was 300 tribute payers, reduced in '79 to thirty. Ixumul, chief town of the province in 1579, was then taxed as for 400; it is close to, or perhaps once the same as Tihotzuco, which joined with Cisteil in the great uprising of 1731. Of the only other town on either list, Kanpocolché, we are told by its grantee in 1579 that to his knowledge the population had been cut in half.

For many years the head of the ' indios rebeldes ' in back of Bacalar has been General May; it is understood that his successor-to-be is a Cochuah, by name.

Chauac-há (Choaca), or ' Long Water.'

Of this once great province we are only now able to map two towns, and those but in approximation: the capital Chauac-há and the port Conil, or Conitzá. The expulsion of Montejo's force in 1527 has been told in the previous pages. The land was arable, not stony, giving two crops a year, with plantations of copal. Offshore are the famed fresh-water springs rising from the sea. The public buildings at Chauac-há were of stone, the private houses of strong wood, thatched. The Spanish reports agree in alloting high intelligence to these people of the coast regions, both Chauac-há and the Tazees, and as using " very correct language."

We are told that in 1529 Chauac-há had 3000 houses, and in 1543 when Montejo attempted to found the new town of Valladolid near the Indian city, there were only 1000 houses. After the revolt of '46 the incoming friars burned the native town to drive the inhabitants inland to the vicinity of the coming convents at Chaan-cenote and Tizimín, and the official Valladolid Relation says there were only *twenty houses left* in the ancient town in 1579. Urrutia received it in grant, and reports his tribute payers as thirteen, due " to the removals and the sumptuous stone convents the Indians were impressed to build "; this was in '79, his earlier tribute having been 200. Another writer speaks of a time previous, with 250 houses, and 600 to 700 population.

The port town of Conil is said by one writer to have had 5000 houses; in '79 Díaz Alpuche, then 75 years old, says he witnessed the town burnings and that nearly all the people died of grief or destitution; that it was all done " by the official order " of the Auditor López, in support of the friars' plan of removals for doctrination and church attendance. In '79 it was still taxed for Contreras in 80 payers.

The only other town name that has come down to us is that of Samyol; in '79 Sarmiento says that his predecessor Cieza received from 900, but he only has from 160. Its location is lost.

The Tazees.

The name is most probably a corruption of Tah-Itzáes, ' among those of the Itzá.' The chiefdom shared with Chauac-há in reputation for high civil order and polity, free from any tyranny. Its capital was Chaan-cenote, named for the beauty of the land at its chief cenote, with 600 on its first tax list. Surrounding it were five other towns, including Temasa with 400; then came friar Francisco Aparicio and without warning burned all five towns over the heads of the people, totally destroying all five, including a good church in Temasa, and driving all the people in around Chaan-cenote. There is no report on these five burned towns for 1549, but when Urrutia received the grant he had 900 tribute payers for his support and income, which were reduced in 1579 to 300. He further says that when Aparicio burned Temasa, with its 170 houses, and the rest, he did not even give time to remove the household goods; that he burned all the fruit trees, and so " within eight days " the head men and many others died. The rest were then made to work on a monastery fit to accommodate 100 friars, to serve actually for *four*.

Kantunil once had 120, was taxed for 50 in '49, and in '79 there were but 2 to pay and provide living for the grantee Bellido.

Dohot is a site now wholly lost. The people, numbering 600 in '49, were removed to near the convent at Tizimín, and less than 100 were left in '79.

Of Sinsimché Sarmiento tells us in '79 that it was once a place of great population, numbering 600, and was taxed on his predecessor for 80, but "now, because of the heavy tributes, I have only 8 left."

Two other towns, now entirely lost to the map, had paid Cieza 900 in '49, reduced in '79 to 150.   Of all this removal Diaz Alpuche tells us it was by the *orders* of Tomás López, " coming with power thereto from the Audiencia " (corresponding to our Supreme Court in such matters) of Guatemala. This López was one of the committee to which Landa's appeal against Bishop Toral was referred in Spain, resulting in his absolution of " any wrong or usurpation of power," and his return in 1573 as Bishop.

The Cupuls.

The region we have up to now surveyed became in later days the Territory of Quintana Roo, covered in the Díaz-Molina days with " exploitation grants " to some half dozen concessionaires, shown on the Espinosa map, but who found it profitless.   That map aids us chiefly in its almost total lack of even settlements marked, but also in the different trail complexes such as those at the probable site of Conil, Chaan-cenote, Kantunil, Chemax, the two Muyils, Tabi and Ixmul.   A thousand years ago we know it to have been in full flower as ancient Itzá territory: Tulum alive, Cobá with its branching system of great built up stone roads that we have only learned about in the past few years, and the great sac-be, or ' white road ' of stone almost certainly from Tulum or P'ole to Cobá; then as now known from Cobá to near Chichén, and then Itzamal, thus linking all the great Itzá sacred places.

What happened after the incoming of the Mexicans soon after that, we have still to learn; difficulties were certainly foreshadowed, but that it was still populous even after the rise of the Xius and the fall of Mayapán, and up to the coming of the Spanish invaders, the atrocities of Pacheco constantly told of and even referred to by Landa as something wherein the friars " were protecting the Indians," and then the torches of Aparicio, Guevara and Villalpando, and the Ordinances of Tomás López, is certain.   But passing from this region where even the great monasteries at Chaancenote and Chikincenote, among the Tazees and the Cochuahs, were early abandoned when the drive for conquest and conversion had died down, we next come to the regions actually ' made Spanish,' and marked by the railway lines of today: Campeche, Muna, Peto, Valladolid and Tizimín, outside of which impenetrability and a practical independence under the Indian leaders was grudgingly allowed. The civil power and administration became settled under Mérida, Valladolid and Salamanca de Bacalar, and under that protection the political functionaries, the grantees and their successors the ' científico ' hacendados of the Díaz period, and the clergy settled down.

All this continued until our own great machine age, with its thousand acre farms and tractors, began to need fuel (oil and Sisal hemp) to threaten us with a tenant farm régime, and our own ' dust-bowl ' with *its* threatened depopulation, put the final pressure on the screws of exploiting the Indian of Yucatan, and Mexico proper, for the amassing of wealth by those in control, through the sale of things extracted for the foreign trade. In no whit was there any difference from the protests to Montejo in 1543 for leave to sell off their Maya slaves to Cuba, to buy the ' luxuries ' from abroad. The only difference was that this last turn of the screws broke the screws themselves, and set the Indian on his strength to become again a man and a producing, educated, economic citizen of his own country.

Fortunately for our present purpose, the Tax List of 1549 followed a geographical course from one province or chiefdom to the next, with occasional slips at the overlappings; also most of the grantees had more than one town, helping us in a sufficiently close location of names that have disappeared from our map, or from the 1579 reports themselves. Many places named in '49 were lost, ' removed ' or their people driven away or absorbed, in '79. In this connection the basic and destructive, merciless evil of the ' removal ' system cannot be appreciated except by remembering the universal ' community ' system of agriculture, not only native to the Indian (and not realized by ourselves, as ' individualists '), but necessary particularly in Yucatan with its thinly covered limestone and corn its staple.

To a town lot pertained a cropping lot outside; each town had its *ejido* territory in common, that of Ebtun near Valladolid (for instance) comprising no less than twenty-seven *ejidos*, each with its own special name; all such *belonged* to that community. Every townsman had the right to select his coming milpa site for clearing, planting and harvesting for two, rarely three years; then the maize had exhausted the soil nitrogen below the profit level of cultivation, and he selected another site. On these community rights the life of the people depended, and they *were* respected; but they also meant the possession of a goodly town-owned region, proportioned to the population needs. The towns had to be moderately sized, but also reasonably close set; on the balance of these two factors the whole life of the whole country depended.

It is obvious that when half a dozen such town centers, with a total of perhaps 1800 households (man, wife, children and young married couples living as by custom the first few years with the father-in-law) were suddenly uprooted from the soil in which they not only rested the social order but drew physical life itself, and with houses and possessions burned, were suddenly driven to ' the city,' famine, despair and death were inevitable. Add to this the labor of tearing down their old stone buildings or pyramids to build what were described as veritable fortresses fit to hold several thousand soldiers instead of the few friars for whose use they were erected, it is little wonder that first the natives died off, and then as inevitable retribution, the monasteries themselves decayed as did the Missions in California, from the identical causes. Excessive concentration of every kind, whether of great cities, trade monopolies however supported—privately or governmentally, or bureaucracies, must go on drawing from the weaker outposts until they too must die, from lack of more resources to ' tax.' But the medial processes are not pleasant, even to read of; neither are they a work of civilization. In the chiefdom of the Cupuls we see this working process, in the raw.

Allotment of *encomiendas* or town grants was made in Mérida in 1542, and in Valladolid in 1544, at once on its removal from the unhealthy Choaca location to the site of the ancient Saci. The 1549 List, besides ten towns in Tabasco, taxes 175 under the jurisdiction of Mérida or Valladolid, to some 100 grantees. Valladolid at its founding had forty Spaniards, its citizens, each entitled to his share of the whole population in the region covered by the eastern half of our map. Not all these forty names appear in the Tax List, and for whatever reason the reports of only twenty-four grantees appear in '79. In all the eastern region we have 69 towns listed, of which 60 are among the Cupuls; nine towns taxed in '49 are not reported in '79, but we have instead five that were apparently not taxed in '49.

Of the 60 Cupul towns we can list one-half as ' survivals,' that are left on the map; the other half we only know as Cupul from their being in the Cupul section of the List. They were either burned or otherwise directly *de*populated, or else abandoned. But from the double record in '49 and '79 we can reconstruct the picture. As to locations we are further helped by tributes of salt and/or fish being called for in '49, showing nearness to one or another coastline. The population for every town taxed in '49 is fixed by the levy of one *manta* or triple breadth of cloth per year from each head of a household; this is then to be compared with the statements of how much less the grantee in '79 was getting; at times additional figures are supplied; in all this we usually have concrete figures at both dates, but at times the statement: " reduced to less than half," etc.

Thirteen of our surviving towns show an annual tribute of 5000 mantles reduced to 1100 in the thirty years between Landa's arrival and his death. Five towns not mentioned in '49 are reported in '79 as having gone down from 2040 to 786; also Chocholá as gone to half. Nine towns mentioned in '49 as paying 2630 mantles per year, have become ' non-survivals ' in '79.

Thirteen neighboring towns were burned and the people removed to Popolá, taxed in '49 at 430; all these towns together went down from 2000 to 900, and finally to 300; today Popolá is *there,* but abandoned.

Tizimín (misnamed Peecemy in '49) stood for 360; Cismopo and six others had the torch applied by friar Guevara, to drive them either to Tizimín or the nearby Temozón, and the tribute fell from 600 to 140. Nabalá with a once great population fell to a third. Yalcón went down in twenty years from 50 to 18. Kaua fell from 360 to half. Cacalchén from 100 to 28. Sotzil and Tecay together, 600 to 200. Xocén, taxed in '49 at 110, once paid 200, then 150, then 30. At Temul out of 460 one-third were left. Of the various towns about Kikil only about half the people were left, in '79. The grantee Juan Cano, the son of Juan, tells us that Tinum covered seven towns, two of which had paid 390 in '49, to his father, whereas in '79 he only received 70 from all together.

Pixoy went from 300 to 100; Casalac from 180 to 35, and Tancuy from 60 to 21. Four towns around Ekbalám, an ancient Cupul capital, were depopulated, and the tribute fell from 600 to 200. Tekanxó from 400 to 190, and two towns on the main highway to the port of Conil, now lost on our map, in '79 had fallen from 400 to 28. And finally, Villanueva tells us that Sicab, close to Valladolid, had fallen from 500 to 240, " due to the forced removals of the people, their flight away into the forests, after the heavy labor " on the building of the great monastery at Sisal. He also tells us that " now 26 surrounding towns come in to Valladolid, for doctrination " and church attendance; on this see the López Ordinances, below.

On our '49 list we find the names of 21 towns, directly reported as ' concentrated ' or else lost on our map, but probably all within the Guevara work of centralization of the ' teaching ' at Tizimín (whose monastery was said to have been one of the most sumptuous in the whole country) and the neighboring Temozón; these 21 towns were in '49 listed for 4290 mantles per year. To this total must be added other *known* towns, by reports, probably concentrated at Valladolid, raising the above figure to 5330 mantles — towns off the map in '79. And yet other data, assignable to ' somewhere in Copul,' raises the total of ' lost towns ' for that chiefdom, on our known and existing reports, to 36, with tribute originally of over 8000 mantles per year.

To these bald figures we are added the following. Juan Cano, the ' old man,' one of Montejo's original company, tells us that he had been granted at the settlement of Valladolid Tinum and six towns near by. That to concentrate the Indians for ' doctrina ' there came Fray Hernando de Guevara, and at once set on fire all the towns, driving everybody to Tinum or Temozón; that he complained of this to the Alcalde Mayor, Ortiz Delgueta, and was non-suited and charged the costs, as the acts were done by " order of the Auditor from Guatemala, Tomás López." The same thing happened under friar Luís de Villalpando, around Valladolid; 13 towns burned and the population moved, to build the Sisal monastery.

Juan Rodríguez, the elder, tells us that five towns were gathered in to Sucopo, now a sorry little hamlet a couple of leagues east of Tizimín, when the present writer saw it in 1917. (Two leagues further into the ' unknown ' I then came on an unlisted ancient site, with stone buildings around a large plaza, still I think unknown even to archaeologists.)

And nearly every single informant in the twenty-five Valladolid Relations of 1579, tells the same story. To which we must add the reports, nine in number, that are known to have been called for by the Instructions sent out from Spain in 1577, but which are missing from the volume in the archives from which the twenty-five Relations were taken and printed. Given then that by the ' married men ' taxed we must understand only heads of a household, and not including the newly married youth who had to work for and with his father-in-law for several years, we have a total *in sight* on our records of some 18,000 households with anywhere from five to ten times the actual number of individuals, in Cupul territory, *after* the decimation by war and flight following the 1546 revolt; and that again following losses we can only guess at from pestilence and the earlier wars of 1527-9, when Montejo was allowed to settle at Chichén Itzá, and then driven from the country when his purposes became understood.

The Chiefdom of Ahkin-Chel.

As we now pass from the eastern to the western half of our map, we find a distinctly marked cleavage, and therewith a great difference in both the quantity and character of the information given us in the Relations. This too, in spite of the fact that both Chels and Cocoms belong in the eastern group, politically. The reader will remember that the first Ahkin-Chel was that son-in-law of a high priest of Mayapán, who after being deeply instructed by the elder man in their writings and wisdom, then after the fall of the city carved for himself his own barony, settling first at Tikoch, where many stone remains are left today. The Cocoms also became by the destruction of the Federation the implacable enemies of the revolting and victorious Xius, a story told in deep colors in all the later history.

Nevertheless the line down the middle of the map divides the jurisdictional authority of Mérida and Valladolid, as self-administering centers under the general provincial government, which until the last century also included the Campeche local administration. From the *Spanish* side of things, this brought them into the western influence, notwithstanding that we are told by the relators that the Chels were highly respected by their neighbors, except those of Ceh-Pech on their western border, with whom they constantly warred; and that the Cocom-Xiu enmities overrode all other factors, on the *Maya* side of things.

The 1549 Tax List, with slight exceptions, from Nos. 1-14 covers Zipatán; 15-35 Ceh-Pech; 36-59 Chel; then Hocabá; 61-70 Cocom; 74-91 Xiu; 92-108 Campeche, Champotón and the Canuls; and then goes through the eastern chiefdoms we have above summarized, to and with ten grants in Tabasco. As we then go through the western group of Relations, dated in 1580-1, and sent in to Mérida direct, we find a constant repetition of ancient historical and native cultural data; in brief, the background of the Xiu influence, of Kukulcán or Quetzalcóatl, the League, the subsequent " evil conduct of the Cocoms," and their surprising importation of *Mexican* mercenaries from Tabasco and Xicalango, these latter finally accepted as ' good Mayas ' by the Xius, and " allowed " to settle on the west coast — the Canuls; finally joining with the Xius in welcoming and then defending Montejo against the Cocoms. The story does not easily make sense. But twelve of these Relations directly credit Gaspar Antonio Chi with aid in their preparation, and five others show his cooperation without actually naming him; in these seventeen are included every one of the nine grantees of towns in Ahkin-Chel, and even the two from Sotuta and Tabi, of the Cocoms. In the quite scanty reports we get from the west coast, Zipatán, the Canuls, and Campeche, he evidently did not aid directly, as he did for practically all the Pech, Xiu, Chel and Cocom towns.

This, together with the constant treatment of the Indians in these reports as lazy, worthless, stupid, ignorant in their *proper* food, medicine, and their use of cold baths and bleeding, simply shows that the whole western division had come to take on Hispanization in thought; and one sees the same difference today between the atmosphere of things in Mérida, and that of Valladolid — where uprisings (even that for Madero against Díaz) always start, just as in Guatemala it is San Pedro Carchá that has to be ' watched out for.'

The threads of this same story, politically, run all through Landa's text, with the hand of Gaspar Antonio Chi again clear. For all that he has thus told us, through the Relations and the work of our Franciscan friar, concerning past Maya history and mythology, and especially of the ancient customs and laws, we are deeply grateful. But the plain simple fact is that in both these contributions we have *the Xiu side of the story* of ' Things in Yucatan. And we lack the Cocom side.

In another respect, directly involving our present summary, we find the demarcation equally marked. In neither the general Mérida Relation nor the twenty-four other individual ones, do we find more than the scantiest reference to the reduction in population, save as sometimes referred to as a result of their bad habits, or their flight back into the forests and hills to the south. About the most we can do is to add up the total taxation as set in 1549, and do without the later figures or data.

Thus among the Chels in '49 Tz'ilám paid Montejo 580 mantles and the rest, plus fish; Tz'tz'ontún 600, and fish; Tekal 420; to the Quiros Chalanté paid 700; two lost places, Cuxbil and Chaltundehad paid 600 and 550. Brizeño had Tikal in '49 for 420 mantles, and still had it in '80, but does not tell his later income. San Martin had Euan in '49 with 320, and Cansahcab in '80, but tells us nothing more. The Sánchez minors held Tixjocapay in '49, for 680 mantles; one son in '80 held Tekantó and Tepacán, where he tells us seven or eight surrounding towns had been moved in, to be near the Tekantó monastery. As a total we can tell that the Chel towns were at the start taxed at least for 5000 mantles, and the only information we are given as to losses in population is where Paredes says he received Sitilpech and Kisil from his father, and the income had gone from 300 down to 120.

The Cocom Chiefdom.

Here again we find the same story to tell. In '49 Sotuta itself paid two grantees together 720 mantles; Chomulná paid Nieto 740; Chilultel 350 to Sánchez, and Chachetunich 70 to one Cea; García received 270 from Vayacus, which later with two other towns was moved to Tabi, García telling us that his income on the three had fallen off from 400 to 150; Tiquinabalon paid Ponce 290, and another town, probably Sahcabá, paid Manrique 300. Finally, Alonso Julian tells that his town of Ixtual, a league from Temax, once contributed 500, but " now only 150; the Indians are stupid and bad."

Through these western Relations generally we are told that the chief ailments are fevers, asthma and *lamparones* or scrofula; we find no mention of syphilis or tuberculosis of the lungs, to both of which the Shattuck report, confirming the testimony of the old Maya medicinal texts, shows almost complete immunity among the Maya. They cured with herbs, bleeding and baths, but were generally in much poorer health than in the old days, owing to the break-up of their ancient customs, and especially their native drink, the **balché,** with its purgative and clearing effects, instead of which the Spanish intoxicants had been forced on them by the prohibition of the **balché** as having been a part of ancient ceremonial uses, and so constantly harped on by Landa, except when now and then he forgets.

The Cocoms in the older days, we are told, traded into Honduras, Tabasco and Mexico; we even are told of *tuchumite* stuffs imported from the Mizteca into Cocom territories.

Ceh-pech.

Twenty-two Ceh-Pech towns are listed in 1549, as follows: Motul 1450; Ixil 280; Maxtunil 500; Mochochá 500; Tixcunchel 220; Ekmul 180; Baca 480; Sauanal 250; Quibil (probably Kini) 480; Yaxkukul 60; Nolo 120; Tixkokob 530; Motul 600; Muxup'ip' 300; Telchac 1030; Yobain 740; Sinanché 320; Euan 320.   All these are known towns today; to them must be added, now off the map, Treveca 160; Texiol 200; Chaltún 130;

Pacat 370; in all a total of 9610 mantles annually, plus the usual beans, honey, wax, and salt and fish from towns near the coast. Of this total 2280 mantles went to Montejo and 1920 to the Crown.

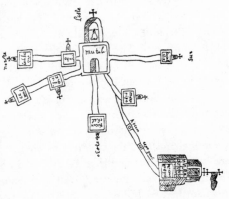

As to causes and conditions Pacheco, to whom we have before referred for his brutalities in the east, says the population has decreased because of pestilences, the Indians themselves being lazy and worthless; he also refers to their having been gathered into towns by the friars " with holy zeal."   Another encomendero tells us that this concentration was " good for their souls but bad for their bodies."   At Sinanché we are told the same — concentration and pestilences; population decreased at Chuburná, Mocochá (but now increasing again); Buctzotz, one of largest towns, now greatly decreased.

Hocabá-Humún.

This small province (if either it or Chakan, wherein lies Mérida, were really ever independent chiefdoms) seems to have played a very minor part in Maya affairs; so also here in this connection.   Of ancient Acanceh with its marvelous facade (now at last destroyed) we hear nothing, even from Landa.   In the uprising of 1546 at Valladolid, it joined the Xius and Canuls in aiding Montejo against the Cupuls and other eastern Mayas.

Monasteries were built at both Hocabá and Humún, and the first of these was taxed in 2400 mantles, 1200 each to Pacheco and Alvarez while Cusamá (probably the town of that name near Acanceh, if not that in Zipatán) gave the Crown 900 mantles, besides salt.

The Xius of Mani.

All of which brings us to the chiefdom of the western hegemony, yet with a quite surprising tax situation. Corresponding well to the dense settlement shown on the map, Molina Solis lists 57 Xiu towns, most of which are known and inhabited today. But in the list for '49 only 16 are named, and of these Yaxá 460 (4 leagues to south in the sierra) is reported as since depopulated to be sent to Oxkutzcab, although many fled back to the forests; Ateque 140 and Cisnuache 360 are in doubt as to location, as is also the identity of Hayan, which was taxed 390 to one grantee and another 360 to a second. After this our list reads Maní 970 and Ticul 790, both to the Crown; then Tekit 400; Mamá 440; Muna 350; Sacalum 220; Pencuyut 250; Yotholín 160; Tekax 940; Izuná 60. Then Xul far down in the sierra 630, and Cantemoy near Peto 310: a total of only 7290 for the whole district. Oxkutzcab does not appear in the list, but Pacheco tells us it had 1200 residents.*

Of specific information, Muñoz Zapata estimates the population (meaning certainly the family heads) when the taxes were levied, at 50,000, " now much reduced by the removals for *doctrina.*" Bote tells us his three towns are losing, and that the children die young. Julian again tells us the Indians are stupid and bad, and that Tetzal had dropped from 500 to 108, and Ixtual from 400 to 90. Practically all the above reports on the western region, down to here and also including the next, Chakán, are substantially one in matter, with a great deal of information as to history and ' things of the country,' manifestly coming from Gaspar Antonio himself. Most of them also refer, for further details, to the report of the cosmographer Francisco Domínguez, and his report prepared in 1566 — the same year in which Landa in Spain wrote his book.

Chakán.

For this district, which besides Mérida included both Mayapán, and also Acanceh on the Hocabá border, with 23 other towns in the list given by Molina Solís, we have but the one long general report, at Mérida, and signed

---

* The following paragraphs from the elder Montejo's instructions, given to his son, in Chiapas, in 1540, probably throw light on this:

" You shall make partition to one hundred citizens, and not less, because the provinces are large and the Indians many, and it is necessary that the citizens resist and subdue them; and this (Ti-ho) must be the chief city of all. And after you have made the partitions, and what I have taken for myself, you will leave various towns without assigning them, for persons suiting to his Majesty's service; for so it is done with all the grants in these new lands."

" Also, you shall make the entries duly of those towns I have taken as for myself and in his Majesty's name, and my part which is in the province of Tutul Xiu with all attached thereto, the town of Telchac with all attached thereto, the town of Campeche with all attached thereto, and the town of Champotón with all attached thereto."

directly by both Martín de Palomar and "Gaspar Antonio Chi." The information is all general (this is in 1580, Mérida not having been allotted as a grant in '49), and as told in the other Chi documents.

The foregoing thus gives us a *listed*, known, taxation in 1549 of some 29,000 mantles for these six interior districts, between the Cupul border and the line of west coast provinces. How to account for the absence of so many known towns from the very definite list of '49, in both the east and especially the west, is difficult. The towns were certainly there, and it is equally difficult to think of their being ignored by Montejo's soldiers in their applications for exploitable and helpless economic fodder. But with those still to follow in Zipatán, the Canuls and Campeche, they reach a *recorded* total of well over 50,000 Mayas, for whom " the taxes began by the aid of those at Maní," in 1542, as so frankly confessed by Juan Xiu, as above.

Zipatán.

This district was chiefly the home of fisherfolk and salt gatherers, and played some part economically, and less politically. Of its past native history and relationships it is safe to say we know nothing. Sihunchén was a friars' concentration point for shore people, but it fell from a one-time tax of 80 mantles to 10.

In '49 Samahil was taxed for 400; Ucú 250; Timucuy 160; Yabucú 130 before the people were moved to Hunucmá; Tetis 210, and Caucel, the capital, 150. Besdies these we have Acalaxán 250; Muca 250, Aquimihil 150; Taubain 150; Atimzizibique 200, and Alinacama 180 — all lost names. Finally the first name on the '49 List, Ayucalco, allotted to Montejo himself, and which from its size and tax of 860 we should probably identify as Hunucmá, this name not appearing itself listed. A total of 3640 mantles, with salt or fish, or both, in every case.

The region was not regarded as healthy, although now it plays a larger part owing to the passage through of the railroad and other trade factors due to the nearness of Mérida and its port, once at Sisal in Zipatán, and later changed to Progreso.

The Canuls, Campeche and Champotón.

In our Tax List, immediately following the Xiu towns, and before those of the Cupuls, are 25 others that clearly belong to these three chiefdoms. Campeche being however the jurisdictional capital for this region, we have no Relations corresponding to those returnable at Mérida and Valladolid, leaving us only with the earlier population figures, and no means of knowing the falling off in the term of our present inquiry. They should however be added here to complete the record of the full 1549 taxation, and are as follows.

For the **Ah-Canul** chiefdom: Calkiní the capital 70; Maxcanú 260; Halachó 200; Becal 100; Pomuch 130; Pocboc 250; Tuchica, probably the place where the younger Montejo was forced to halt on his march from Campeche to Mérida, 360; Nocacao, on the road from Becal to Maní, and after passing lake Yibá, 100. The important modern town of Hecelchakán, the seat of the present Federal Normal School for the whole peninsula, is not named, but since all the rest are identifiable it may be represented by the largest of the above towns, Tuchica with its 360 tribute payers. A total tax in '49 of 1470 mantles, with salt in no instance save at Pomuch.

For the towns of **Campeche**: the capital itself, taxed for the Crown in 630 mantles, with the usual additions, and with both salt and fish; Chulilá 360; Quinlacao, probably for Kinlacán, 300; Sahcabchén, southwest of Bolonchen-ticul, 350; and Ticul, probably for Bolonchen-ticul, 480. A total of 2280.

For **Chakán-putún,** or **Champotón:** the city itself, to the Crown for 420, with fish; and Sihó, probably the one in this province, to Triana, a citizen of Campeche, in 400. Then in company with this Sihó four other towns only placeable by their position: Con or Tecon, also Triana, 480, with salt; then three towns to one Ricalde, Ixcacauché 360, with salt; Sisia, 420; Enasir, 130. Assuming the location of these six towns in Champotón, from the data we have as above, we have as a total, 2110.

One other name occurs, ten places earlier than this Sihó, and named Sihot, taxed at 210, and probably the town found in the Ah-Canul territory.

For the remaining chiefdoms on our list of seventeen districts, namely Tixchel, Chetumal and the country of the Guaymiles, and finaly the independent kingdom of the Itzás, Tah-Itzá around Lake Petén, we have no data in either of our present sources. All this region has been left quite severely alone by the governmental authorities, and its Itzá-Mayas greatly feared by the border inhabitants, with an ever-present threat of a new uprising. A status of practical ' self-dependence,' at Xkanhá and two other centers, was even recognized by definite convention at one time.

The Ordinances of Tomás López.

Of the Royal Audience of the Confines, promulgated in 1552.

Coming from the Royal Audiencia in Guatemala, at the request of the Friars in Yucatan, and decreed for the conduct and treatment of the Indians.

In exercise of the power of our Emperor, vested in me, I command you, the caciques, chief men and people, as follows:

No cacique shall be absent from his town, save for the temporal or spiritual good, or as called by the padres, for over 50 days, on pain of loss of office.

The Indians must not live off in the forests, but come into the towns together, in good strong houses, under pain of whipping or prison.

To avoid difficulties in doctrination, no Indian shall change from one town to another without permission of the local Spanish authorities.

Since many of the chiefs and older men, in the respect they hold by their ancient descent, call the people into secret meetings to teach their old rites and draw them from the Christian doctrine, in their weakness of understanding, all such actions and meetings are prohibited.

The caciques shall not hold gatherings, nor go about at night, after the bells are sounded for the souls in purgatory.

Every cacique or chief of a town shall carry in mind the list of all the people. Every man of the common people absenting himself from his town for over 30 or 40 days, save in public service or with the padres, even with permission from his cacique, shall be punished by 100 blows and 100 days in prison.

Every town, within two years, must have a good church, and one only, to which all may come. Nor may any cacique build any other church than the one, under pain of 100 blows.

Every town shall have schools where the Indians shall be taught the necessity of baptism, without which no one can enjoy God. The schools shall be built by the town, and the caciques shall compel them thereto, in the form and manner required by the padres, and at places designated by them.

On the days for doctrination, one shall go through the towns, bearing a cross and cloth, to call all people together, where all shall gather in order, those of each town by themselves.

If any one, after having heard the holy word and left his false doctrines, shall return to these, he shall be imprisoned to await the due punishment to be ordered by the Royal Audiencia.

No Indian shall undertake by himself to preach the holy word save by express license of the religious fathers.

No baptised person shall possess idols, sacrifice any animals, draw blood by piercing their ears or noses, nor perform any rite, nor burn incense thereto, or fast in worship of their false idols.

No Indian baptised, shall return to be baptised a second time.

Many Indians having been told that their children will die if baptised, I command that all children be brought for baptism.

* The full Spanish text of these Ordinances will be found as an appendix to volume II of Ancona's *Historia de Yucatan*, Barcelona, 1889; and later reprint in Mérida.

Matrimony being in great respect among the Indians, I ordain that no one shall have more than one wife, and that an adulterer shall receive 100 blows, and other punishments if he does not amend.

No cacique shall have to do with a female slave.

No one shall be so daring as to marry secretly.

No one shall marry twice, on penalty of branding with a hot iron in a figure 4 on the forehead.

No purchase gifts shall be made to the woman's parents, nor shall the youth be required by them, as by their old customs, to remain and serve in their father-in-law's house for two or three years.

No one shall give a heathen name to his children.

All people must bend the knee before the sacrament, recite the prayers fixed when the Ave is rung, and reverence the cross and images.

Every one, man or woman, must go to the church both morning and evening, and say an Ave and Paternoster with all reverence.

At meals all shall say grace before and after, and on retiring at night cross themselves and recite the prayers the fathers will teach them.

No one shall cast grains of corn for divination, nor tell dreams, nor wear any marks or ornaments of their heathendom, nor tattoo themselves.

So lacking in charity and care even for their wives or husbands, or family, are the Indians, that I command that all shall care for them when sick, etc.

Where much sickness comes to a town, it shall be reported, and the fathers shall have those at hand for instruction in holy dying.

All inheritances shall be properly cared for.

There shall be no holding in slavery, and all so held shall be set free. But I allow to the caciques, principal men or other powerful Indians to hire people for their service, all of whom shall be reported to the padres and taken to them for doctrination.

The custom of banquets to large numbers is so common, and so destructive of Christianity, that I order that no general banquets be given by any one save at marriages or like fiestas, but then no more than a dozen people may be invited.

No dances shall be held except in daytime.

God gave us time for work, and time for his service; whereby I order the keeping of all church fiestas, as and in the manner fixed by the religious fathers.

All preparation of their ancient drinks is prohibited, and the caciques, principal men, and even the encomenderos are ordered within two months to gather and burn all utensils or cups used therein, on penalty of 50 pesos fine if they allow more to be made.

Towns must be in the Spanish fashion, have guest-houses, one for Spaniards and another for Indians. Also marketplaces to avoid all traveling about to sell or buy. Nor shall any merchant, Indian, Mexican, Mestizo or Negro, be lodged in any private house.

Proper weights and measures shall be provided within two months, on penalty of 20 pesos gold.

I command the raising of cattle to be introduced among the Indians.

The chief tribute of the country being cotton mantles, I order that teaching for this be given.

I order that all women wear long skirts and over them their huipiles; and that all men wear shirts and go shod, at least with sandals.

Since the Indians are always wandering the woods to hunt, I order that all bows and arrows are to be burned. But each cacique shall hold two or three dozen bows, with arrows, for special occasions, or necessity as against tigers.

Good roads from town to town shall be kept in order.

No negro, slave or mestizo shall enter any village save with his master, and then stay more than a day and night.

Proclamation.

Required to be made by every chief of an expedition to the Indians at the moment of disembarking.*

I, N. N., servant of the high and mighty kings of Castile and León, the conquerors of the barbarian peoples, being their messenger and captain, notify and inform you:

That God, our Lord, One and Eternal, created the heaven and the earth, and a man and woman, from whom you and we all the people who shall come after us. But because of the multitude thus begotten out of them in the past five thousand and more years since the world was created, it was necessary that some should go to one place and others to another, and divide into many kingdoms and provinces, since in one alone they could not sustain themselves.

All these people God gave in charge to one who was called St. Peter, that he might be lord and superior of all the people of the world, that all should obey him and he should be the head of the entire human lineage, wherever men might be and live, and under whatever law, sect or belief, giving to him the entire world for his service and jurisdiction.

And since he commanded him to fix his seat in Rome, as the place best fitted to rule the world, he also promised him that he might be and establish his seat in any other part of the world, and judge and govern all nations, Christians, Moors, Jews, Gentiles and of whatever other sect or belief they might be. Him he named *Papa*, Father and Ruler of all men. This St. Peter was obeyed and held as Lord, King and Superior of the Universe by those who lived at that time, and so it has been with all those who since then have been chosen to the pontificate, and so it has continued until today, and will continue until the world shall end.

One of the previous pontiffs, whom I have spoken of as Lord of the world, made donation of these islands and mainlands of the ocean, to the Catholic kings of Castile, who were then Don Fernando and Doña Isabel, of glorious memory, and to their successors our Lords, together with all that is in them, as is contained in certain writings covering this as is stated (and which you may see if you desire). So that his Majesty is king and lord of these islands and mainlands, by virtue of the said donation; and since certain islands, being almost all to whom this notice has been given, have received his Majesty as such king and lord, and have obeyed and served, and do serve him as his subjects, as is their duty, with goodwill and with no resistance, so with no delay, having been informed of what is stated, did they obey the religious men whom he sent to preach and instruct them in the Holy Faith.

All of their free and accepting will, without reward or any conditions, turned Christians and so are, and His Majesty received them with joy and benignity, and thus commanded that they should be treated the same as his other subjects and vassals; and you are held and obligated to do the same.

Finally, as I best can, I beg and require that you understand well this I have told you, take it to your understanding and deliberation in its proper time, and recognize the Church as Mistress and Superior of the world and Universe, and the Supreme Pontiff, called *Papa*, in his name, and his Majesty in his name, as Superior and lord, king of the islands and mainlands, by virtue of said donation, and that you consent that these religious Fathers declare and preach this to you.

If so you do, you will do well, and what you are held and obligated to do, and his Majesty and I in his name will receive you with all love and affection, and will leave to you your wives and children, free and without servitude, that you may do with them and yourselves whatever you wish and see fit, freely, as has been done by nearly all the inhabitants of the other islands. Besides this, His Majesty will grant you many privileges and exemptions, and will show you many mercies and grace.

If you do not do this, and maliciously set delays, I assure you that with God's aid, I shall enter with power among you, and shall make war on you on all sides and in every way I can, and subject you to the yoke and obedience of the Church and of his Majesty; and I shall take your wives and children and make them slaves, and shall sell them as such and dispose of them as his Majesty shall command; and I shall take your property and shall do you all the harm I can, as to vassals who will not obey, and refuse to receive their lord, and resist and contradict him.

I protest that the deaths and harm which shall thereby come, will be by your fault, and not that of his Majesty, nor ours, nor of these gentlemen who came with me.

And as I say and require of you, I ask that the secretary present give me the signed testimonial.

* The Spanish text of this proclamation will be found as an appendix to volume I of Ancona's *Historia de Yucatan;* see also Stephens, *Travels in Yucatan*, II, 446.

Identification of Plant Names mentioned in Landa's text

tixzula: lirio; probably Hymenocallis americana, Jacq. (Molina Solis).

ixlaul: laurel; Stemmadenia insignis, Miers.

nicte: the generic name for Plumerias.

yerbamora or nightshade; **pahalcan:** Solanum nigrum, L.

doradilla; **muchcoc:** Selaginella, lapidophylla, Spring.

yaxpahalche: Piper Gaumeri, Trel.

zarzaparilla; **coceeh:** Smilax mexicana, Griseb.

"kind of hemp": **halal?** Scirpus validus, Vahl.

ixim: maize; Zea mayz, L.

beans, frijoles; **buul:** Phaseolus vulgaris, L.

peppers: Capsicum genus.

" root, growing like the turnip . . . is the fruit ": **chicam?**; jícama; Pachyrhizus erosus L.

"root which grows like the turnip, short, fat, and round": **chicam**, jicama; Pachyrrhizus erosus, L.

"root that grows under the earth"; peanut? Arachis hypogaea, Schlecht, Cham.

"there are two other kinds of good roots they use as food":

  a—**iz**, camote, sweet potato; Ipomoea batatas L.

  b—**maxcal, macal**, yam; Dioscorea alata L.

"tree with fruit like round gourds": jícara? **luch**; Crescentia cujete, L.

"smaller gourds": **lec?** Lagenaria siceraria, Standl.

"incense tree": **pom**, copal; Protium copal, Engl.

"handsome tree that grows by wells": **yaxche**, ceiba; Ceiba pentandra, L.

kulche: cedar; Cedrela mexicana, M. Roemer.

"sort of yellowish tree": **ya**, sapote; Achras sapota L.

brasil; **chacte:** Caesalpinia platyloba, Wats.

zoon: Guaiacum sanctum L.

"causes sores": **chechem**; Metopium Brownei Jacq.

"tree with double thorns": **subim**, cornezuelo; Acacia Collinsii, Safford.

"use for tying in building": **hol**; Hibiscus tiliaceus L.

"another . . . of which they make bows and lances": **chulul ?**; Apoplanesia paniculata, Presl.

"for pillows is superior to tow": **piim**; Ceiba aesculifolia HBK.

"wine-tree which the Indians esteem so highly": **balche**; Lonchocarpus longistylus, Pittier.

niiche: grapes; Coccoloba uvifera L.

abal: plums; Spondias mombin L., or S. purpurea L.

bananas: platanos; Musa paradisiaca L., or M. sapientum L.

"very large tree that bears a large, longish fruit": **chacal haas**; Calocarpum mammosum L.

ya: sapote; Achras sapota L.

ox: ramón; Brosimum alicastrum, Sw.

"another (tree) exceedingly beautiful which bears a fruit like large eggs": **put**, papaya; Carica papaya L.

uayam: guaya; Talisia olivaeformis HBK.

pichi: guayava; Psidium guajava L.

on: aguacate; Persea americana, Mill.

"this tree bears a small, tasty, yellow fruit": **chucum?** Pithecolobium albi-
    cans, Kunth.

"there are artichokes that are very spiny and ugly": **chacuob**, pitahaya;
    Cereus undatus, Haw.

"small, rather spiny tree bearing a fruit shaped like a slender cucumber":
    chom? Bromelia karatas L.

"small tree . . . bearing spiny pods like chestnuts": **kuxub**, achiote; Bixa
    orellana L.

"one kind (of palm) serves for the thatching of the houses": **xaan**, huano;
    Inodes japa, Standl.

"the other is a low, spiny palm": **tuk?** Acrocomia mexicana, Karw.?

"the other kind (of cotton tree) . . . lasts five or six years"; **taman**; Gos-
    sypium barbadense L or G. Schottii Watt, Wild and Cult.

It should be noted that the pronunciation of all Maya words is as in Spanish,
with the following exceptions: **c** is always hard; **x** is sounded like *sh* in English, **Xiu** being like *Shu*. The letter **k** and the stop consonants **p t ch** and **tz**,
when marked by an apostrophe, as **p' t' ch' tz'**, are preceded by a muscular
tension and then sounded explosively, the usual technical term being ' glottal
stop.' Thus **tz'** sounds to the English ear as if it were **dz**, and is usually so
written in Yucatan, as in the town **Dzitás**, near Chichen Itzá. The Mayance
languages lack our ' sonants ' **d**, hard **g**, **j**, **z**, as also **f**; Yucatecan Maya also
lacks the **r**. Double vowels are to be sounded as such, with accent on the first.

A CATALOGUE OF SELECTED DOVER BOOKS
IN ALL FIELDS OF INTEREST

A CATALOGUE OF SELECTED DOVER
BOOKS IN ALL FIELDS OF INTEREST

CONDITIONED REFLEXES, Ivan P. Pavlov. Full translation of most complete statement of Pavlov's work; cerebral damage, conditioned reflex, experiments with dogs, sleep, similar topics of great importance. 430pp. 5⅜ x 8½. 60614-7 Pa. $4.50

NOTES ON NURSING: WHAT IT IS, AND WHAT IT IS NOT, Florence Nightingale. Outspoken writings by founder of modern nursing. When first published (1860) it played an important role in much needed revolution in nursing. Still stimulating. 140pp. 5⅜ x 8½. 22340-X Pa. $3.00

HARTER'S PICTURE ARCHIVE FOR COLLAGE AND ILLUSTRATION, Jim Harter. Over 300 authentic, rare 19th-century engravings selected by noted collagist for artists, designers, decoupeurs, etc. Machines, people, animals, etc., printed one side of page. 25 scene plates for backgrounds. 6 collages by Harter, Satty, Singer, Evans. Introduction. 192pp. 8⅞ x 11¾. 23659-5 Pa. $5.00

MANUAL OF TRADITIONAL WOOD CARVING, edited by Paul N. Hasluck. Possibly the best book in English on the craft of wood carving. Practical instructions, along with 1,146 working drawings and photographic illustrations. Formerly titled *Cassell's Wood Carving*. 576pp. 6½ x 9¼. 23489-4 Pa. $7.95

THE PRINCIPLES AND PRACTICE OF HAND OR SIMPLE TURNING, John Jacob Holtzapffel. Full coverage of basic lathe techniques— history and development, special apparatus, softwood turning, hardwood turning, metal turning. Many projects—billiard ball, works formed within a sphere, egg cups, ash trays, vases, jardiniers, others—included. 1881 edition. 800 illustrations. 592pp. 6⅛ x 9¼. 23365-0 Clothbd. $15.00

THE JOY OF HANDWEAVING, Osma Tod. Only book you need for hand weaving. Fundamentals, threads, weaves, plus numerous projects for small board-loom, two-harness, tapestry, laid-in, four-harness weaving and more. Over 160 illustrations. 2nd revised edition. 352pp. 6½ x 9¼. 23458-4 Pa. $6.00

THE BOOK OF WOOD CARVING, Charles Marshall Sayers. Still finest book for beginning student in wood sculpture. Noted teacher, craftsman discusses fundamentals, technique; gives 34 designs, over 34 projects for panels, bookends, mirrors, etc. "Absolutely first-rate"—E. J. Tangerman. 33 photos. 118pp. 7¾ x 10⅝. 23654-4 Pa. $3.50

ART FORMS IN NATURE, Ernst Haeckel. Multitude of strangely beautiful natural forms: Radiolaria, Foraminifera, jellyfishes, fungi, turtles, bats, etc. All 100 plates of the 19th-century evolutionist's *Kunstformen der Natur* (1904). 100pp. 9⅜ x 12¼.   22987-4 Pa. $5.00

CHILDREN: A PICTORIAL ARCHIVE FROM NINETEENTH-CENTURY SOURCES, edited by Carol Belanger Grafton. 242 rare, copyright-free wood engravings for artists and designers. Widest such selection available. All illustrations in line. 119pp. 8⅜ x 11¼.
23694-3 Pa. $4.00

WOMEN: A PICTORIAL ARCHIVE FROM NINETEENTH-CENTURY SOURCES, edited by Jim Harter. 391 copyright-free wood engravings for artists and designers selected from rare periodicals. Most extensive such collection available. All illustrations in line. 128pp. 9 x 12.
23703-6 Pa. $4.50

ARABIC ART IN COLOR, Prisse d'Avennes. From the greatest ornamentalists of all time—50 plates in color, rarely seen outside the Near East, rich in suggestion and stimulus. Includes 4 plates on covers. 46pp. 9⅜ x 12¼.   23658-7 Pa. $6.00

AUTHENTIC ALGERIAN CARPET DESIGNS AND MOTIFS, edited by June Beveridge. Algerian carpets are world famous. Dozens of geometrical motifs are charted on grids, color-coded, for weavers, needleworkers, craftsmen, designers. 53 illustrations plus 4 in color. 48pp. 8¼ x 11. (Available in U.S. only)   23650-1 Pa. $1.75

DICTIONARY OF AMERICAN PORTRAITS, edited by Hayward and Blanche Cirker. 4000 important Americans, earliest times to 1905, mostly in clear line. Politicians, writers, soldiers, scientists, inventors, industrialists, Indians, Blacks, women, outlaws, etc. Identificatory information. 756pp. 9¼ x 12¾.   21823-6 Clothbd. $40.00

HOW THE OTHER HALF LIVES, Jacob A. Riis. Journalistic record of filth, degradation, upward drive in New York immigrant slums, shops, around 1900. New edition includes 100 original Riis photos, monuments of early photography. 233pp. 10 x 7⅞.   22012-5 Pa. $7.00

NEW YORK IN THE THIRTIES, Berenice Abbott. Noted photographer's fascinating study of city shows new buildings that have become famous and old sights that have disappeared forever. Insightful commentary. 97 photographs. 97pp. 11⅜ x 10.   22967-X Pa. $5.00

MEN AT WORK, Lewis W. Hine. Famous photographic studies of construction workers, railroad men, factory workers and coal miners. New supplement of 18 photos on Empire State building construction. New introduction by Jonathan L. Doherty. Total of 69 photos. 63pp. 8 x 10¾.
23475-4 Pa. $3.00

YUCATAN BEFORE AND AFTER THE CONQUEST, Diego de Landa. First English translation of basic book in Maya studies, the only significant account of Yucatan written in the early post-Conquest era. Translated by distinguished Maya scholar William Gates. Appendices, introduction, 4 maps and over 120 illustrations added by translator. 162pp. 5⅜ x 8½.
23622-6 Pa. $3.00

THE MALAY ARCHIPELAGO, Alfred R. Wallace. Spirited travel account by one of founders of modern biology. Touches on zoology, botany, ethnography, geography, and geology. 62 illustrations, maps. 515pp. 5⅜ x 8½.
20187-2 Pa. $6.95

THE DISCOVERY OF THE TOMB OF TUTANKHAMEN, Howard Carter, A. C. Mace. Accompany Carter in the thrill of discovery, as ruined passage suddenly reveals unique, untouched, fabulously rich tomb. Fascinating account, with 106 illustrations. New introduction by J. M. White. Total of 382pp. 5⅜ x 8½. (Available in U.S. only)   23500-9 Pa. $4.00

THE WORLD'S GREATEST SPEECHES, edited by Lewis Copeland and Lawrence W. Lamm. Vast collection of 278 speeches from Greeks up to present. Powerful and effective models; unique look at history. Revised to 1970. Indices. 842pp. 5⅜ x 8½.   20468-5 Pa. $8.95

THE 100 GREATEST ADVERTISEMENTS, Julian Watkins. The priceless ingredient; His master's voice; 99 44/100% pure; over 100 others. How they were written, their impact, etc. Remarkable record. 130 illustrations. 233pp. 7⅞ x 10 3/5.   20540-1 Pa. $5.95

CRUICKSHANK PRINTS FOR HAND COLORING, George Cruickshank. 18 illustrations, one side of a page, on fine-quality paper suitable for watercolors. Caricatures of people in society (c. 1820) full of trenchant wit. Very large format. 32pp. 11 x 16.   23684-6 Pa. $5.00

THIRTY-TWO COLOR POSTCARDS OF TWENTIETH-CENTURY AMERICAN ART, Whitney Museum of American Art. Reproduced in full color in postcard form are 31 art works and one shot of the museum. Calder, Hopper, Rauschenberg, others. Detachable. 16pp. 8¼ x 11.
23629-3 Pa. $3.00

MUSIC OF THE SPHERES: THE MATERIAL UNIVERSE FROM ATOM TO QUASAR SIMPLY EXPLAINED, Guy Murchie. Planets, stars, geology, atoms, radiation, relativity, quantum theory, light, antimatter, similar topics. 319 figures. 664pp. 5⅜ x 8½.
21809-0, 21810-4 Pa., Two-vol. set $11.00

EINSTEIN'S THEORY OF RELATIVITY, Max Born. Finest semi-technical account; covers Einstein, Lorentz, Minkowski, and others, with much detail, much explanation of ideas and math not readily available elsewhere on this level. For student, non-specialist. 376pp. 5⅜ x 8½.
60769-0 Pa. $4.50

GEOMETRY, RELATIVITY AND THE FOURTH DIMENSION, Rudolf Rucker. Exposition of fourth dimension, means of visualization, concepts of relativity as Flatland characters continue adventures. Popular, easily followed yet accurate, profound. 141 illustrations. 133pp. 5⅜ x 8½.
23400-2 Pa. $2.75

THE ORIGIN OF LIFE, A. I. Oparin. Modern classic in biochemistry, the first rigorous examination of possible evolution of life from nitrocarbon compounds. Non-technical, easily followed. Total of 295pp. 5⅜ x 8½.
60213-3 Pa. $4.00

PLANETS, STARS AND GALAXIES, A. E. Fanning. Comprehensive introductory survey: the sun, solar system, stars, galaxies, universe, cosmology; quasars, radio stars, etc. 24pp. of photographs. 189pp. 5⅜ x 8½. (Available in U.S. only)
21680-2 Pa. $3.75

THE THIRTEEN BOOKS OF EUCLID'S ELEMENTS, translated with introduction and commentary by Sir Thomas L. Heath. Definitive edition. Textual and linguistic notes, mathematical analysis, 2500 years of critical commentary. Do not confuse with abridged school editions. Total of 1414pp. 5⅜ x 8½. 60088-2, 60089-0, 60090-4 Pa., Three-vol. set $18.50

DATE DUE			
FEB 3 1988			
MAR 4 1988			